T0305460

Global Divergence in Trade, Money and Policy

# Global Divergence in Trade, Money and Policy

*Edited by*

Volbert Alexander

*University of Giessen, Germany*

and

Hans-Helmut Kotz

*Deutsche Bundesbank, Frankfurt, Germany*

**Edward Elgar**
Cheltenham, UK • Northhampton, MA, USA

Published by
Edward Elgar Publishing Limited
Glensanda House
Montpellier Parade
Cheltenham
Glos GL50 1UA
UK

Edward Elgar Publishing, Inc.
136 West Street
Suite 202
Northampton
Massachusetts 01060
USA

A catalogue record for this book
is available from the British Library

**Library of Congress Cataloguing in Publication Data**

Global divergence in trade, money and policy / edited by Volbert Alexander and Hans-Helmut Kotz.
    p.cm.
    "This book is a compilation of papers from a conference about 'Asymmetries in Trade and Currency Arrangements in the 21st Century' held as one of the main biennial conferences of the Athenian Policy Forum at Deutsche Bundesbank (Frankfurt, Germany) in July 2004."
    Includes bibliographical references and index.
    1. International trade—Congresses. 2. Foreign exchange—Congress. 3. Monetary unions —Congresses. I. Alexander, Volbert. II. Kotz, Hans-Helmut.
HF1379.G584 2006
337—dc22                                                        2006007959

ISBN-13: 978 1 84542 773 3
ISBN-10: 1 84542 773 4

Printed and bound in Great Britain by MPG Books Ltd, Bodmin, Cornwall

# Contents

PART FOUR: MONETARY POLICY ISSUES

PART FIVE: ACCESSION COUNTRIES AND EMU

# List of Contributors

**Bala Batavia** is Professor of Economics at DePaul University, Chicago, IL, USA.

**Ansgar Belke** is Professor of Economics at the University of Hohenheim, Germany.

**Daniel Gros** is Director of the Center for European Policy Studies, Brussels, Belgium.

**Marc D. Hayford** is Associate Professor of Economics at the Loyola University, Chicago, IL, USA.

**Dr. Minoas I. Koukouritakis** is Lecturer at the Department of Economics at the University of Crete, Rethymno, Greece.

**Nicholas A. Lash** is Professor of Finance at the Loyola University, Chicago, IL, USA.

**A.G. Malliaris** is Walter F. Mullady, Sr. Professor of Economics and Finance at the Loyola University, Chicago, IL, USA.

**Ronald McKinnon** is William D. Eberle Professor of Economics of International Economics at Stanford University, CA, USA.

**George Michalopoulos** is Lecturer at the Department of Accounting and Finance at the University of Macedonia, Thessaloniki, Greece.

**Dr. Leo Michelis** is Lecturer at the Department of Economics at the Ryerson University, Toronto, Ontario, Canada.

**Parameswar Nandakumar** is Professor of Business Economics at the Indian Institute of Management Kozhikode, India.

**Fernando A. Noriega-Ureña** is Professor of Economics at Universidad Autónoma Metropolitana, México, D.F.

**Carlos A. Rozo** is Professor of Economics at the Universidad Autónoma Metropolitana-Xochimilco, México, D.F.

**Dominick Salvatore** is Professor of Economics at Fordham University, New York City, USA.

**Dr. Gunther Schnabl** is *Privatdozent* in the Department of Economics at the University of Tuebingen, Germany.

**Cheick Wagué** is Associate Professor of Economics at the South Stockholm University, Södertörn, Sweden.

# Preface

Though the rapid growth in worldwide information technologies and in the globalization of markets supports harmonization and integration between countries substantial differences still exist in all parts of the world. Undoubtedly these differences in economic power, institutional structures, per capita income and welfare between countries and regions are the reason for important international tensions today and will be a substantial problem for many decades ahead.

The volume 'Global Divergence in Trade, Money and Policy' tries to analyse aspects and implications of such differences. It rests on a conference about 'Asymmetries in Trade and Currency Arrangements in the 21st Century' held as one of the main biennial conferences of the Athenian Policy Forum at Deutsche Bundesbank (Frankfurt, Germany) in July 2004. After a rigorous referee process ten papers out of more than forty presented at this conference were selected and carefully revised. Other papers were published in major international journals.

First of all the organizers want to thank the Board of Governors of Deutsche Bundesbank for hosting the conference in a perfect way. The Bundesbank not only provided conference facilities for the whole bulk of sessions but also hosted nearly all participants in its guesthouses. All meals, receptions and a wonderful conference dinner were financed and organized by the Bundesbank's staff. In particular, Prof. Kotz, Member of the Board of Deutsche Bundesbank, supported the organization before and during the conference in a perfect way.

Substantial financial support came from the Alumni Network of the Department of Economics of the University of Giessen and from P. Hanker, CEO of the Volksbank Mittelhessen.

The conference program was enriched by a speech of Prof. Papademos, Vice President of the European Central Bank, about 'Monetary Policy in an Enlarged Europe' and by a panel discussion with distinguished panelists: Sven Arndt, Claremont McKenna College, George von Furstenberg, Indiana University, Marianne Kager, Chief Economist of the Bank of Austria, Hans-Helmut Kotz, Member of the Board of the Deutsche Bundesbank and Dominick Salvatore, Fordham University discussed the topic 'EU-Enlargement – The Problems Ahead'. The discussion was chaired by Volbert Alexander, University of Giessen.

We are indebted to George von Furstenberg, Indiana University for an extremely efficient help during the preparation of the program, the selection of the papers and the publishing process for the present volume. Chris Paraskevopoulos, President of the Athenian Policy Forum and Professor of Economics at York University, Toronto (Canada) supported the organizers with helpful information.

Last but not least we gratefully acknowledge the help of the staff of the Institute of Money, Credit and Banking, University of Giessen (Germany). In particular, Carsten Lang did an excellent job in preparing the layout of the book. Perfect cooperative and constructive behaviour of all authors in rewriting the papers for the publication and the extremely professional help of the publisher made our work easy.

Volbert Alexander
Hans-Helmut Kotz

# The Evolution and Development of the Athenian Policy Forum

> Our constitution... is called a democracy because power is in the hands not of a minority but of the greatest number.

Thucydides II, 37

> We Athenians, in our own persons, take our decisions on policy or submit them to proper discussions: for we do not think that there is an incompatibility between words and deeds; the worst thing is to rush into action before the consequences have been properly debated.

Thucydides II, 40

(Thucydides (460–400 BC) – Pericles' Funeral Oration)

The Athenian Policy Forum (APF) – for more than a decade now – has been promoting conferences and other scholarly activities on the broad themes of economic integration, globalization and the structural changes that have been taking place in the world economy over the turn of the twentieth and twenty-first centuries. Three main principles have guided the discussion all along:

Firstly, from the start there has been an emphasis on the concerns of relatively smaller players caught up in the globalization process. For example, Greece within the European Union (EU), or Mexico and Canada (both 'small' economically relative to the USA) within NAFTA. To this end the themes of globalization, 'unequal development' and 'asymmetry', as developed in previous publications, will be maintained.

Secondly, there has been a serious commitment to an open debate, reflecting as many different shades of political and economic opinion as possible. Inspired by the ancient Greek and Athenian tradition of thoroughly and properly debating important issues in public with clarity, and without obfuscation, the APF is aspiring to meet that standard. Such pluralism is sufficiently rare in both academic discussions and decisions on policy these days to warrant special mention.

Thirdly, we adhere to the principle of 'positive sum game' where everybody is a winner, and not to that of 'zero sum game,' where one gains at the expense of everybody else.

In pursuing its objectives internationally, the APF is promoting conferences, commissioned studies, symposia, invited presentations, occasional papers and now its own journal.

The program of activities of the APF includes the following THREE distinct initiatives, namely:

## 1  THE CONFERENCE PROGRAM

Several conferences, on a biennial or regional basis, have been held so far, with great success. In fact, so far in this young century we have held conferences in the following nine cities: Brussels (BELGIUM), Izmir (TURKEY), Athens (GREECE), Antwerp (BELGIUM), Leuven (BELGIUM), Thessaloniki (GREECE), Xanthi (GREECE), Chicago (USA), Cambridge (UK), London (UK) and now Frankfurt (GERMANY). I hope that you will agree with me that, over a period of about four years, having APF conferences in eleven major cities of the world is truly a remarkable achievement.

In fact, the timing could not be any better, given the recent developments at a global and regional scale coupled with the largest enlargement of the EU in 2004, and the stated commitment to create the Free Trade Area for the Americas (FTAA) by 2005. In addition I do believe that a 'new paradigm' is emerging and the APF is ready, once again, to reaffirm its serious commitment to an open debate, reflecting, as far as possible, every shade of political and economic opinion.

## 2  THE APF PRESS PUBLISHING HOUSE

The APF Press is the publishing arm of the APF. By the end of 2005 approximately 20 titles (mainly out of these conferences) – 16 economic and four non-economic – will have been published by the APF Press.

# 3 THE JOURNAL OF ECONOMIC ASYMMETRIES

I am pleased to report that the long-standing objective of the APF, the launching of its own journal, is now a reality.

We are very proud to announce *The Journal of Economic Asymmetries (JEA)* and to introduce it to its academic and policy audience.

The concept of asymmetries is very central to our research agenda. We interpret asymmetries broadly as economic relationships between trading partners with unequal market power, and also in the narrow technical sense of dissimilar information between trading agents.

The APF has recognized that equitable and efficient international trading and monetary integration schemes between unequal partners could not be achieved with policies of 'one size fits all'. In a series of conferences and published volumes, the APF documented how trade, agriculture, labor, financial and industrial policies must be modified to take these differences into account. The adaptation or modification of such policies may be defined as asymmetric policy responses.

As it is pointed out in the latest APF Press volume:

> The concept of asymmetries was introduced into economics in the early 1970s by Nobel Laureates Joseph Stiglitz, George Akerlof and Michael Spence who replaced the then standard assumption of equally informed agents by the assumption that some agents know more while others know less. They coined the term 'asymmetrically informed' agents to describe dissimilar information between economic agents. The Athenian Policy Forum has extended this notion of asymmetries to many aspects of economics, such as trade, monetary policies, financial institutions, growth, investment, public policy, competitiveness and others to highlight the differences, dissimilarities and nonuniformities that may exist between two economies.

Finally, for updates on all three distinct initiatives of the APF – Conference Program, Publishing House and Academic Journal – and other exciting activities of the APF visit our two websites: APF [www.apforum.org] and APF Press [www.apfpress.com] respectively.

Chris Paraskevopoulos
President of the Athenian Policy Forum

# Introduction

Modern information technologies and the increased openness of markets between countries have changed the world in many respects. If decisions in one part of the world are influenced by information from all other parts, countries and their economies are connected more closely and international relations become more intensive. Within such a globalized world competition between systems, structures and institutions increases: A strong pressure emerges for efficient arrangements in order to survive the global competition. Inefficient national production processes and bureaucratic organizations are outperformed and then replaced by foreigners leading to severe negative consequences for domestic employment and welfare. This intensive competition covers all parts of economic and political life: monetary and fiscal policy, banking systems, production processes, market regulations, exchange rate systems etc. The fall of nearly all former communist countries clearly shows that in a globalized world political and legal systems that are inefficient have no chance to survive.

One important consequence of the developments briefly described above is the increase in worldwide productivity. Unproductive arrangements are removed and inefficient national systems preserved during decades or centuries by protection and discrimination against foreigners now become subject to international competition. After a sometimes very painful transition period this leads to an increase in output and welfare. New developments and inventions in technology, organization and production processes are available for nearly all countries within a short period of time improving the quality of capital stocks and reducing inefficient market regulations. Inevitably this productivity pressure leads to a greater harmonization of production processes, structures and legal arrangement and to a convergence to the most efficient solutions.

The effects of globalization are relevant for all countries and economies independent of their current level of economic development. High developed economies are massively influenced as well as less developed countries. The productivity pressure and the dependence on international competition hits economies that cannot be more unequal. Huge divergences exist between high and less developed countries in nearly all fields shaping the basic fundaments of their economies: Skilfulness of the labour force, quality of the capital stock, production and distribution structures, financial intermediation (banking systems and deepness of financial markets), natural resources, soundness of the legal and political systems and economic as well as political power.

In contrast to the positive effects of globalization the increase in international competition and an acceleration in productivity pressure exerted on basically unequal partners can create an explosive mixture. If strong developed countries use their superior economic power to impose regulations on weak countries that are not accepted by the latter political tensions will emerge. If powerful international enterprises dominate markets in other countries by overtaking firms or by dumping prices these countries may not realize the gains from globalization because of high unemployment. As a result globalization is increasingly interpreted as a process resulting in a loser position of the home economy and in a winner position of strong foreign countries. The danger emerges that loser countries will step out of this international competition by introducing protection again resulting in a decrease in global wealth.

The role divergences play in a globalized world can be discussed for many fields of the economy. They have a strong influence on international trade, on the question of optimal exchange rate systems and on the effectiveness of national and international financial markets. They also play a crucial role for banking systems and monetary policy issues and for problems related to the introduction and development of monetary unions. Perhaps the most important effect divergences between different economies have lies in the minds and attitudes of people: While economists or policy makers from countries with a strong currency treat a currency board established in a traditionally unstable economy as a possible anchor of stability experts from the unstable country focus on the loss of an independent national monetary policy as a consequence of a currency board system. While Americans and Europeans stress the efficiency aspect of foreign direct investments Mexicans only may have an interest in patronizing or even exploitation implications coming along with such activities. The danger emerges that without a mutual knowledge of the way of thinking or of the mentalities prevailing in different parts of the world a common, constructive discussion of important issues becomes more and more difficult.

The interaction between globalization processes on one and basically different current situations on the other side is of central importance for this book. In particular, asymmetric positions are analysed between different economies (USA versus Mexico, core European versus peripheral European countries, countries inside the European Union versus accession countries), between different currencies (the US dollar versus East Asian currencies), between different financial markets in the core versus the peripheral European states, between different types of banks (inside the USA and between USA and Mexico) and between more powerful and less powerful central banks. A further main objective of this book is the attempt to discuss the problems involved from different perspectives by including contributions from countries like Mexico, Greece and India. This may help to understand how differently the process of globalization is regarded and valued in countries characterized by completely different current situations.

Part One refers to 'Problems of International Trade'. According to Salvatore ('Currency Misalignments and Trade Asymmetries among Major Economic Areas') the main reason for trade asymmetries among major economic areas like the USA, Europe and East Asia lies in massive currency misalignments. The present international monetary system consisting of a variety of different exchange rate regimes is not able to prevent large volatilities of exchange rates and international financial crises. Wide and persistent misalignments of exchange rates and huge trade imbalances exist and no efficient economic policy coordination among the leading economies is promoted. The large trade deficit of the USA and the corresponding surpluses in East Asia including Japan and China require a fundamental change in consumption and savings behaviour in the USA in the long run. Currently the high US consumption is only possible because of massive capital inflows to the USA leading to an overvalued US dollar. The main reason for this capital inflow is a high productivity growth in the USA because of a more widespread use and adoption of information technology than in the Euro area and East Asia.

An increase in US savings is not easy to achieve because of the well–known attitudes of US consumers and might only be achieved in the long run. To reduce the misalignment problem and the imbalances of trade flows in the short run Salvatore favours macroeconomic policy coordination between the USA, Europe and Japan in order to bring their currencies smoothly to their long–run equilibrium level. The enforcement of the IMF objective to avoid manipulating exchange rates could be of considerable help.

In Chapter 2, 'Free Trade and Poverty', Noriega–Ureña discusses problems of international trade from a completely different perspective. As he points out underdeveloped countries have enforced their export activities, have opened their economic borders and have made many steps towards a free international trade system. In the end this strategy was not succesful: Many underdeveloped economies were confronted with increasing poverty and income inequalities. Therefore, the author presents a very fundamental criticism of the general belief that more free trade is welfare–increasing by constructing a model of a small, technologically weak and open economy. His main conclusions are that trade deficits cannot be solved by devaluations but only by internal reforms reducing the technological gap between domestic and foreign production processes. In addition, the stimulation of exports by a devaluation reduces domestic consumption because of worse terms of trade leading to higher poverty. Economic policy should be concentrated on necessary internal reforms and should not rely on the positive effects of international trade and of exports, in particular.

This result is in sharp contrast to the assumptions and conclusions contained in Salvatore's chapter where free international trade with no obstacles and distortions is an important source of higher welfare for all countries. However, a common implication in both chapters is the increasing scepticism that domestic problems can be solved by optimal international agreements. Both authors point out that the sustainable solutions for problems like the trade-balance deficit of the USA or the technological gaps in underdeveloped economies only can be reached by internal changes in consumption behaviour and structural reforms of production processes.

In Part Two ('Exchange Rate Aspects and Financial Markets') McKinnon and Schnabl discuss in Chapter 3, the problems of the relation between East Asian currencies on the one hand and the US dollar on the other hand. The crucial difference between strong global and weak local currencies comes from the existence or non-existence of deep foreign markets. As a consequence firms and banks dealing with local currencies are always confronted either with a maturity or a currency mismatch. They are vulnerable to large revaluations or devaluations against the strong foreign currency. Therefore, a free-float system leads to high risk so that many East Asian countries try to peg their currencies against the dollar. The authors support more formal commitments for a peg of the yuan and the yen to the dollar and expect similar pegs for the small currencies and a greater monetary stability in this region. It should be noted here that in the long run this proposal will only be successful if inflation rates are kept low in East Asian countries. Otherwise the danger of currency crises remains high.

In Chapter 4, 'Integration and Convergence of Financial Markets in the European Union' Batavia Nandakumar and Wagué deal with characteristics of financial markets in core EU nations like Germany, France, Spain, advanced small economies (Sweden, Denmark, Ireland, Finland) and less advanced small nations like Portugal and Greece. It is shown empirically how these different types of financial markets are interconnected by using covered interest parity, uncovered interest rate parity, real interest rate parity and by the Feldstein-Horioka index as measures of integration. The authors show that large core nations are strongly integrated with the EU market but weakly linked globally. Small advanced countries are integrated with the EU market and globally to a medium extent. Small less advanced economies are integrated with the EU but not globally. The importance of studies about financial integration becomes obvious in the light of the EU accession of East European countries in the near future.

Many asymmetries exist in banking systems inside and between countries. A huge bulk of literature centres around differences between private and public banks and between the universal banks of the Central European type and the separate banking system in the UK and the USA. Part Three ('Asymmetries in Banking Sectors') is focuses on two aspects representing the general topic of the book: The role of small, discriminated banks inside a country and the relation between a weak national banking system and powerful foreign banks.

In Chapter 5, 'Asymmetries in US Banking: The Role of Black-owned Banks' the central issue Lash discusses are questions about the functions small, black-owned banks have in the US banking system. In particular, banks of this type are considered to serve black communities, foster growth and development in their communities and in this way are necessary for providing banking services to low-income, minority communities. According to the author there is no clear proof for an important productive contribution to economic development mainly because of the small size of black-owned banks, insufficiently skilled managements and existing discriminations.

As pointed out above the expansion of powerful firms and banks into markets of other countries is a typical characteristic in a globalized world. A very sensitive type of expansion are takeovers of foreign firms or banks. In Chapter 6, 'The Extranjerización of the Mexican Banking Sector: Expectations and Results' Rozo discusses positive and negative effects of the takeover of Mexican banks by Spanish, US, UK and Canadian banking corporations. Today around 80 per cent of the total assets of the Mexican banking system are controlled by foreigners. From a Mexican point of view this massive transfer of banking assets to foreign owners has a positive and a negative effect: The health and the capitalization level of Mexican banks have increased leading to a sounder asset fundament and a reduced probability of a banking crisis. On the other side the new ownership has not increased the volume of credit outstanding implying that a better supply of financial services for the Mexican economy is not achieved.

The crucial question arises: Will the more solid capital situation of the Mexican banking system lead to a better supply of financial services in the future? If the negative effect of the stagnation of the credit volume is permanent the acceptance of foreign ownerships in Mexico will decrease.

Part Four ('Monetary Policy Issues') focuses on two aspects of asymmetries among central banks. The first aspect centres around the question of leader–follower relations among major central banks; the second aspect concentrates on optimal reaction strategies of central banks. Belke and Gros in Chapter 7 ('Asymmetries in Trans-Atlantic Monetary Policy Relationship? ECB versus FED') present an empirical investigation about the leadership of the FED and discuss the problems of leader–follower relations in the broader context of a central bank reacting to global information. It becomes obvious that a clear proof for the hypothesis that the FED's policy dominates the ECB is difficult to find. They conclude that only for very limited time periods (September 2001) the ECB really followed the FED.

Hayford and Malliaris in Chapter 8 ('Rethinking Monetary Stabilization in the Presence of an Asset Bubble: Should the Response be Symmetric or Asymmetric?') very critically discuss the question if and how a central bank should react to asset bubbles. The main finding is that monetary policy should react in an asymmetric way: neutral in stock market booms unless inflation is caused and with a substantial monetary ease after a stock market bust. One implication of this study is that a simple Taylor rule treating expansionary and restrictive monetary policy equally cannot be an optimal strategy.

Part Five ('Accession Countries and EMU') concludes and deals with problems of monetary integration in Europe. In Chapter 9, 'The Internationalization of the Euro: Trends, Challenges and Risks' Michalopoulos describes the current situation of the euro as an international means of payment and vis-à-vis the dollar, in particular. He then discusses the necessary steps to make the euro a fully-fledged international currency and problems for its use coming from the limited financial market integration in the EU. His main conclusion is that the euro has a real disadvantage against the dollar in the long run because of the general economic governance and the decentralized political decision process in Euroland.

In Chapter 10, 'Linkages in the Term Structures of the EU Accession Countries' Michelis and Roukouritakis examine interest rates in the central and East European accession countries (including Malta and Cyprus). Presenting empirical evidence for linkages in the term structure of interest rates in the so–called EU accession countries the authors contribute substantially to the question of monetary convergence. Their main finding is that there is a weak short run and long run interdependence among the term structures of the new EU countries and that these countries have followed independent monetary policies.

Volbert Alexander
Hans-Helmut Kotz

PART ONE


PROBLEMS OF
INTERNATIONAL TRADE

# 1. Currency Misalignments and Trade Asymmetries among Major Economic Areas

## Dominick Salvatore

---

## 1  INTRODUCTION

One of the most serious problems facing the present international monetary system is the large and persistent misalignments among the world's leading currencies (dollar, euro and yen). Currency misalignments disrupt the pattern of specialization and trade based on comparative advantage and can lead to adoption of dangerous protectionist measures. The problems created by large and persistent currency misalignments are not amenable to correction by adopting any of the various proposals advanced to reform the present international monetary system. Correcting currency misalignments and overcoming the serious asymmetries and problems that they create requires instead the elimination of the structural imbalances that exist in the United States, the European Monetary Union (EMU), Japan and emerging markets in East Asia, particularly China.

Section 2 of this chapter briefly reviews the characteristics and functioning of the present international monetary system. Section 3 identifies the major shortcomings of the present international monetary system – the most important of which being currency misalignments. Section 4 then reviews the proposals advanced to overcome this problem and examines the reasons why none of them are likely to eliminate currency misalignments. Section 5 identifies the structural imbalances in the world's major economic areas that are the fundamental cause of currency misalignments, and it shows that only by eliminating them can currency misalignments be eliminated and the serious problems that they create be solved. The proposals previously advanced for improving the operation of the international monetary system may be of some use only as short-run, stop-gap measures to buy time and allow fundamental reforms and structural adjustments to be introduced and to begin to bear fruits.

## 2  CHARACTERISTICS AND OPERATION OF THE PRESENT INTERNATIONAL MONETARY SYSTEM

The present international monetary system has four main characteristics:

1.  There is a wide variety of exchange rate arrangements. According to the new de facto classification to which the IMF (2004) officially moved in 1999, at the end of 2001, 40 countries had no legal tender of their own (these include the 12 EMU countries), eight had a currency board (among which, Bulgaria, Hong Kong, Estonia and Lithuania), 41 had a conventional fixed peg (among which are China, Malaysia and Saudi Arabia), five had a horizontal band (among which are Denmark and Hungary), four a crawling peg, six a crawling band, 43 had managed floating (among which are India, Indonesia, Russia Federation and Thailand), and 39 an independent floating (among which are Brazil, Canada, Japan, Korea, Mexico, Poland, United Kingdom, United States and Switzerland), for a grand total of 186 countries (Figure 1.1 provides a schematic view of the new IMF classification of exchange rate regimes, while Table 1.1 shows the distribution and evolution over time of exchange rate regimes among developed countries, all developing countries, and emerging markets).
2.  Countries have almost complete freedom of choice of exchange rate regimes. All that is required by the 1978 Jamaica Accords (which formally recognized prevailing exchange rate arrangements) is that a nation's exchange rate actions not be disruptive to trade partners and the world economy.
3.  Exchange rate variability has been substantial. This is true for nominal and real, bilateral and effective, short-run and long-run exchange rates. The IMF (2004) estimated that exchange rate variability has been about five times larger during the period of flexible (i.e., since 1971) than under the preceding fixed exchange rate or Bretton Woods System. Exchange rate variability of 2–3 percent per day and 20–30 percent per year has been common under the present system. Exchange rate variability has been larger than originally anticipated, does not seem to be declining over time, and is for the most part unexpected.
4.  Contrary to earlier expectations, official intervention in foreign exchange markets (and therefore the need for international reserves) has not diminished significantly under the present and more flexible exchange rate system as compared with the previous fixed exchange rate system. Nations have intervened in foreign exchange markets not only to smooth out day-to-day movements, but also to resist trends, especially during the 1970s and since the mid-1980s (Salvatore, 1994).

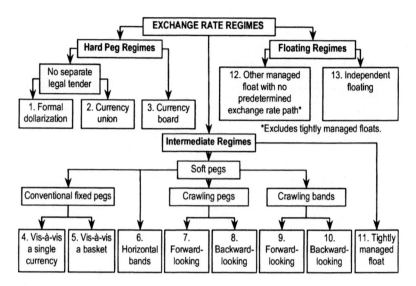

*Figure 1.1   De facto classification of exchange regimes*

The period of more flexible exchange rates since 1971 has been characterized by far greater macroeconomic instability in the leading industrial countries than during the previous fixed exchange rate or Bretton Woods period. The system was jolted by two rounds of large oil price increases (1973–4 and 1979–80), which resulted in double-digit inflation and led to recessions (as industrial nations sought to break the inflationary spiral with powerfully tight monetary policies). The period also saw the rapid growth of the eurodollar market and the liberalization of capital controls. The resulting sharp increase in international capital flows, as well as the institutional changes and adjustments following the collapse of the Bretton Woods System in 1971, rather than the prevailing flexible exchange rates, were the primary cause of the large macroeconomic instability suffered by the leading industrial countries, however. Indeed, it is now widely agreed that no fixed exchange rate system could have survived the combination of oil shocks, portfolio shifts, and structural and institutional changes that the world faced during the past three decades (see Salvatore, 1994). It must also be remembered that the present managed exchange rate system was not established deliberately as the result of an international agreement, but was instead forced upon the world by default as the result of the collapse of the Bretton Woods System because of lack of an adequate adjustment mechanism and dollar overvaluation.

Table 1.1 Evolution of exchange rate regimes by country

| | 1990 | 1991 | 1992 | 1993 | 1994 | 1995 | 1996 | 1997 | 1998 | 1999 | 2000 | 2001 |
|---|---|---|---|---|---|---|---|---|---|---|---|---|
| **Developed Countries** | | | | | | | | | | | | |
| Hard pegs[a] | 0.0 | 0.0 | 4.2 | 4.2 | 4.2 | 4.2 | 4.2 | 4.2 | 4.2 | 50.0 | 50.0 | 54.2 |
| Intermediate regime[b] | 73.9 | 73.9 | 50.0 | 54.2 | 54.2 | 54.2 | 62.5 | 58.3 | 58.3 | 12.5 | 12.5 | 4.2 |
| Of which: soft pegs[c] | 73.9 | 73.9 | 50.0 | 50.0 | 50.0 | 50.0 | 58.3 | 58.3 | 58.3 | 12.5 | 12.5 | 4.2 |
| Floating regimes[d] | 26.1 | 26.1 | 45.8 | 41.7 | 41.7 | 41.7 | 33.3 | 37.5 | 37.5 | 37.5 | 37.5 | 41.7 |
| Total | 100.0 | 100.0 | 100.0 | 100.0 | 100.0 | 100.0 | 100.0 | 100.0 | 100.0 | 100.0 | 100.0 | 100.0 |
| **Developing Countries** | | | | | | | | | | | | |
| Hard pegs[a] | 18.4 | 18.8 | 21.8 | 17.7 | 18.0 | 18.0 | 18.0 | 20.4 | 20.4 | 20.4 | 21.0 | 21.6 |
| Intermediate regime[b] | 68.4 | 65.2 | 57.1 | 59.5 | 57.1 | 59.6 | 57.8 | 52.5 | 47.5 | 45.1 | 45.7 | 43.8 |
| Of which: soft pegs[c] | 62.5 | 58.0 | 50.0 | 53.2 | 47.8 | 49.1 | 49.1 | 46.9 | 43.8 | 38.9 | 37.0 | 34.0 |
| Floating regimes[d] | 13.2 | 15.9 | 21.2 | 22.8 | 24.8 | 22.4 | 24.2 | 27.2 | 32.1 | 34.6 | 33.3 | 34.6 |
| Total | 100.0 | 100.0 | 100.0 | 100.0 | 100.0 | 100.0 | 100.0 | 100.0 | 100.0 | 100.0 | 100.0 | 100.0 |
| **Emerging Market Countries[e]** | | | | | | | | | | | | |
| Hard pegs[a] | 6.7 | 10.0 | 9.7 | 9.4 | 9.4 | 9.4 | 9.4 | 12.5 | 12.5 | 12.5 | 15.6 | 15.6 |
| Intermediate regime[b] | 76.7 | 66.7 | 64.5 | 75.0 | 68.8 | 81.3 | 78.1 | 56.3 | 53.1 | 40.6 | 37.5 | 34.4 |
| Of which: soft pegs[c] | 63.3 | 53.3 | 51.6 | 62.5 | 53.1 | 59.4 | 62.5 | 50.0 | 46.9 | 34.4 | 28.1 | 25.0 |
| Floating regimes[d] | 16.7 | 23.3 | 25.8 | 15.6 | 21.9 | 9.4 | 12.5 | 31.3 | 34.4 | 46.9 | 46.9 | 50.0 |
| Total | 100.0 | 100.0 | 100.0 | 100.0 | 100.0 | 100.0 | 100.0 | 100.0 | 100.0 | 100.0 | 100.0 | 100.0 |

Notes:
[a] Comprises arrangements with another currency as legal tender (i.e., dollarization), currency unions, and currency boards.
[b] Comprises soft pegs plus tightly managed floating regimes.
[c] Comprises conventional fixed pegs vis-à-vis a single currency or a basket, horizontal bands, and crawling pegs and crawling bands.
[d] Comprises independently floating regimes and managed floating with no predetermined exchange rate path, excluding tightly managed floats.
[e] Includes 32 countries and territories: Argentina, Brazil, Bulgaria, Chile, China, Colombia, Czech Republic, Ecuador, Egypt, Hong Kong, SAR, Hungary, India, Indonesia, Israel, Jordan, Korea, Malaysia, Mexico, Morocco, Nigeria, Pakistan, Panama, Peru, Philippines, Poland, Russia, Singapore, South Africa, Sri Lanka, Thailand, Turkey, and República Bolivariana de Venezuela.

4

# 3 SHORTCOMINGS OF THE PRESENT INTERNATIONAL MONETARY SYSTEM

The present international monetary system does, however, face some important shortcomings. These are

1. the large volatility of exchange rates,
2. the wide and persistent misalignments of exchange rates and huge trade imbalances,
3. the failure to promote greater coordination of economic policies among the leading economic areas, and
4. the inability to prevent international financial crises or to adequately deal with them when they do arise.

Let us briefly examine each of these shortcomings.

There is little disagreement that exchange rates have exhibited large volatility since the establishment of the present managed exchange rate system. There is also no question that large exchange rate volatility, by adding to transaction costs, has affected the volume and pattern of international trade. These costs, however, are not very large and are not greater than those faced by firms in many other markets, as in the metal and agricultural sectors (IMF, 2004). Firms engaged in international trade also seem to have learned how to deal with volatility by pursuing hedging and diversification strategies quickly and at little cost. The IMF (1984a, 2004) concluded that exchange rate volatility did not seem to have had a significantly adverse effect on international trade. Measures could, of course, be devised to reduce exchange rate volatility, but the costs of these measures would in all likelihood not justify the benefits resulting from them.

Much more serious and damaging to the flow of international trade and investments than excessive exchange rate volatility are the wide and persistent exchange rate misalignments. These refer to the departure of exchange rates from their long-run, competitive equilibrium levels. An overvalued currency has the effect of an export tax and an import subsidy on the nation and, as such, it reduces the international competitiveness of the nation and distorts the pattern of specialization, trade, and payments. A significant exchange rate misalignment that persists for years could not possibly be hedged away (as can the risks arising from exchange rate volatility) and can impose significant real costs on the economy in the form of unemployment, idle capacity, bankruptcy, and protectionist legislation. Indeed, currency misalignments can be regarded as the most serious problem facing the present international monetary system.

The most notorious example of exchange rate misalignment was the overvaluation of the US dollar during the 1980s. According to the Board of Governors of the US Federal Reserve System, from 1980 to its peak in February 1985, the dollar appreciated by about 40 percent on a trade-weighted basis against the currency of the 10 largest industrial countries. This resulted in the huge trade deficit of the United States and equally large combined trade surplus of Japan and Germany. It also resulted in increasing calls for and actual trade protectionism in the United States. The Council of Economic Advisors (1986, 1987) estimated that the 1985 US trade deficit was $60 to $70 billion greater (about twice as large) than it would have been had the dollar remained at its 1980 level, and that this deficit cost about two million jobs in the United States. Despite the fact that by the end of 1988 the international value of the dollar was slightly below its 1980–1981 level (so that all of its overvaluation had been eliminated), large global trade imbalances remained and did not show signs of declining rapidly. Economists have borrowed the term 'hysteresis' from the field of physics to characterize the failure of trade balances to return to their original equilibrium once exchange rate misalignments have been corrected.

More recent major misalignments of the dollar have occurred since the mid-1990s. This is evidenced by the fact that the euro was worth $1.17 at its debut on January 1, 1999, fell to a low of $0.85 in June 2001, rose to a high of $1.36 in December 2004 and it was $1.30 in February 2005. Similarly, the dollar was worth 83.7 yen in April 1995, rose to a high of 144.7 yen in August 1998, fell to 105 yen in January 2000, then rose to 134 yen in February 2002, before falling to 103 yen in January 2005 (see Figures 1.2 and 1.3). Clearly, whatever the equilibrium exchange rate, such wild fluctuations of the dollar exchange rate imply major exchange rate misalignments between the dollar and the euro, on the one hand, and the dollar and the yen, on the other, over the past six to ten years. For example, the dollar was estimated to be overvalued by about 20-25 percent with respect to the euro in the summer of 2001 and by 15–20 percent with respect to the yen in the summer of 2004. Furthermore, the sharp growth in the US trade deficit with China from $33.7 in 1995 to $124.1 in 2003 is a reflection of a major structural imbalance between the two countries. There is, of course, no theory that postulates that trade must be balanced bilaterally, but such huge and rapidly growing US trade deficits with respect to East Asia (China, Hong Kong, Taiwan, Korea, Malaysia, Singapore), which totaled $224 billion out of the total US trade deficit of $549 billion in 2003, is proof that the dollar is grossly overvalued with respect to East Asian currencies.

The third shortcoming of the present international monetary system is that it failed to promote greater coordination of macroeconomic policies among

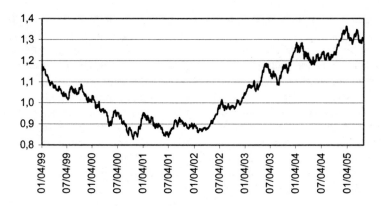

*Figure 1.2    Daily exchange rate of USD/Euro*

*Source:* Federal Reserve Statistical Release – Foreign Exchange Rates Historical Data.

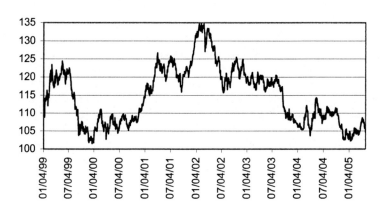

*Figure 1.3    Daily exchange rate of Yen/USD*

*Source:* Federal Reserve Statistical Release – Foreign Exchange Rates Historical Data.

the leading industrial countries. To a large extent this was due to their very different inflation-unemployment tradeoffs in the major economies. Policy coordination under the present system has taken place only occasionally and has been very limited in scope. One such episode was in 1978 when Germany agreed to serve as 'locomotive' to stimulate growth in the world economy. This experiment came to an abrupt end, however, when Germany, fearing a resurgence of inflation, backtracked. Another episode of limited policy coordination was the Plaza Agreement of September 1985, under which the G-5 countries (United States, Japan, Germany, United Kingdom, and France) intervened in foreign exchange markets to induce a gradual depreciation or soft landing of the dollar in eliminating its large overvaluation. Successful international policy coordination can also be credited for greatly limiting the damage from the 1987 world stock market crash, for preventing the 1994–1995 Mexican crisis from spreading to or having a lasting damaging effect on other emerging markets, and for avoiding an economic crisis as a result of the terrorist attack of September 11, 2001 in the United States. Although important and mostly successful, these instances of international macroeconomic policy coordination were sporadic and limited in scope rather than continuous and institutionalized.

Finally, the present international monetary system has been unable to prevent international financial crises, such as the one that hit Mexico in 1994–5, South-East Asian emerging economies in 1997–8, Russia in summer 1998, Brazil at the beginning of 1999, and Argentina and Turkey in 2000–2002. An international financial system that is prone to frequent and deep international financial crises and that require immediate and massive financial resources to prevent its spreading to other nations is certainly not a very good system. The challenge is how to prevent or minimize the number and depth of financial crises and how to resolve those that do occur without falling into the moral hazard trap. This refers to the situation where investors go after very high returns while disregarding risks in investing in emerging markets, convinced that the IMF will bail them out in case of a financial crisis – thus making returns private and losses public.

A number of measures have been proposed and some steps have already been taken to avoid or minimize such crises in the future, thus greatly strengthening the architecture of the present international monetary system and improving its functioning. These include:

1.  increasing transparency in international monetary relations,
2.  strengthening banking and financial systems,
3.  promoting greater private sector involvement, and
4.  providing adequate financial resources to emerging markets to prevent them from being affected by financial crises elsewhere (i.e., to avoid contagion – see IMF, 2004; Salvatore, 1998, 1999; Task Force Report, 1999; Eichengreen, 1999, 2003; Reagle and Salvatore, 2000; Fisher, 2003).

Fully implementing the above measures would go a long way toward reducing the occurrence of financial crises and limiting their contagion when they do occur. In the final analysis, however, we must recognize that some international financial instability and crisis may be the inevitable result of liberalized financial markets and the cost that industrial and emerging market economies need to pay for the benefits that they both receive from liberalized financial markets.

Of the four shortcomings of the present international monetary system, the most serious is the large and persistent misalignments among the world's major currencies. Resolving this problem will also help minimize the occurrence and the gravity of future financial crises, reduce excessive exchange rate volatility, and even reduce the need for international policy coordination. But, as discussed in the next section, eliminating exchange rate misalignments cannot be accomplished by the adoption of any of the proposals that have been advanced for reforming the present international monetary system, but it requires correction of the structural imbalances that exists in the major economies today (discussed in Section 5).

## 4 PROPOSALS FOR IMPROVING THE FUNCTIONING OF THE INTERNATIONAL MONETARY SYSTEM

Several proposals have been advanced to reduce exchange rate volatility and avoid large exchange rate misalignments as well as to deal with increased international financial instability. One proposal first advanced by Williamson (1986) is based on the establishment of *target zones*. Under such a system, the leading industrial nations estimate the equilibrium exchange rate and agree on the range of allowed fluctuation. Williamson suggests a band of allowed fluctuation of 10 percent above and below the equilibrium exchange rate. The exchange rate is determined by the forces of demand and supply within the allowed band of fluctuation and prevented from moving outside the target zones by official intervention in foreign exchange markets. The target zones would be soft, however, and would be changed when the underlying equilibrium exchange rate moves outside of or near the boundaries of the target zone. Although not made explicit, the leading industrial nations agreed on some such 'soft' target or 'reference zones' for the exchange rate between the dollar and the yen and between the dollar and the German mark in the Louvre Accord of February 1987 (but with the allowed band of fluctuation much smaller than the 10 percent above and below the par value advocated by Williamson). During the early 1990s, however, this tacit agreement was abandoned in the face of strong market pressure, which saw the dollar depreciating heavily with respect to the mark and the yen.

Critics of target zones believe that target zones embody the worst characteristics of fixed and flexible exchange rate systems. As in the case of flexible rates, target zones allow substantial fluctuation and volatility in exchange rates and can be inflationary. As in the case of fixed exchange rates, target zones can only be defended by official interventions in foreign exchange markets, thus reducing the monetary autonomy of the nation. In response to this criticism, Miller and Williamson (1988) extended their blueprint to require substantial policy coordination on the part of the leading industrial nations so as to reduce the need for intervention in foreign exchange markets to keep exchange rates within the target zones (Williamson seems, however, to have since moved away from this extension).

Other proposals for reforming the present international monetary system are based exclusively on extensive *policy coordination among the leading countries*. Two of the most discussed proposals are the ones advanced by McKinnon (1988) and Mundell (2000). In McKinnon's proposal, the United States, Japan, and Germany would fix the exchange rate among their currencies at their equilibrium level (determined by purchasing-power parity (PPP)) and then closely coordinate their monetary policies to keep exchange rates fixed. A tendency for the dollar to depreciate vis-à-vis the yen would signal that the United States should reduce the growth rate of its money supply, while Japan should increase it. The net overall increase in the money supply of these three countries would then be expanded at a rate consistent with the non-inflationary expansion of the world economy. Mundell envisions that with even greater inflation convergence, a monetary union among the dollar, euro and yen areas, and eventually a single world currency, could be established.

Another proposal advocated by the IMF Interim Committee (1996) was based on the development of objective indicators of economic performance to signal the type of coordinated macro policies for nations to follow, under the supervision of the Fund, in order to keep the world economy growing along a sustainable non-inflationary path. These objective indicators were the growth of GNP, inflation, unemployment, trade balance, growth of the money supply, fiscal balance, exchange rates, interest rates, and international reserves. A rise or fall in these objective indicators in a nation would signal, respectively, the need for restrictive or expansionary policies for the nation. Stability of the index for the world as a whole would be the anchor for non-inflationary world expansion. This proposal for reforming the international monetary system, which was pushed by the US Treasury in the mid–1980s, was, however, short–lived.

This type of close macroeconomic policy coordination is virtually impossible under present conditions, however. For example, during the 1980s and 1990s, and again since 2003, the United States seem unable or unwilling to reduce its huge budget deficit substantially and rapidly, the EMU has been unwilling to stimulate its economy sufficiently even though it faced a high rate of unemployment, Japan has been very reluctant to dismantle its protectionistic policies to allow much more imports from the United States so as to help correct the huge trade imbalance between the two nations, and so has China more recently. As long as these nations have different inflation-unemployment tradeoffs, effective and substantial macroeconomic policy coordination is practically impossible. In fact, these nations consider the ability to choose different inflation-unemployment tradeoffs to be an important advantage of the present international monetary system over the previous Bretton Woods system.

There are also other more practical obstacles to successful and effective international macroeconomic policy coordination. One is the lack of consensus about the functioning of the international monetary system. For example, the United States may believe that a monetary expansion would lead to an expansion of output and employment, while the EMU may believe that it will result primarily in inflation. Another obstacle arises from the lack of agreement on the precise policy mix required. This results from the fact that different macroeconometric models give widely different results as to the effect of a given fiscal expansion. There is then the problem of how to distribute the gains from successful policy coordination among the participants and how to spread the cost of negotiating and policing agreements. Empirical research reported by Frankel and Rockett (1988), Frenkel et al., (1991) and McKibbin (1997) indicate that nations gain from international policy coordination about three-quarters of the time but that the welfare gains from coordination, when they occur, are not very large.

Another class of proposals for reforming the architecture of the present international monetary system is based on the premise that huge international capital flows in today's highly integrated international capital markets are the primary cause of exchange rate instability and global imbalances afflicting the world economy. These proposals are, therefore, based on *restricting international speculative capital flows*. Tobin (1978, 1996) proposed to accomplish this with a flat transaction tax, which, therefore, becomes progressively higher the shorter the duration of the transaction, in order 'to put some sand in the wheels of international finance'. Dornbusch and Frankel (1987) would instead have reduced financial capital flows internationally with dual exchange rates - a less flexible one for trade transactions and a more flexible one for purely financial transactions not related to international trade and investments. By restricting international 'hot' money flows through capital market segmentation or the decoupling of asset markets, Tobin and Dornbusch and Frankel believed that the international financial system could be made to operate much more smoothly and without any need for close policy coordination by the leading industrial countries – which they regarded as neither feasible nor useful.

Critics of these proposals, however, point out that it is next to impossible to separate 'non–productive' or speculative capital flows from 'productive' or non-speculative ones related to international trade and investments (Dornbusch and Frankel subsequently moved away from their proposal). We might add that capital is fungible, so that evasion of such a transaction tax or more volatile exchange rates would greatly limit these efforts. Chile, among developing nations, has experimented with restricting speculative capital flows throughout most of the 1990s, but there are some questions as to how successful such a policy was (see Edwards, 2000). Finally, there is Mundell's (2000) utopian *single world currency proposal*. With a single world currency, of course, there would be no balance of payments or exchange rate problems. But nations would have no control over their money supply and be unable to conduct any type of national monetary stabilization policy. This would certainly be unacceptable to the United States, the EMU, Japan and most other large nations. In short, having a single world currency, as advocated by Mundell, would be like 'throwing away the baby with the bath water'.

It is clear that none of the proposed reforms of the present international monetary system discussed above or by others (see IMF 1984b, 1987; Kenen, 2001; Eichengreen, 1999; Bretton Woods Commission, 1994; Mussa, 1995; Fratianni et al., 1997; Frankel, 1999; Clarida, 2000; Salvatore 2000a, b; IMF, 2004) would eliminate currency misalignments among the currencies of the leading economic areas and the serious problems that they create. Furthermore, while misaligned exchange rates can be regarded as the immediate cause of prevailing global trade imbalances, they are themselves the result of internal structural disequilibria in the leading economic areas (United States, EMU, Japan, and China). It is these structural disequilibria, and not exchange rate misalignments themselves, that are the fundamental cause of the huge global trade imbalances that exist in the world today, and it is these structural disequilibria that must be corrected to avoid currency misalignments in the future and improve the functioning of the present international monetary system.

## 5   STRUCTURAL IMBALANCES AND CURRENCY MISALIGNMENTS

Tables 1.1–1.3 show the structural disequilibria facing the United States, the Euro Area and Japan, and it is these that are the fundamental causes of the large trade imbalances and currency misalignments between the dollar, on the one hand, and the euro, the yen, and the Chinese yuan, on the other, which represent the most serious shortcoming and problem with the functioning of the present international monetary system.

From Table 1.2, we see that the US trade deficit has increased sharply over the past decade and has reached the unsustainable level of $549.3 billion, or 5 percent of the GDP, in the United States in 2003. These huge and rapidly increasing trade deficits are the result of inadequate savings in the United States and its much more rapid growth relative to the Euro Area and Japan over the past decade. Table 1.3 shows that the savings rate in the United States declined by four percentage points (from 17 percent to 13 percent of GDP) from 1995 to 2003, while the investment rate remained more or less unchanged (at about 18.5 percent of GDP) from the beginning to the end of the period considered, so that US net borrowing from abroad was equal to 5.4 of its GDP in 2003. This led to a grossly overvalued dollar exchange rate and to the large and unsustainable trade deficit (the counterpart of the net borrowing from abroad) of the United States.

From Table 1.2, we see that more than half of the US trade deficit is now with China and the other emerging markets of East Asia and Japan, and it is the currencies of these countries or areas that exhibit large undervaluation with respect to the US dollar. After being undervalued by as much as 20–25 percent in the summer of 2001, the euro appreciated with respect to the US dollar and now, after reaching a value of about $1.30 in January 2005, can be regarded as overvalued by 10-15 percent. The US trade deficit with the Euro Area can now be regarded as due primarily to inadequate savings in the United States and anemic growth in the Euro Area (see Table 1.3). The appreciation of the euro with respect to the dollar since the beginning of 2002 is now putting pressure on Euro Area exports to the United States and to the emerging markets of East Asia, whose currencies also depreciated with respect to the dollar (to which they remain mostly pegged). This is bad news for the Euro Area, whose growth has been anemic during the past decade and whose exports may come under further pressure during 2005 and 2006 as a result of the lagged and J-curve effects of the recent euro appreciation.

Although savings and investment are in near balance in the Euro Area (see Table 1.3), it faces serious structural problems, which have kept its growth rate well below its potential and much lower than the growth rate in the United States since 1995 (see Table 1.4). The restructuring that has taken place in the Euro Area during the past decade has clearly been inadequate and its economy, especially its labor market, remains excessively rigid. In addition, the Euro Area has not pursued the creation of a 'new economy' sufficiently aggressively and it has thus not been able to harvest as much benefits as the United States has from it. From 1995 to 2003, the average annual growth rate was 2.1 for the real GDP and 0.9 percent for labor

*Table 1.2    Trade imbalances of leading industrial countries and areas (in billions of US dollars)*

| Country/Area | 1995 | 1996 | 1997 | 1998 | 1999 | 2000 | 2001 | 2002 | 2003 |
|---|---|---|---|---|---|---|---|---|---|
| United States | -174.2 | -191.0 | -198.1 | -246.7 | .346.0 | -452.4 | -427.2 | -482.9 | -549.4 |
| US with respect to | | | | | | | | | |
| Western Europe | -15.2 | -24.7 | -23.6 | -34.9 | -52.1 | -64.7 | -69.6 | -92.5 | -104.8 |
| Japan | -59.9 | -48.7 | -57.3 | -65.4 | -74.8 | -83.0 | -70.6 | -71.8 | -67.7 |
| East Asia | -64.1 | -69.4 | -84.8 | -117.9 | -137.4 | -163.6 | -183.6 | -178.0 | -200.1 |
| China | -33.8 | -39.6 | -49.7 | -57.0 | -68.7 | -83.9 | -83.2 | -103.2 | -124.0 |
| Euro Area | - | - | - | - | 63.7 | 13.3 | 65.1 | 139.8 | 142.2 |
| Japan | 131.8 | 93.6 | 101.6 | 122.4 | 123.3 | 116.7 | 70.2 | 93.8 | 106.4 |

*Source:* Survey of Current Business and IMF: IFS, various issues.

*Table 1.3    Trade imbalances of leading industrial countries and areas (in billions of US dollars)*

| Country/Area | 1995 | 1996 | 1997 | 1998 | 1999 | 2000 | 2001 | 2002 | 2003 |
|---|---|---|---|---|---|---|---|---|---|
| United States | | | | | | | | | |
| Savings | 17.0 | 17.3 | 18.1 | 18.3 | 18.1 | 18.0 | 16.4 | 14.7 | 13.0 |
| Investment | 18.7 | 19.1 | 19.9 | 20.3 | 20.6 | 20.8 | 19.1 | 18.4 | 18.4 |
| Net lending | -1.7 | -1.8 | -1.8 | -2.0 | -2.6 | -2.7 | -2.6 | -3.7 | -5.4 |
| Euro Area | | | | | | | | | |
| Savings | 20.7 | 20.5 | 21.0 | 21.7 | 21.8 | 21.8 | 21.4 | 21.3 | 20.2 |
| Investment | 20.2 | 19.6 | 19.7 | 21.0 | 21.4 | 22.0 | 21.0 | 20.0 | 19.9 |
| Net lending | 0.5 | 0.9 | 1.3 | 0.7 | 0.4 | -0.2 | 0.4 | 1.3 | 0.3 |
| Japan | | | | | | | | | |
| Savings | 30.2 | 30.9 | 29.8 | 29.8 | 28.6 | 28.8 | 27.8 | 26.7 | 27.1 |
| Investment | 28.2 | 29.2 | 28.7 | 26.8 | 26.0 | 26.3 | 25.7 | 23.9 | 24.0 |
| Net lending | 2.0 | 1.4 | 2.2 | 3.0 | 2.5 | 2.5 | 2.1 | 2.8 | 3.1 |

*Source:* IMF, World Economic Outlook, various issues.

productivity in the Euro Area, as compared with 3.2 percent and 2.2 percent, respectively, in the United States. This has kept the rate of unemployment much higher in the Euro Area than in the United States over the past decade (see Table 1.4).

Thus, the fundamental disequilibrium facing the Euro Area is inadequate restructuring of its economy, which dampens the growth of labor productivity and GDP, and keeps its unemployment rate much too high. The appropriate long-term policy for the Euro Area is, thus, to speed up the restructuring of its economy, liberalize its labor markets more rapidly, and encourage a faster adoption and spread of the new ICT (information and communications technology). Labor, however, has generally resisted deep reforms and it has so far been successful in preventing European governments from introducing the necessary reforms. This may be understandable – Europe is justifyingly proud of its high wages and its social protection achievements and seems unwilling to compromise them. It must also be kept in mind that it is difficult to introduce reforms and restructure the labor market when the economy is growing slowly. Furthermore, the benefits of restructuring generally come only over time, while most of the costs are paid upfront. The longer the restructuring is delayed, however, the more the Euro Area falls behind the United States in real per capita income. In fact, after rapidly reducing the gap in PPP real per capita income from less that 40 percent in 1950 to 75 percent in the early 1970s, the Euro Area average per capita income slipped back to 66 percent of US income in 2003.

Since Europe's fundamental problem is mostly structural rather than cyclical in nature, a more expansionary monetary policy (as many advocate) on the part of the European Central Bank (ECB) would provide only a limited stimulus to growth in the Euro Area. Furthermore, with the precise mandate to target only inflation, the statutes of the ECB would have to be changed to permit it to use monetary policy to also pursue the goals of growth and employment (as the FED does), and this is by no means easy to do because it requires a change in the Maastricht Treaty itself.

The problem in Japan is also structural and mostly of an internal nature, thus requiring, for the most part, domestic policies to correct. Specifically, Japan has been in a serious financial and economic crisis for the entire past decade and faces serious structural imbalances. Domestic deflation rather than international disturbances is the primary cause of the large undervaluation of the yen with respect to the dollar and thus of the large Japanese trade surplus vis-à-vis the United States. Japan simply saves too much and consumes and invests domestically too little (see Table 1.3). Japan has followed three policies to overcome its deflationary problem. It has carried out a very powerful expansionary monetary policy, which has kept nominal interest rates at a practically zero level (with real rates negative because of domestic deflation). It has adopted an equally powerful expansionary fiscal policy (with an average annual budget deficit of 6.2 percent of GDP from 1995 to 2003 – and 7.4 percent from 2000 to 2003 – and a public debt equal to 157.3 percent of GDP in 2003). Finally, Japan has intervened in foreign exchange markets in a massive way to prevent a further yen appreciation, so as not to discourage its exports and the growth of the economy. In fact, Japan foreign exchange dollar reserves increased from $116 billion in 1995 to $439 billion at the end of 2003. Yet, until 2003,

Japanese growth has remained very subdued in spite of the sharp increase in its exports to China.

*Table 1.4      Unemployment rate and growth of real GDP and labor productivity*

| Country/Area | 1995 | 1996 | 1997 | 1998 | 1999 | 2000 | 2001 | 2002 | 2003 |
|---|---|---|---|---|---|---|---|---|---|
| United States | | | | | | | | | |
| Real GDP | 2.5 | 3.7 | 4.5 | 4.2 | 4.4 | 3.7 | 0.5 | 2.2 | 3.1 |
| Labor productivity | 0.3 | 2.0 | 2.4 | 2.1 | 2.8 | 2.2 | 0.7 | 3.9 | 3.4 |
| Unemployment rate | 5.6 | 5.4 | 4.9 | 4.5 | 4.2 | 4.0 | 4.8 | 5.8 | 6.0 |
| Euro Area | | | | | | | | | |
| Real GDP | 2.3 | 1.4 | 2.4 | 2.8 | 2.8 | 3.7 | 1.7 | 0.9 | 0.5 |
| Labor productivity | 1.8 | 1.0 | 1.7 | 0.8 | 0.8 | 1.4 | 0.1 | 0.5 | 0.4 |
| Unemployment rate | 10.5 | 10.7 | 10.8 | 10.2 | 9.4 | 8.4 | 8.0 | 8.4 | 8.8 |
| Japan | | | | | | | | | |
| Real GDP | 1.9 | 3.4 | 1.9 | -1.1 | 0.1 | 2.8 | 0.4 | -0.3 | 2.7 |
| Labor productivity | 1.7 | 2.9 | 0.9 | -0.8 | 0.6 | 3.2 | 0.8 | 0.9 | 3.4 |
| Unemployment rate | 3.2 | 3.4 | 3.4 | 4.1 | 4.7 | 4.7 | 5.0 | 5.4 | 5.3 |

*Source:* OECD, *Economic Outlook*, June 2004.

Clearly, Japan's fundamental disequilibrium is internal rather than external. It is due to Japan's excessive savings and/or inadequate domestic investments and consumption. Only by stimulating domestic investments and consumption can Japan eliminate its structural problem. Indeed, if anything, Japan should open up its economy more widely to imports and allow the yen to appreciate further with respect to the dollar, thus eliminating its remaining overvaluation (now estimated to be in the range of 10-15 percent) with respect to the US dollar. It is true that it is not easy to get the Japanese to save less and spend more, and for Japanese firms to increase the rate of domestic investments (you can bring the horse to the water but you cannot force it to drink), but with the problem basically internal, the appropriate solution must also be primarily internal. Increasing domestic investments would also deal with the problem created by the expected higher future costs of providing for Japan's rapidly aging population.

The remaining serious structural imbalance in the world economy today arises from the overvaluation of the dollar with respect to the Chinese yuan, now estimated to be in the 30-40 percent range. This is the cause of the huge and rapidly growing and unsustainable US trade deficit with China (see Table 1.2). China has maintained its currency pegged at 8.3 yuan to the dollar since 1994 despite skyrocketing trade surpluses with the United States. It has done so by massive official purchases of US dollars, which increased its official reserves from $70 billion in 1995 to over $400 billion at the end of 2003 (Eichengreen, 2004). To render the US trade deficit with China more manageable, China should revalue its currency by 30-40 percent. This would also be useful to reduce China's explosive growth of over 8.5 percent per year over the past decade and contain its inflationary pressures. It would also allow the other emerging markets of East Asia (Hong Kong, Korea, Malaysia, Singapore, and Taiwan) to similarly revalue their currencies vis-à-vis the US dollar – something that they have been unwilling to do as long as China does not revalue its currency first because of strong competitive pressures from China. A yuan revaluation would also (and for the same reason) probably induce Japan to allow the yen to appreciate further. Thus, a revaluation of the yuan is crucial to eliminate a major structural imbalance in the world economy and improve the functioning of the present international monetary system.

# 6   CONCLUSIONS

Since the misalignment problem among the world's leading currencies is primarily the result of internal structural imbalances in the United States, the Euro Area, Japan and China, the medium- and long-run solution to the problem must be sought internally in these economies or areas. The most serious problem facing the United States is grossly inadequate domestic savings in the face of rapid domestic growth. The rapid growth of the United States during the past decade was based on a more flexible economic structure and the more widespread use and adoption of the information technology (the new economy) than in the Euro Area and Japan. This led to huge capital inflows to the United States, an overvalued exchange rate, and huge and growing trade deficits. The medium- and long-run solution to this problem is for the United States to adopt policies to stimulate domestic savings (BIS, 2004). This is not easy to do because US consumers and firms have become addicted to living with increasing levels of debt and it is difficult to break the habit. An increase in the US savings rate would reduce the need for capital inflows, reduce or eliminate the dollar misalignment and reduce its trade deficit to a sustainable level.

Since this will take time (years) to achieve and, in any event, the trade deficit responds with a time lag that can be as long as two years or more to exchange rate changes, there is a need for short- to medium-term policies to bridge the gap. It is here that the proposals to reform the present international monetary system can be most useful. These could include some macroeconomic policy coordination, exchange rate changes, and intervention in foreign exchange markets on the part of the United States, the Euro Area, and Japan in order to steer the exchange rates among their currencies toward their long-run equilibrium level. Although extensive formal macroeconomic policy coordination among the major economies is almost impossible (for the reasons discussed above), some informal and weaker form of macroeconomic policy coordination (of the type successfully applied, for example, after the stock market collapse of 1987) together with some coordinated intervention in foreign exchange markets (as needed) should be possible. The IMF should also fulfill its obligation to enforce Article IV, Section 1 (Paragraph iii) that stipulates that each member shall 'avoid manipulating exchange rates ... in order to prevent balance of payments adjustment or to gain unfair competitive advantage over other members' and demand (for example, through its annual review of member countries) that the United States, the Euro Area, Japan, and China take stronger measures to correct their structural disequilibria as soon as possible.

## REFERENCES

BIS (2004), *Annual Report*, June.
Bretton Woods Commission (1994), *Bretton Woods: Looking to the Future*, Washington, DC: Bretton Woods Commission.
Clarida, Richard H. (2000), 'G3 Exchange Rate Relationships: A Recap of the Record and a Review of Proposals for Change', *NBER Working Paper*, No. 7434.
Council of Economic Advisors (1986), *Economic Report of the President*, Washington, DC: Government Printing Office.
Council of Economic Advisors (1987), *Economic Report of the President*, Washington, DC: Government Printing Office.
Dornbusch, Rudiger and Jeffrey A. Frankel (1987), 'The Flexible Exchange Rate System: Experience and Alternatives', *NBER Working Paper*, No. 2464.
Edwards, Sebastian (2000), 'Interest Rates, Contagion and Capital Controls', *NBER Working Paper*, No. 7801.
Eichengreen, Barry (1999), *Toward a New International Financial Architecture*, Washington, DC: Institute for International Economics.
Eichengreen, Barry (2003), 'Restructuring Sovereign Debt', *Journal of Economic Perspectives*, **17** (4), 75–98.
Fisher, Stanley (2003), 'Financial Crises and Reform of the International Financial System', *Review of World Economics*, **1**, 1–37.
Frankel, Jeffrey A. and Katharine Rockett (1988), 'International Macroeconomic Policy Coordination When Policy Makers Do Not Agree on the Model', *American Economic Review*, **78** (3), 318–340.
Fratianni, Michele U., Dominick Salvatore, and Jurgen von Hagen (eds) (1997), *Handbook of Macroeconomic Policies in Open Economies*, Westport CT: Greenwood Press.
Frenkel, Jacob A., Morris Goldstein, and Paul R. Masson (1991), *Characteristics of a Successful Exchange Rate System*, *IMF Occasional Paper*, No. 82.
IMF (1984a), *Exchange Rate Volatility and World Trade*, Washington, DC: IMF.

IMF (1984b), 'The Exchange Rate System: Lessons of the Past and Options for the Future', *IMF Occasional Paper*, No. 30.

IMF (1987), 'Strengthening the International Monetary System', *IMF Occasional Paper*, No. 50.

IMF (1996), *Interim Committee Report*, Washington, DC: IMF.

IMF (2004), 'Evolution and Performance of Exchange Rate Regimes', *IMF Occasional Paper*, No. 229.

Kenen, Peter B. (2001), *The International Financial Architecture*, Washington, DC: Institute for International Economics.

McKibbin, Warwick J. (1997), 'Empirical Evidence on International Economic Policy Coordination', in M. Fratianni, D. Salvatore, and J. von Hagen (eds) (1997), *Handbook of Macroeconomic Policies in Open Economies*, Westport, CT: Greenwood Press, 148–176.

McKinnon, Ronald I. (1988), 'Monetary and Exchange Rate Policies for International Financial Stability: A Proposal', *Journal of Economic Perspectives*, **2** (1), 83–103.

Miller, Marcus H. and John Williamson (1988), *Targets and Indicators: A Blueprint for the International Coordination of Economic Policy*, Washington, DC: Institute for International Economics.

Mundell, Robert (2000), 'A Reconsideration of the Twentieth Century', *American Economic Review*, **90** (3), 327–340.

Mussa, Michael (1995), 'The Evolving International Monetary System and Prospects for Monetary Reform', *Journal of Policy Modeling*, **17** (5), 493–512.

Reagle, Derrick and Dominick Salvatore (2000), 'Forecasting Financial Crises in Emerging Market Economies', *Open Economies Review*, **11** (3), 247–259.

Salvatore, Dominick (1994), 'The International Monetary System: Past, Present, and Future', *Fordham Law Review*, May, 1975–1988.

Salvatore, Dominick (1998), 'International Capital Flows, Current Account Deficits and Financial Crises in Emerging Market Economies', *International Trade Journal*, Spring, 5–22.

Salvatore, Dominick (1999), 'Could the Financial Crisis in East Asia Have Been Predicted?', *Journal of Policy Modeling*, **21** (3), 341–348.

Salvatore, Dominick (ed.) (2000a), *The Euro, the Dollar, and the International Monetary System*, Special Issue of the *Journal of Policy Modeling*, **22** (3), 275-279.

Salvatore, Dominick (2000b), 'The Present International Monetary System: Problems, Complications, Reforms', *Open Economies Review*, **11** (1), 133–148.

Task Force Report (1999), *Safeguarding Prosperity in a Global Financial System – The Future of International Financial Architecture*, Washington, DC: Institute for International Economics.

Tobin, James (1978), 'A Proposal for International Monetary Reform', *Eastern Economic Journal*, July/October, 153–159.

Tobin, James (1996), 'A Currency Transaction Tax, Why and How', *Open Economies Review*, **7** (1), 493–500.

Williamson, John (1986), 'Target Zones and the Management of the Dollar', *Brookings Papers on Economic Activity*, **1**, 165–174.

# 2. Free Trade and Poverty

## Fernando A. Noriega-Ureña

## 1 INTRODUCTION

During the past twenty years underdeveloped economies have enforced their export leading activities, but in terms of product per capita and income distribution the results of these efforts were in contrast to the positive effects expected by the neoclassical tradition. For underdeveloped countries free trade and free capital mobility did not produce the theoretically expected results. The increase in poverty and inequality clearly showed that free trade is not the royal avenue to well-being. On the contrary, free trade seems to be the reason for a significant increase in poverty and inequality.

To show and analyze some basic features of underdeveloped countries vis-à-vis the rest of the world, we construct a model of a small, technologically weak and open economy. This economy is able to fix by itself the following three exogenous variables: the nominal wage, the nominal exchange rate and the money supply. A specific aim of the model is the explanation of mechanisms of how the exchange rate determines production, employment and prices levels, as well as distribution and poverty phenomena. The specific analytic environment corresponds to an export–oriented economy.

The model contains the following basic features of underdeveloped economies: Against the rest of the world they are considered to be small and price takers due to their production size. Their production is irrelevant for the formation prices in international markets. Their imports mainly consist of inputs and capital goods necessary for their production. This is a necessary implication of their technological weakness and their dependence on industrialized countries. Because they need inputs and capital goods produced by the rest of the world for their internal economic activity, their production is highly inelastic to exchange rate fluctuations. In contrast, their imports of consumption goods are highly elastic.

In order to find an alternative explanation for the observed results mentioned above, the model is based on the following assumptions:

1. Labor mobility between the domestic economy and the rest of the world is zero.[1]
2. The domestic economy is represented by two agents: a consumer and a producer; further by two non–durable products: the internal one and the imported one, and by two production factors necessary for any production: domestic labor force and import product.
3. In order to meet her needs any consumer demands both the domestic product and the import good. The same consumer is labor supplier in the domestic production process. There is a positive gross substitutability between the national and the imported product for consumption.
4. The producer demands the imported product as the only physical input that he transforms into the final domestic product. He also demands the labor supplied by the consumers, in order to organize the production process and to accomplish production itself. The producer supplies the final domestic product, not only for domestic consumption, but also for exports to the rest of the world.
5. The producer does not use its own product as an input.
6. There are no durable goods in the world economy, so that the domestic and the external economic processes take place in only one period.

## 2 THE MODEL

### 2.1 Accounting Features

Let the consumer behavior in the domestic economy be given by:

$$\max U = f(Q_c, Q_m, S) \quad \text{s.t.} \tag{2.1}$$

$$\Pi + WL_s = PQ_c + \varphi P_m Q_m \tag{2.2}$$

Here the preferences are represented by a well–behaved utility function $f(\bullet)$, and $Q_m$ refers to the product imported for internal consumption from the rest of the world; $P_m$ represents the price of the imported product, and $\varphi$ the nominal exchange rate expressed in terms of a number of domestic monetary units per monetary unit of the rest of the world. The other variables are: $Q_c$ is the domestic consumption of domestic product, $S = (\tau - T_o)$ is the demanded time for leisure, $P$ is the price of the domestic product, $W$ is the nominal wage, $L_s$ is the supplied time for labor, and $\Pi$ are the profits perceived by the consumers who own the domestic firms.

The firm's economic behavior is defined by the maximization of its profit rate, subject to a strictly concave production function (diminishing returns to scale) regarding $(L_d - L^*)$, so that:

$$\max (1 + \pi) = \frac{PQ_0}{(WL_d + \varphi P_m Q_{\min I})} \quad \text{s.t.} \quad (2.3)$$

$$Q_0 = g[(L_d - L^*), Q_{\min I}]; \quad g' > 0, g'' < 0 \quad (2.4)$$

In (2.3) and (2.4) $Q_{\min I}$ is the quantity of external products internally used as an input for production. The term $L^*$ represents the quantity of labor employed by the firm in order to organize all its processes. The bigger the number of contracts realized by the firm in order to employ labor and to sell the products, the higher $L^*$ will be. In other words, the size of $L^*$ always corresponds directly to the size of the internal product market.

It is necessary to state that $L^*$ neither will imply increasing return effects nor indivisibilities, since in the macroeconomic equilibrium of the model $L^*$ will be shown to be completely flexible. $L^*$ makes possible the profit rate maximization, ensuring economic meaningful results.

Once defined $Q_x = Q_s - Q_c$, being $Q_x$ the exported quantity of domestic products, and $Q_c$ the locally consumed domestic products, the balance of the internal economy is given by:

$$W(L_d - L_S) = PQ_x - \varphi P_m [Q_m + Q_{\min I}] \quad (2.5)$$

Equation (2.5) shows that the trade deficit has the same size like unemployment. The rest of the world then will have a surplus and a positive excess demand for labor. If there was limited labor mobility between the two economies, the economy with surplus would be confronted with immigration, and the deficit economy with emigration. However, following assumption (1), the deficit in (2.5) would not be solved completely by labor mobility. In this context it is nearly impossible for a small, open economy to solve its unemployment only by allowing the exchange rate to fluctuate freely until its international trade is balanced. As will be shown, the free flotation of the exchange rate would only influence the balance and employment in a transitory way, that is to say in the short period, because the deficit condition is a problem of structural transformation of its productive apparatus. The trade deficit is only the countable expression of the technological weakness of the local economy against the rest of the world. It is a problem that cannot be solved exclusively by the exchange rate.

Since the analyzed economy does not correspond to a general equilibrium system, $P_m$ is given by the rest of the world. The right expression of (2.5) is not a demand surplus in a Walrasian sense, derived from the difference between the demand and supply of the same product or service; it is the difference in value between exports and imports. The equality in (2.5) will depend on the magnitude of $\varphi$. It will be shown that the domestic economy consists of a domestic product market, a labor sector, a demand for the foreign product, and a monetary sector. As a consequence it will be possible to determine production, employment, distribution and prices, if the nominal wage $W$, nominal exchange rate $\varphi$ or money supply are predetermined by exogenous criteria. If money supply $M^s$ is fixed, $W$ and $\varphi$ are subject to the degrees of freedom.

## 2.2   Supply and Demand Functions

In our model we only need to know the fractions of income assigned to each of the two existing products because the consumer's maximization behavior consists in distributing his income between goods in an optimal way. So let $\gamma$ and $\zeta$ be two positive parameters representing the consumer's preferences, such that $1 > (\gamma + \zeta) > 0$. Considering that $S = (\tau - L_s)$ the optimum fractions of income the consumer assigns to $Q_c$, $Q_m$ and $S$, respectively, is given by:

$$(\Pi + W\tau) = \gamma(\Pi + W\tau) + \zeta(\Pi + W\tau) + (1 - \gamma - \zeta)(\Pi + W\tau) \qquad (2.6)$$

We obtain the following expressions, which correspond exactly with the results of a standard maximization exercise:

domestic demand for the internal product:

$$Q_c = \gamma\left(\frac{\Pi + W\tau}{P}\right) \qquad (2.7)$$

domestic demand for the external product:

$$Q_{cm} = \zeta\left(\frac{\Pi + W\tau}{\varphi P_m}\right) \qquad (2.8)$$

leisure demand:

$$S = (1 - \gamma - \zeta)\left(\frac{\Pi + W\tau}{W}\right) \tag{2.9}$$

labor supply:

$$L_s = (\gamma + \zeta)\tau - (1 - \gamma - \zeta)\left(\frac{\Pi}{W}\right) \tag{2.10}$$

Due to the differences between the traditional maximization problem and the one proposed here, the modeling of the firm's behavior requires a detailed procedure. Our maximization problem is defined as follows:

$$\max(1 + \pi) = \frac{PQ_0}{(WL_d + \varphi P_m Q_{\min t})} \quad \text{s.t.} \tag{2.3}$$

$$Q_s = (L_d - L^*)^\alpha Q_{\min t}^\beta \; ; 1 > \alpha + \beta > 0; \; \alpha,\beta \in \Re^+ \tag{2.11}$$

defined for every $(L_d - L^*) \geq 0$.

Considering the first order conditions, we obtain the marginal relationship of technical substitution (2.12), the sum of factors elasticities equal to one (2.13), and using the production function (2.14):

$$\frac{\alpha Q_{\min t}}{\beta(L_d - L^*)} = \frac{W}{\varphi P_m} \tag{2.12}$$

$$\alpha \frac{T_d}{(L_d - L^*)} + \beta = 1 \tag{2.13}$$

$$Q_s = (L_d - L^*)^\alpha Q_{\min t}^\beta \tag{2.14}$$

After solving this system, we obtain:

labor demand:

$$L_d = \left(\frac{1 - \beta}{1 - \alpha - \beta}\right)L^* \tag{2.15}$$

internal demand for the external product that will be used as input:

$$Q_{\min i} = \left(\frac{\beta}{1-\alpha-\beta}\right)\left(\frac{W}{\varphi P_m}\right)L^{\cdot}$$  (2.16)

domestic product supply:

$$Q_s = \frac{\alpha^{\alpha}\beta^{\beta}}{(1-\alpha-\beta)^{\alpha+\beta}}\left(\frac{W}{\varphi P_m}\right)^{\beta}(L^{\cdot})^{\alpha+\beta}$$  (2.17)

As can be shown in (2.15), the demand for labor by the firm is independent of the real wage and of any price. It is, therefore, demonstrated that firms do not demand labor as a function of real wages, but as a result of the size of its output market. This size is represented by $L^*$, which has to be solved by the macroeconomic solution of the model. It is also apparent that the demand of imported input as well as the product supply of domestic products depend on prices, although important differences exist regarding the traditional theory. This is also true for (2.16): Though there is an inverse relationship with the price, a price increase or a rise of the exchange rate will not necessarily bring down the quantity of the goods sold. It can be the case that the growth in the market of the domestic product (reflected in $L^*$) will increase the demand for the imported input though its price has risen.

In (2.17), the quantity produced by the firm is positively related with the real wage. The growth of real wages will cause the expansion of the product supplied. In effect it is substantially different from the results of neoclassical theory. According to neoclassical theory the firm increases its production when a decrease in real wages is observed. It implies that whenever the market is confronted with a contraction in demand, the firms are encouraged to produce more goods. This is in contradiction to the logics of our model, which could be called a TNLM model (Theory of Nonexistence of Labor Market model).

In contrast to the fact that labor supply depends on $W$ (according to (2.14)) it is shown in (2.15) that labor demand is independent of this variable. This implies again that the labor sector is not a 'market', as it is treated in traditional theory. As a consequence, $W$ (or ceteris paribus $W/P$) does not regulate the employment level, neither is it determined by the relationship between supply and demand of labor. The nominal wage $W$ serves as a distributive variable that is exogenously determined by negotiations. Therefore, the 'labor market' does not exist and cannot be part of the analytical structure explaining the operation of a capitalist economy without raising serious conceptual errors.

## 2.3  Monetary Sector

Our economy is characterized by the existence of domestic money and foreign currency. They are introduced through two channels: First, by the money supply generated by the central bank in order to cover the domestic transactions in national output. Second, the foreign currencies enter the economy through the firm's revenues for its exports. $M^s$ is given to the firms as a special credit by the central bank; the firm then pays to the consumers the wages and profits not only with the domestic money but also with the foreign currency, and also pays the imported goods to the rest of the world. Whereas domestic transactions can be settled with both domestic money and foreign currencies, the rest of the world only accepts the foreign currency. There are no earnings for the intermediation in the monetary exchange transactions.

The equilibrium in the monetary sector is permanent and instantaneous, and represented by the following equation:

$$M^d = M^s \qquad (2.18)$$

The money supply is identical to the value of the domestic transactions for the internal product:

$$M^s = PQ_c \qquad (2.19)$$

The balance equation of the monetary system has on the left side as sources domestic currency ($M^s$) and of foreign currency ($D_{iv}$), and on the right side the uses of these sources:

$$M^s + D_{iv} = PQ_c + \varphi P_m(Q_{cm} + Q_{mint}) \qquad (2.20)$$

The exports are the only channel to get foreign currency:

$$M^s + PQ_x = PQ_s \qquad (2.21)$$

## 2.4  Domestic Market of Internal Product

Starting from optimal plans and the conditions of the rest of the world economy we have to calculate the reduced forms of the functions above depending on the interaction between consumers and firms.

This market is determined by the domestic and foreign demand for and supply of the internal product. The demand surplus of this market is given by:

$$(Q_c + Q_x) - Q_s = 0 \tag{2.22}$$

The external demand for domestic product (exports function) is represented by the following expression:

$$Q_x = \psi\left(\frac{\varphi Y^*}{P}\right) \tag{2.23}$$

The term $Y^*$ in (2.23) represents the level of nominal income of the rest of the world economy; the price $P$ and the exchange rate are the same as in the previous functions. The parameter, $\psi$, $1 > \psi > 0$, is assumed to represent the preferences of the consumers of the rest of the world, and it allows to specify the fraction of income that consumers dedicate to the demand of the domestic product.

Replacing (2.7), (2.16), (2.17), (2.21) and (2.23) in (2.22), and solving for $L^*$, we arrive at:

$$L^* = (1 - \alpha - \beta)\left[\tau + \frac{\psi Y^* \varphi}{W} - \left(\frac{1-\gamma}{\gamma}\right)\frac{M^s}{W}\right] \tag{2.24}$$

This expression shows that $L^*$ is fully flexible and its magnitude is directly related to the domestic and external effective demand for the domestic product. This guarantees the permanent equilibrium in the product market. When there is a higher demand for the domestic product, $L^*$ will be much higher. The function (2.24) will always satisfy the function (2.22). This means that the firm will not produce more nor less than the market demands. When they produce more than demanded, they will realize losses, the same is true for the opposite case. Therefore, the permanent equilibrium in the market for the domestic product makes clear real firms' behavior. It must be said now that the permanent equilibrium in that market does not lead to full employment. As a matter of fact, the model is able to show a situation of positive unemployment and a simultaneous permanent equilibrium.

## 2.5 Price Level and Non-inflationary Character of Wages

Equation (2.24) is fundamental for the solution of all endogenous variables in the system of structural parameters (preferences, technology and the endowment $\tau$), and exogenous variables $W$ and $\varphi$, and of the predetermined $M^s$. Replacing (2.24) in (2.7) and inserting the result in (2.19), we obtain the following expression for the domestic price level:

$$P = \frac{W^\alpha (M^s + \psi Y^* \varphi)(\varphi P_m)^\beta}{(\alpha^\alpha \beta^\beta)\left[W\tau + \psi Y^* \varphi - \frac{1-\gamma}{\gamma} M^s\right]^{\alpha+\beta}} \qquad (2.25)$$

This function corresponds to the reduced form of $P$. It shows that while the demand for the internal product is higher than its supply, $P$ will be higher, too.

Concerning the relation between $P$ and $W$, it is inspired by the traditional theory a common assumption, that an increase in nominal wages causes inflation; as a consequence it is assumed that to control inflation the growth of nominal wages has to be avoided or kept below the expected inflation rate.[2] However, in our model, the wage $W$ is in general not inflationary. Only under very peculiar conditions a $W$ growth causes inflation, which reduces the relevance of the neoclassical tradition dramatically.

The following inequalities are the cornerstone of the main argument of the analysis:

$$\text{a) } \frac{\psi Y^* \varphi}{M^s} \le \frac{1-\gamma}{\gamma} \quad \text{or} \quad \text{b) } \frac{\psi Y^* \varphi}{M^s} > \frac{1-\gamma}{\gamma} \qquad (2.26)$$

The slope of equation (2.25) with $W$, $\varphi$ or $M^s$ as exogenous variables crucially depends on the expressions (2.26a) and (2.26b). Both expressions show on the left–hand side the proportion between the value of the foreign demand for the domestic product to the domestic demand for the domestic product. On the right–hand side the proportion between the fraction of consumers' income stemming from transactions in exports divided by the fraction of income stemming from transactions in the domestic product is defined. In the case of dominating domestic markets we will have (2.26a); on the other hand, if the foreign market dominates domestic transactions we will have (2.26b). It becomes obvious that the equality condition possible in (2.26a) only represents a trivial case that is not durable and of very limited importance in the context of our analysis.

The shape of (2.25) for a situation where a dominance of the domestic market can be observed makes clear, ceteris paribus, that the growth of wages will in general be deflationary. Whenever $W$ increases, keeping constant the nominal exchange rate and the money supply, $P$ will decrease. This implies, as shown in Figure 2.1, that W is not inflationary if the wage growth is not financed by the money supply but is a consequence of a redistributive decision from the firm:

Such a decision of the firm alters the structure of the demand; the domestic market is strengthened and the level of employment goes up. Although we have a decrease in the profit rate, lots of benefits occur because the higher relative price of imports leads to more consumption of internal or domestic products.

Neoclassical theory tells us that whenever nominal wages grow with the

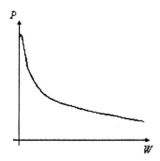

*Figure 2.1    The relation between the price level and wages*

same rate as the value of the marginal productivity of the labor, they will not cause inflation. Only when the growth rate of nominal wages is higher will inflation be caused.[3] This assumption may be misleading because in the TNLM model it is demonstrated that the relationship between wages and productivity in the neoclassical sense does not have any appropriate analytic foundation, since it is derived from a behavior of firms that does not represent rational behavior in a relevant way. In addition, $W$ in the neoclassical theory is considered to be a price, not a distributive variable. Therefore, if wages grow positively or negatively as a result of an exogenous shock, the real conditions of the system are kept constant since all other prices are adjusted in the same proportion. This implies that after an inflationary process caused by $W$, no production and employment conditions are changed though the level of nominal prices has increased.

However, as shown in Figure 2.1, $P$ reaches an absolute maximum in a point very near to the $W$ axis. Between zero and the maximum, there are only very few values of $W$ accompanied by an increase in $P$; this implies that a wage increase is only inflationary inside that range. The neoclassical postulate of a positive relationship between wages and prices is only relevant in a very limited way. In the more general case the relationship between $W$ and $P$ is always negative.

It is possible to conclude that the relationship between the domestic price level and the nominal wages in an open economy with fixed exchange rates and exogenous money supply is generally inverse provided that the domestic market dominates: a higher nominal wage leads to a lower price level.

A similar result is obtained when we analyze the case of an economy dominated by the exports of its own product supply; a system represented by (2.26b). The shape of the $P$ function in this case is shown in Figure 2.2.

Geometrically, the function in this figure has the following characteristics:

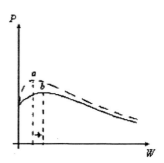

*Figure 2.2    The relation between the price level and wages with*
*domestically produced exports*

in comparison to Figure 2.1 its maximum is located further to the right, the higher the dependence on exports. Figure 2.2 shows two curves. The dotted one has a maximum at $a$, the continuous one a maximum in point $b$. The higher the dependence of the economy on exports, the positive relation between $W$ and $P$ covers a wider range on the $W$ axis. If wages in the dotted curve are between zero and $a$, they will cause inflation, even in the case when they are not financed with an additional money supply. Only if $W$ is bigger its increase will have a deflationary effect on $P$. When the dependence on exports becomes higher, the range of inflationary effects of wage increases is higher, too. This is shown in Figure 2.2 by an arrow between the two maxima $a$ and $b$.

This analytical conclusion is particularly important for those economies that have experienced growth rates of exports high above the growth rates of their domestic production and have not reached a very significant progress in bringing down production costs relative to the rest of the world. Since the underdeveloped world is generally characterized by rather low wages, it is very likely that inflationary effects of an increase in $W$ become more and more important. As a consequence it is necessary to stabilize the domestic price level and the exchange rates in order to implement growth. This implies that for growing purposes the substitution of the external market in favor of domestic production will result in an increasing tendency to control wages in order to achieve inflation targets and exchange rate stability, except in the case when a dynamic technological progress takes place in a very short period of time.

## 2.6 Labor Sector: Effective Demand and Employment Level

The TNLM model has shown clearly that the poor and inadequate concept of a neoclassical 'labor market' has no relevance for an open economy. As a result of the reduced form of the model, the demand for labor depends on the effective demand for the domestic product, and therefore depends positively on $W$. When $W$ does not function as a price, it is not able to serve as a mechanism for the regulation of the employment level. The wage $W$ plays the role of distributive variable, confirming the classical and Marxian approach.

Labor demand can be derived from the substitution of (2.24) in (2.15), and has the following expression:

$$L_d = (1-\beta)\left[\tau + \frac{\psi Y^* \varphi}{W} - \left(\frac{1-\gamma}{\gamma}\right)\frac{M^s}{W}\right] \qquad (2.27)$$

This equation shows that the employment level depends on the effective demand for the domestic product. From (2.27) we see that the weight of each of the two markets will be crucial for the influence exogenous variables exercise on $L_d$. It also is possible to demonstrate by (2.27), that the influence of the exchange rate on the employment level will be positive. The money supply has a negative and $W$ an ambiguous influence.

### a) Employment level and wage
The inverse relation between $W$ and $\Pi$ implies that when $W$ diminishes, income is shifted toward profits and therefore people who possess the property rights of firms become better off. On the other hand, increases in $W$ will lead to a more progressive income distribution with an increase in the employment level.

At this point, it is crucial to answer the following question: What is the relation between $W$ and $L_d$ in all these cases, and under what circumstances can we make sure that employment grows together with consumption demand?

Figures (2.3a) and (2.3b) show the possible relevant cases:

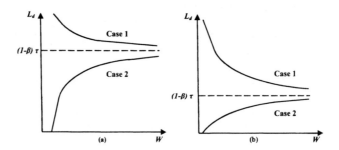

*Figure 2.3    Labor supply and wages with small and large β*

The difference between (a) and (b) is determined by the magnitude of the parameter $\beta$, which determines the degree of dependence of the domestic economy on imported input. This can be treated as a proxy of the technological dependence in the model.

Figure (2.3a) represented an economy with small $\beta$. Figure (2.3b) corresponds to a high $\beta$. Since the magnitude of this parameter reflects the degree of technological dependence from the rest of the world, (2.3b) corresponds to a much more dependent economy.

*Case 1: An economy highly dependent on its exports*
The two asymptotic curves in each quadrant represent the magnitude $(1 - \beta)\tau$, the maximum employment level that can be reached in the system. The ones marked with 'Case 1' characterize the situation of an economy whose main impulse for economic activity comes from its exports. The 'Case 2' economies refer to a situation where economic activity is mainly based on its domestic market.

From Figure 2.3 it becomes obvious that in an economy characterized by Case 1 and (a) or (b), the firms hire more labor when the labor supply is cheaper. This is typical for the neoclassical situation. As a consequence a small and open economy depending more on exports than on domestic markets has to follow wage reduction policies in order to preserve or to expand its employment level. This is typical for those economies who have concentrated on the development of assembly plants as a central part of their productive activities during the last 30 or 40 years.[4] To maintain their competitiveness they have operated systematically with wage reductions. Since the inputs this type of economies have bought from other countries are determined by international prices and in order to keep profit rates on internationally attractive levels, they use the only available source in the domestic economy to knock down costs: the wages. These economies, instead of having reduced or even overcome their technological dependence, have increased it (in the context of the model $\beta$ has grown). Like a vicious circle it then becomes more and more necessary to maintain low wages in order to preserve employment levels and their international competitiveness.

### Case 2: An economy highly dependent on its domestic market

Now we analyze the case of those economies which produce the overwhelming part of their output in domestic markets depending on the purchasing power of domestic consumers, although these economies use foreign currencies in order to finance the purchases of their imported inputs. In this scenario labor demand will be defined as a positive function of the real wage, implying that ceteris paribus an increase in the employment level can be reached by an increase in $W$. This case shows a situation contrary to the one postulated by neoclassical theory. The higher $W$, the higher the employment level. In addition, if the same initial level of wages exists in two economies where the first one is technologically less dependent than the other one (as shown by (a) and (b)), the first one has a greater possibility of increasing its employment level by an increase in $W$. This is due to technological dependence.

The size of the domestic market in economies characterized by Case 2 strongly depends on the purchasing power of domestic consumers and its size is bigger the smaller the part of production necessary to finance the import. The positive relationship between wages and employment means that the increase in $W$ will initiate progressive developments in the distribution of the monetary income among consumers. Therefore, the growth in the employment level will be accompanied by a tendency toward a more equal income distribution.

It is shown that an underdeveloped economy facing the situation to be strongly dependent on its exports in order to assure its output level, is condemned to decrease its consumption level and to concentrate its income in more and more. On the contrary, underdeveloped economies depending mainly on their domestic markets have real possibilities to increase their welfare and to improve their income distribution.

### b) Employment level and money supply

The growth of money supply $M^s$, leaving unaffected all the other exogenous variables, has a negative effect on labor demand. The size of this effect, however, will depend on the parameter $\beta$ and $W$. The lower is $\beta$, the flatter will be the slope of (2.27). Similar to the $\beta$ effect the slope of the function will be flatter when $W$ is bigger. Therefore, the negative effects of an increase in $M^s$ on the employment will be less important.

It becomes obvious that an expansive monetary policy without an appropriate wage and exchange rate policy will have a negative effect on the employment level. The transmission mainly goes via the level of $P$. However, this does not imply that an expansive monetary policy has recessive effects, in general. We only can say that the effect of monetary policy on the employment level is negative.

**c) Labor supply**
The reduced form of the labor supply strictly depends on the domestic conditions of the economy. This implies that $L_S$ positively depends on $W$ and negatively depends on the money supply, as is shown in the following expression:

$$L_s = \tau - \left(\frac{1-\gamma-\zeta}{\gamma}\right)\frac{M^s}{W} \tag{2.28}$$

It is important to stress the absence of the exchange rate and of the level of income of the rest of the world in (2.28). This means that the supply of labor in the domestic economy exclusively depends on domestic conditions. Variations in the level of the total exports or in exchange rates will not affect labor supply, except for the case that monetary authorities decide to adjust the levels of $M^s$ and $W$ to impulses from the rest of the world. Without this policy labor supply stays independend from all variables characterizing the relationship between the domestic economy and the rest of the world.

**d) Unemployment**
The function for the excess demand for labor, a proxy for unemployment, is given by:

$$L_d - L_s \leq 0. \tag{2.29}$$

Substituting (2.27) and (2.28) in (2.29), we obtain the following weak inequality:

$$\left(\frac{1-\beta}{\beta}\right)\psi Y^* \varphi W^{-1} - \frac{\zeta-\beta(1-\gamma)}{\beta\gamma} M^s W^{-1} \leq \tau \tag{2.30}$$

(2.30) can be interpreted as follows: With a given wage the left–hand side of equation (2.30) shows that the employment level depends exclusively on the effective demand for domestic output. Whenever the expression of parameters multiplied with $M^s$ is positive, the relation between $M^s$ and the unemployment level will be inverse, which implies that a smaller money supply necessary for transactions in domestic consumption the higher unemployment will be. A positive sign of this quotient crucially depends on $\zeta$ representing the propensity to consume imported goods. If $\zeta < (1 - \beta)$, the monetary supply is positively correlated with the employment level. If $\zeta > (1 - \beta)$, the money supply has an inverse relationship to the employment level. On the contrary the wage rate $W$ has a positive influence. This implies that a constant decrease in $W$ leads to an increase in unemployment.

The link between $W$ and the employment level can be positive, negative or zero. If $W$ grows with a smaller rate than the money supply and at the same time the money supply is increased faster than the exchange rate, the employment level rises with a positive influence on the domestic market and without a regressive redistribution of income. If on the other hand the exchange rate goes up, leaving everything else constant, employment also grows because of an increase in the foreign demand for the domestic product, weakening the domestic market.

Another possible scenario is given by a situation of equal growth rates of exports, $M^i$ and $W$, leaving the exchange rate constant: in this case the employment level remains constant, the income distribution changes in favor of people depending mainly on the salary revenues. The import of inputs then will grow more than the total demand for domestic goods, with a substitution effect in favor of labor.

This analysis makes clear that the relation between unemployment and the wage level and its flexibility is not only subject to the limit possibilities of the neoclassical theory; multiple employment levels can correspond to every level of real wages. This implies that every employment level is consistent with countless levels of real wages. In (2.30) the three degrees of freedom (neglecting $Y^*$) assure that independent of the adjustment rule assumed for $W$ in a regime of full flexibility, the change of its magnitude is not able to guarantee that full employment will be reached. On the contrary, it is obvious that in starting from a hypothetical situation of equality in (2.30), that means starting from full employment, a decrease in any component of the effective demand will contract the employment level without any automatic mechanism to restore full employment. Involuntary unemployment then will emerge, even when the relative prices in the system have not changed.

## 2.7   Poverty Caused by Increases in Exports

We define poverty as the situation stemming from the decrease in per capita income available for final consumption. To analyze the role of the external sector we treat the export and import functions as one subsector of the economy similar to the labor market. It is clear that surpluses or deficits with the rest of the economy can exist although some other markets are in a permanent equilibrium as has been shown above.

### a) Exports

Substituting (2.25) in (2.23), we obtain the following equation for the reduced form of the export function:

$$Q_x = (\alpha^\alpha \beta^\beta) \left( 1 + \frac{M^s}{\psi Y^* \varphi} \right)^{-1} \left( \frac{W}{\varphi P_m} \right)^\beta \left[ \tau + \frac{\psi Y^* \varphi}{W} - \left( \frac{1-\gamma}{\gamma} \right) \frac{M^s}{W} \right]^{\alpha+\beta} \quad (2.31)$$

We can see that exports are not only a function of external variables and of the exchange rate, but also of domestic variables like the monetary supply and the wage level.

According to the standard theory, exports of internal products depend positively on the exchange rate, but the effect increases with an exchange rate increase. This indicates that economies whose competitiveness depends on devaluations have to devaluate more and more drastically to achieve the same impact on its exports.

### b) Imported inputs

Our TNLM model has the ability to build up some extreme cases underdeveloped countries suffer from today because of the changes that drive the international division of labor. One of them is the increasing importance of the processing industry whose fundamental features consist of the transformation of imported goods with the help of domestic labor and in re-exporting theses goods with a very small value added generated domestically. It is possible to represent this case in our model in a perfect way, equalizing export and import values with the added value necessary for the transformation. However, despite of its increasing importance this case is not completely representative of the situation in underdeveloped countries mainly in underdeveloped Latin American countries. Although the processing industries have expanded quickly throughout the region, the Latin American underdevelopment is characterized basically by a production process that is not able to produce the domestic output without the imported goods. This is the clearest expression of a technological dependence.

Substituting function (2.24) in (2.16) the following expression is obtained:

$$Q_{min\,i} = \beta \left[ \frac{W\tau}{\varphi P_m} + \psi \frac{Y^*}{P_m} - \left( \frac{1-\gamma}{\gamma} \right) \frac{M^s}{\varphi P_m} \right] \quad (2.32)$$

It becomes apparent by simple inspection that the function is undoubtedly positively related to $W$ and negatively related to $M^s$. On the other hand, the relationship of $Q_{mint}$ with $\varphi$ is not clear. The latter one depends on indirect relations between the exports and the domestic market influencing the activity level.

To sum up, it should be stressed here that in an economy whose activity level is basically determined by the domestic market, the exchange rate is positively related to imports used as input. Secondly, it can be observed that when an axis for the activity level is measured in export growth, the relation between the exchange rate and the import of inputs is negative. This is because devaluations enable the economy to substitute these inputs by labor and exports tend to grow less quickly in these economies than in those guided by the domestic market.

Once again the point should be stressed that the analyzed relationships reveal an enormous distance to those characterized by neoclassical theory.

## c) Imports for consumption

The function of the imports for consumption is one of the simplest of the whole model. As a reduced form it depends exclusively on the money supply and on the exchange rate. Wages are eliminated.

Considering that the supply of the domestic product is given by the following function:

$$Q_s = (\alpha^\alpha \beta^\beta)\left(\frac{W}{\varphi P_m}\right)^\beta\left[\tau + \frac{\psi Y^* \varphi}{W} - \left(\frac{1-\gamma}{\gamma}\right)\frac{M^s}{W}\right]^{\alpha+\beta}, \qquad (2.33)$$

we can verify easily that the sum of $Q_c$ and $Q_x$ is always equal to (2.33). This means that the added demand for the domestic product is always equal to its supply.

When substituting (2.33), (2.32) and (2.24) in the definition of $\Pi$, we obtain:

$$\Pi = \frac{1}{\gamma}M^s - W\tau \qquad (2.34)$$

Finally, by substituting (2.34) in (2.7) we arrive at the reduced form of the function of the demand for external products used for domestic consumption:

$$Q_{cm} = \frac{\varsigma}{\gamma}\frac{M^s}{\varphi P_m} \qquad (2.35)$$

We can see that although the wage determines the individual consumers' demand for imported product, the effect of $W$ is indirect in the (2.35).

The relation between $Q_{cm}$ and the exchange rate shows negative sign. It defines an equilateral hyperbola, similar to that of any habitual function known as a Marshall–type demand function.

### d) Poverty grows as fast as exports

Let us now assume that the authorities responsible for managing the exchange rate development decide to manipulate the price of the foreign currency and to use it as a competitiveness target; or let us assume that an exchange rate flotation is put into existence in order to avoid a commercial deficit. As analyzed above this leads to a constant devaluation of the home currency depending on the technological gap. With this devaluation, the following phenomena will be produced:

1.  The demand for exports grows less than proportional to the rise in the price of foreign currency.
2.  Domestic consumption of the domestic product will decrease.
3.  Domestic consumption of the imported product will decrease.
4.  The imports of inputs will increase less than proportional to the devaluation rate.
5.  The effective demand for the domestic product will increase, and with it the employment level
6.  There will the following inflationary impulse: The level of prices $P$ will grow less than proportional to the devaluation.
7.  Real wages have to go down in order to explain the contraction of domestic demand for domestic and imported products, thus reducing the per capita consumption and causing an increase in poverty.

The effect of the devaluation on the activity level will be positive: the production and employment levels will be increased, and the exports, in particular. On the other hand, there will be serious effects on social welfare: total domestic consumption will go down. As a consequence the domestic market will contract, and exports will expand more quickly than domestic products, partly due to this contraction. The real wage will decrease because of the inflationary effect of the devaluation, and in spite of the increase in employment, per capita consumption inevitably will fall. The main conclusion is that the export–favoring model for underdeveloped economies has the following characteristics: The increase in employment is accompanied by a decrease in the welfare of all consumers of the local economy. Figure 2.4 shows this effect graphically using all the above information.

# 3   CONCLUSIONS

First, it is an empirical fact that the structural reason for the current trade deficits in underdeveloped economies cannot be solved by a devaluation; sooner or later they will have to devalue again. In any case, the local economy re-appreciating its exchange rate suddenly is not able to overcome its technological deficiency.

Secondly, it is also known every effort to stimulate exports by a devaluation will lead to worse terms of trade which is accompanied by decreasing consumption levels. As a consequence the domestic social cost of obtaining any additional unit of foreign currency will constantly increase.

To sum up, the correction of the trade deficit or the gain of international competitiveness through a devaluation will be socially very expensive and will be unable to solve the primary reasons for that deficit. The solution necessarily lies inside the domestic institutional structures.

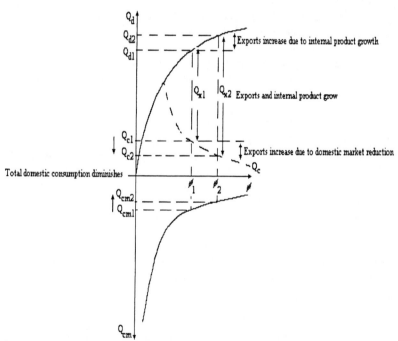

*Figure 2.4   Employment and welfare effects of a devaluation*

In addition to the analytic possibilities of the model, we can conclude that the problem described above can only be solved by an endogenous technological transformation of the domestic production process. In this respect market forces are totally useless in solving this problem.

It is important to say here that the effects of decreases in $P_m$ lead to similar phenomena as studied above. A sustained increase of exports under technological disadvantage unavoidably will lead to an increase in poverty.

To develop a small and open economy in a way that domestic markets are substituted by foreign markets and to use this as a decisive way to determine its activity level implies that wages must be punished in order to achieve competitiveness and to control inflation. The consequences of this way are an increasing income concentration, a sustained increase in poverty and, in spite of the free flotation, a recurrent tendency to deficits with the external sector. Although the deficit is abolished immediately if a free float is put in validity without obstacles, it leads to a drop in the wages in order to avoid inflation and unemployment. This is a structural tendency that is increased systematically. Therefore, the best option for any small, open economy will be to strengthen its domestic market.

Any exchange rate policy cannot correct the technological gaps against the rest of the world. The only possibility to correct it consists of a policy of public intervention characterized by a support of investments in high-priority areas of the production process, and in strengthening the labor supply qualitatively. The free market does not have the capacity to renovate and to strengthen the technology of the production process of an economy like the one analyzed in the model.

The autonomy of the wage, exchange rate and monetary policies crucially depends on the degree of openess of an economy. Economies whose activity level basically depends on its domestic market show wide possibilities of implementing policies designed to correct structural problems like the technological one with a long–term perspective. In contrast, economies highly dependent on exports increase their dependence on wage and monetary policies very quickly in order to keep their international competitiveness by manipulating the exchange rate.

Exchange rate policies lead to redistribution effects and they are much more significant in economies highly dependent on their exports. Their deegres of freedom for other corrections are practically zero.

# NOTES

[1]    It is a fact that migration from poor countries toward the rich ones is much more significant. The flow of illegal immigrants into industrialized countries clearly show a characteristic feature of industrialized economies: they establish increasing obstacles to limit free labor mobility. Industrialized economies do not have a lot of interest in receiving something more than the goods they supply from the underdeveloped world, and their labor force is not willing to move to the underdeveloped world because of lower wages. Therefore, the labor mobility between the industrialized and underdeveloped economies is not significant.

[2]    In fact, differentiating the equation representing the equality between the marginal productivity of labor and the real wage, and dividing the original equation by the result, it can be shown that inflation emerges when the growth rate of money wages exceeds the rate of growth of labor productivity. This is shown in Blanchard and Fischer (1989), pp. 542–546.

[3]    The model of supply dynamics, proposed by Tobin (1972) and included in Blanchard and Fischer (1989), pp. 542–546, clearly shows the neoclassical conception of this problem. There is no place in it for another argumentation but only for the one linking wages in a positive way to the marginal productivity of labor. These and other facets of the problem are extensively discussed in Jossa and Musella (1998), pp. 1–141.

[4]    For example, the economies of Southeast Asia.

# REFERENCES

Blanchard, Olivier and Stanley Fischer (1989), *Lectures on Macroeconomics*, Cambridge, MA: The MIT Press.

Jossa, Bruno and Marco Musella (1998), *Inflation, Unemployment and Money*, Cheltenham, UK and Northamton, MA, USA: Edward Elgar.

Tobin, James (1972), 'Wealth, Liquidity and the Propensity to Consume', in B. Strumple, J. Morgan and E. Zahn (eds.), *Human Behavior in Economic Affairs: Essays in Honor of George Katona*, Amsterdam: Elsevier.

PART TWO:


EXCHANGE RATE ASPECTS
AND FINANCIAL MARKETS

# 3. The East Asian Dollar Standard, Fear of Floating, and Original Sin

## Ronald McKinnon and Gunther Schnabl

### 1  MORE EXCHANGE RATE FLEXIBILITY IN EAST ASIA?

Before the 1997–98 Asian crisis, the East Asian economies, Hong Kong, Indonesia, Korea, Malaysia, Philippines, Singapore, Taiwan, and Thailand had pegged their exchange rates to the dollar. Although these smaller East Asian countries used a variety of exchange rate systems, their common peg to the dollar provided an informal common monetary standard that enhanced macroeconomic stability in the region. China joined the system in 1994 with a hard peg to the dollar. Only Japan was a 'pure' floater with wide fluctuations in the yen/dollar exchange rate.

With the advent of the 1997–98 Asian crisis, the common East Asian monetary standard fell apart. Although China and Hong Kong retained their dollar pegs, the debtor countries, Indonesia, Korea, Malaysia, Philippines and Thailand were forced to float. Even the creditor countries which were not attacked, Taiwan and Singapore, engineered moderate depreciations. And, Japan, as the outlier, let the yen float downward substantially over 1997 through mid–1998 and thus aggravated the crisis for the other East Asian economies (McKinnon and Schnabl, 2003).

The lesson drawn from the currency attacks on the debtor economies by the International Monetary Fund (IMF) and many other commentators was (is) that the pre-1997 system of 'soft' dollar pegs itself was at fault. Before 1997, because of high–risk premia, the interest rates in the East Asian debtor economies were much higher than on dollar or yen assets. Domestic banks were tempted to accept low-interest dollar (or yen) deposits instead of relatively high-interest baht deposits. And this temptation to risk foreign exchange exposure was all the greater because the baht/dollar exchange rate was (softly) fixed.

So, this critique runs, if the exchange rates of the debtor economies had been fluctuating more randomly, the Thai (or Korean, or Indonesian, or Malaysian, or Philippines) banks would see greater risk and be less prone to short-term overborrowing in foreign exchange in the first place. Further, by introducing more flexibility in exchange rates *ex ante*, the critics of soft dollar pegging contend that large discrete depreciations become less likely *ex post,* i.e., after some political or economic disturbance that provokes an attack.

This line of reasoning against restoring soft dollar pegs has been so persuasive that academic commentators and international agencies fear a return to the pre-1997 regime. For emerging markets open to international capital flows, Fischer (2001, pp. 5–10) has argued that soft pegs are not sustainable. Post-crisis, he sees most emerging markets moving toward more flexible exchange rates.

Against this by-now-conventional wisdom, we shall argue in favor of dollar pegging – at least for East Asia. Indeed, we argue that the IMF's 'worst' fears could well be realized: low-frequency dollar pegging (as in Malaysia) will follow the path of high-frequency pegging, and exchange rate volatility will diminish. The informal East Asian dollar standard could be accidentally resurrected by national central banks acting independently.

## 2 LOW-FREQUENCY DOLLAR PEGGING AND THE COMMON NOMINAL ANCHOR

The rationale for exchange rate stabilization in the East Asian countries springs from both international goods and capital markets.

### 2.1 Trade Invoicing

To discuss the rationale for the return to the pre-crisis exchange rate arrangements, let us discuss low-frequency dollar pegging first. Based on monthly observations from 1980, Figure 3.1 shows that all East Asian countries except Japan stabilized the dollar values of their currencies up to the 1997–98 crisis – and, with the major exception of Indonesia, could be returning to such pegging in the near future. With base 100, the various country panels in Figure 3.1 use the same vertical scale for dollar exchange rates (except for Indonesia) so that the observer can more easily compare proportional changes.

East Asian countries used a variety of exchange rate systems ranging from a currency board hard peg in Hong Kong to a sliding or crawling peg in Indonesia before 1997. Although these pegs were often not openly admitted or were disguised as currency baskets, the common adherence to the dollar is easy to recognize. After a series of official devaluations before 1994, China

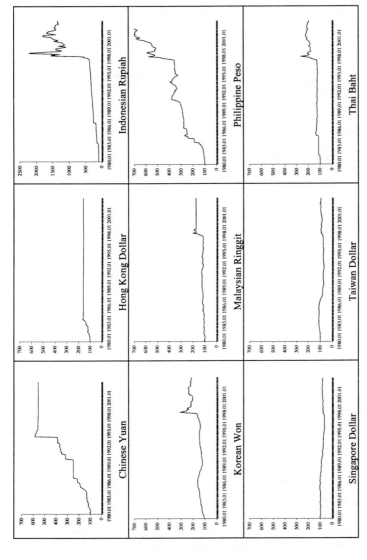

*Figure 3.1  East Asian exchange rate pegs against the dollar, 1980:1–2003:12 (monthly)*

*Source:* IMF: IFS, Central Bank of China. Index 1980:01 = 100. Note different scale for Indonesia.

47

has since maintained a hard, if informal, peg of 8.3 yuan to the dollar and a unified foreign exchange market.[1] Malaysia introduced a fixed exchange rate of 3.8 ringgit to the dollar in September 1998.

The rationale for low-frequency dollar pegging does not primarily arise because of strong trade ties with the United States. The US accounts for only about 23 percent of overall exports of the smaller East Asian economies – and for only 14 percent of their imports. Instead, we focus on the fact that most of East Asian commodity trade is invoiced in dollars.

For instance in 2002, the percentage of Korean imports invoiced in US dollars was 80.6 percent, while the proportion of dollar invoicing of Korean exports was even higher at 86.8 percent – similar to the proportions observed in the preceding two decades. Because the other smaller economies, countries are less industrialized than Korea, their currencies are even less likely to be used in foreign trade, with the proportion of dollar invoicing being correspondingly greater.

Although Japan is the world's second largest industrial economy, the dollar is more widely used in Japanese trade with East Asia than is the yen. As Sato (1999, p. 574) puts it, the East Asian countries are unlikely to use the yen in their foreign trade except when that trade is with Japan. The US dollar predominates in invoicing East Asian trade in general and intra-East Asian trade in particular – as when, say, Thailand trades with Malaysia.

Thus, despite lively discussions as in Kwan (2001) about the possibility of a yen zone in East Asia, the revealed invoicing preferences of Asian importers and exporters indicate the contrary: the area has been, and is, a strong dollar zone – from which the dollar shows no signs of being displaced. This dollar invoicing helps explain why the smaller East Asian economies including China are so anxious to peg to the dollar at both low and high frequencies.

## 2.2    Macroeconomic Stability

Using a much bigger data set going on beyond East Asia, Calvo and Reinhart (2002) showed what they called 'fear of floating' in developing countries on a worldwide scale. Although a small number of Eastern European transitional economies and ex–colonies peg to the euro (Schnabl, 2004), the rest of the developing world pegs 'softly' to the dollar. From monthly data, they showed that exchange rates in developing countries were much less volatile – and interest rates as well as exchange reserves much more volatile – than in the industrial countries.

There are two related aspects to their argument explaining fear of floating. Both are macroeconomic in nature. First, in the absence of capital controls, volatile capital flows could sharply affect nominal exchange rates and, because the domestic price level is relatively sticky, lead to large changes in a country's real exchange rate. Its international competitiveness could fluctuate sharply from one month to the next.

Second, the common low-frequency peg to the dollar helps anchor any one country's price level because such a high proportion of world trade is invoiced in dollars. In non-crisis periods, price increases in the traded goods sector are pinned down. The upward drift of prices in nontradable services is muted because of substitution relationships.[2]

This common dollar anchor was more robust because all East Asian countries except Japan were on it. Then international commodity arbitrage within the whole East Asian dollar zone, and not just with the United States, could better pin down the domestic price level of any one participating country. Indeed, in the great 1997–98 crisis when Indonesia, Korea, Malaysia, Philippines, and Thailand were suddenly forced to devalue – and curtailed imports while trying to stimulate exports – this forced a deflation in the *dollar* prices of goods traded in the region. Thus China and Hong Kong which did not devalue experienced significant deflation in their domestic prices.

## 3   HIGH-FREQUENCY DOLLAR PEGGING AND 'ORIGINAL SIN'

But the nominal anchor argument cannot be used to rationalize *high–frequency* pegging on a daily or weekly basis. Instead we hypothesize that high-frequency pegging reflects the fact that the capital markets of emerging markets are incomplete – the doctrine of 'original sin' as put forward by Eichengreen and Hausmann (1999, p. 3):

> 'Original sin' ... is a situation in which the domestic currency cannot be used to borrow abroad or to borrow long term, even domestically. In the presence of this incompleteness, financial fragility is unavoidable because all domestic investments will have either a currency mismatch (projects that generate pesos will be financed with dollars) or a maturity mismatch (long-term projects will be financed by short-term loans).
>
> Critically, these mismatches exist not because banks and firms lack the prudence to hedge their exposures. The problem rather is that a country whose external liabilities are necessarily denominated in foreign exchange is by definition unable to hedge. Assuming that there will be someone on the other side of the market for foreign currency hedges is equivalent to assuming that the country can borrow abroad in its own currency. Similarly, the problem is not that firms lack the foresight to match the maturity structure of their assets and liabilities; it is that they find it impossible to do so. The incompleteness of financial markets is thus at the root of financial fragility.

In developing countries, in what sense are financial markets incomplete? In the first place, a fixed-interest bond market is typically absent. The reasons are many. On the private side, domestic firms tend to be small, without well–developed accounting systems, and cannot issue bonds in their own name. Firms with longer–term projects cannot issue fixed-interest bonds or mortgages for finance at comparable terms to maturity. Instead, they must roll over short-term bank loans – or, at best, borrow at medium term with variable interest rates tied to short rates.

Even on the government side, developing countries may well have shaky financial histories, inflation and interest rate volatility coupled with exchange controls, that inhibit potential buyers of government bonds from making medium– or long–term commitments. Insofar as a market in government bonds exists into the medium term, interest rates are typically adjusted to reflect some very short–term rate. An ostensible 'one-year' bond might have its interest rate tied to that on overnight treasuries.

In the second place, an active forward market in foreign exchange against the dollar – or any other currency – is also absent in most developing countries. While a missing domestic bond market is obviously bad for domestic capital markets, why should it affect forward transacting by risk-averse traders wanting to hedge their open positions in foreign exchange? Potential market makers such as banks cannot easily cover transactions involving selling the domestic currency forward for, say, dollars because they cannot hold a convenient array of interest-bearing domestic bonds liquid at different terms to maturity. Indeed, domestic interest rates (vis-à-vis foreign) are not available for determining what the proper premium on forward dollars should be.

### 3.1   The Microeconomic Rationale for High-frequency Pegging to the Dollar

Absent an efficient forward market in foreign exchange, risk-averse importers and exporters cannot conveniently hedge. Nor can banks easily cover open positions in foreign exchange.

Suppose first that the private sector of our underdeveloped economy was *not* a net debtor to the rest of the world and its imports and exports were more or less balanced. Then domestic importers could possibly buy dollars forward from domestic exporters at shorter terms to maturity – although such matching would be difficult (high transaction costs) because the domestic forward market for foreign exchange lacks liquidity. Absent liquid domestic money-market instruments at all terms to maturity, banks – who typically act as agents for domestic importers and exporters in the forward exchange markets – could not easily cover themselves.

Now suppose that the private sector is a net short-term debtor, largely in dollars, to the rest of the world. Then, not withstanding the country's government having positive official dollar reserves, the hedging problem for private traders is compounded. Collectively, domestic debtors with future foreign exchange obligations should buy dollars forward to cover themselves. But foreigners collectively are unwilling to sell dollars forward net because they cannot find liquid interest-bearing domestic-currency assets, i.e., bonds, to hold in the interim. Whence the inevitable currency mismatch: economic agents with net foreign exchange (dollar) exposure – usually very short term – cannot hedge even if they wanted to.

To offset the non-existent private market in forward exchange, the government is induced to provide an informal hedge by keeping the exchange rate stable in the short to medium term. Private banks and enterprises can then repay their short-term foreign currency debts, which are largely denominated in dollars, with minimal exchange rate risk. If a country's financial markets are condemned by original sin, its regulatory authorities have strong incentives to undertake high–frequency exchange rate pegging in order to mitigate payments risk.

Alternatively, the same missing-domestic-bond-market argument could be used to justify official intervention to create a 'market' in forward exchange. Presuming that the government has plentiful dollar reserves, it could risk selling dollars forward to individual importers, or to financial institutions, which have forward exchange exposure. Even if the government has the best of intentions, however, this leaves open the question of what the appropriate forward premia on dollars should be for these various individualized contracts.

So, a more neutral and more visible second-best strategy (the first best being to create a domestic bond market!) for reducing foreign exchange risk is for the government to keep the exchange rate from moving much on a day-to-day or week-to-week basis. At higher frequencies of observation than those considered by Calvo and Reinhart (2002), there is 'fear of floating'. Except for the small economies in Eastern Europe attached to the euro, the dollar is the natural currency to which to peg. It is the principal invoice and vehicle currency in East Asia and elsewhere in the developing world. And later we shall show that East Asian countries do peg softly to the dollar at high frequencies.

But pegging to the dollar to limit exchange risk still leaves open two big problems in risk management. The first is the question of extraneous exchange rate fluctuations between the dollar and other major currencies. The second is moral hazard in the sense that economic agents, whether domestic banks or firms, prefer to gamble rather than to hedge their bets in the foreign exchanges. Let us discuss each in turn.

### 3.2   Extraneous Exchange Rate Risk and Double Hedging

The first problem is that of 'extraneous' exchange rate changes between major currencies – as in East Asia when the yen fluctuates against the dollar. A small but significant (about 12 to 13 percent) proportion of Korean imports are invoiced in yen. Let us suppose that in the short and medium terms these yen prices are sticky. Similarly, all dollar prices that Korean importers (or exporters) face are sticky and invariant to fluctuations in the yen/dollar rate. Thus, if the won is pegged to the dollar, Korean importers of yen-invoiced goods are at risk.

Suppose a Korean importer is obligated to pay 100 yen in 60 days. Then any random appreciation of the yen against the dollar within the 60-day interval will increase the won cost of servicing that debt. If the won prices for which the importer can sell his Japanese goods in Korea are sticky, then he could buy forward 100 yen *for dollars* in order to hedge the transaction. Because both Japan and the United States have well–developed bond markets, a well–defined and highly liquid forward inter-bank market between yen and dollars is cheap to use. Thus, the Korean importer, using his bank as his agent, can buy forward all the yen he needs for dollars. And with the won kept predictably stable against the dollar in the spot markets, he can use spot won to buy the dollars 60 days hence when his yen payment is due.

So we have a theory of the optimal – albeit second–best – *double hedge* against currency risk. The bulk of the goods traded by any East Asian emerging market economy are priced to market (sticky priced) in dollars. For these goods, the government's soft pegging against the dollar in the short and medium terms is an informal hedge against exchange risk which compensates for the absence of a forward market between the domestic currency and dollars. However, for that subset of imports or exports which are invoiced in yen, euros, sterling, or some other major currency that fluctuates widely against the dollar, then supplementary hedging in the well–developed forward markets between dollars and the major currency in question is also necessary. As we shall show later, this strategy of reducing exchange risk by double hedging – starting with a peg to just one major international currency – dominates the trade-weighted currency-basket approach involving the developing country in question 'pegging' to several major international currencies with different weights.

### 3.3   The Impossibility of Freely Floating Exchange Rates?

When governments impose tough prudential regulations against banks taking foreign exchange risks, can exchange rates float freely? With either general capital controls or prudential regulations against net foreign exchange exposure by banks in place, we hypothesize that governments have little choice but to peg their exchange rates – perhaps only 'softly' from one day to the next. Why?

The inter–bank spot and forward exchange markets are at the center of foreign exchange trading the world over. In any country, its banks normally have direct access to this international market and are the dealers that match buy and sell orders for the domestic currency. Absent any government intervention, these dealers must continually take open positions – for or against the domestic currency – in order to 'make' the foreign exchange market. In textbooks on international finance, banks are the natural 'stabilizing' speculators when there is confidence in the domestic currency. In a well–behaved market, expectations regarding short-term movements in exchange rates are naturally regressive. That is, when the domestic currency depreciates market makers believe that it will eventually rebound and vice versa. Then a reasonably smooth bank-based float is feasible.

Now suppose that domestic commercial banks are not allowed to take open positions in foreign exchange. Moreover, in the presence of original sin, there is no liquid market in domestic bonds. Then *foreign banks are unwilling to take open positions in the domestic currency.* Thus, with a tightly regulated domestic banking system and/or capital controls, a satisfactory free float is impossible. With no natural market makers in the system, the exchange rate would move so erratically as to be intolerable. In most developing countries, governments recognize this problem – at least implicitly. Day-to-day, the central bank then makes the market often by simply pegging – albeit softly and informally – the domestic currency to the dollar.

In summary, we have two complementary reasons why governments in developing countries usually opt to keep their exchange rates stable on a high–frequency basis:

1. Without a well–organized market in forward exchange (original sin), the government wants to provide an informal forward hedge for importers and exporters.
2. But fear of overborrowing leads many prudent governments to limit net foreign exchange exposure by domestic banks – in the extreme by using capital controls. These regulatory restraints then prevent the banks from being active dealers in stabilizing the exchange rate.

In the industrial countries, these problems are not so acute. Because of a well–developed domestic market in forward exchange, their banks need not be so tightly regulated to prevent foreign exchange exposure. In part because of the active forward exchange market, the problem of containing moral hazard in banks is less – a virtuous circle. So the industrial countries can more easily tolerate a free float – as we shall see. But first consider the exchange rate practices of developing countries in East Asia.

## 4   THE POST-CRISIS RETURN TO HIGH-FREQUENCY PEGGING: A FORMAL EMPIRICAL TEST

Our empirical analysis of high-frequency dollar pegging in East Asia proceeds in two stages. First we test whether the developing countries of East Asia really have, in non-crisis periods, been keying on the dollar more than the yen or euro – and whether basket pegging, where all three currencies are given some weight, was the norm. Was this keying permanently interrupted by the great East Asian crisis of 1997–98? Second, we test for any changes in the volatility of these dollar pegs in the post-crisis period compared to the pre-crisis period.

With Japan being such an important trader and an even more important source of capital in East Asia, post–crisis many authors have proposed pegging to a broader currency basket. For instance, Kawai (2002) has proposed to increase the weight of the Japanese yen in the East Asian currency baskets. Williamson (2000) recommends a 33 percent weight of the Japanese yen.

### 4.1   The Composition of Currency Baskets

Using the regression model developed by Frankel and Wei (1994), we show that the smaller East Asian countries have more or less ignored these recommendations. Instead they have clandestinely returned to high-frequency dollar pegging on a day-to-day basis.

Before the crisis, a few East Asian currencies were *de jure* pegged to a basket of major currencies, but typically the weights assigned to various currencies in the official basket were not announced. To detect the weights of various currencies, Frankel and Wei use an 'outside' currency – the Swiss franc – as a numéraire for measuring exchange rate volatility for any East Asian country (except Japan). These volatilities could then be partitioned among movements in major currencies against the Swiss franc. For example, if changes in the Korean won against the Swiss franc are largely explained by the changes of the US dollar against the Swiss franc, we can conclude that the Korean won is virtually pegged to the US dollar. Alternatively it could be pegged to the Japanese yen or German mark.

To show this, we regress the exchange rates of each of the nine East Asian currencies on the US dollar, the Japanese yen, and the German mark[3] with the Swiss franc as numéraire. Equation (3.1) is the regression model.

$$e_{EastAsiancurrencySwissfranc_t} = \alpha_1 + \alpha_2 e_{DollarSwissfranc_t} + \alpha_3 e_{YenSwissfranc_t} + \alpha_4 e_{MarkSwissfranc_t} + u_t$$
$$(3.1)$$

The multivariate OLS regression is based on first differences of logarithms in these exchange rates. The residuals are controlled for heteroscedasticity which can be assumed to be strong during the crisis and the post-crisis period. The daily data are compiled from Datastream. According to Frankel and Wei, the $\alpha$ coefficients represent the weights of the respective currencies in the currency basket. If the East Asian currency is closely fixed to one of the major currencies appearing on the right–hand side of equation (3.1), the corresponding $\alpha$ coefficient will be close to unity. If a coefficient is close to zero, we presume no exchange rate stabilization against that particular currency.

We run the regression for three periods: pre-crisis, crisis, and post-crisis. The pre-crisis period (869 observations) is from February 1994, when China unified its foreign exchange market, to May 1997. We specify the crisis period (415 observations) to start in June 1997 when the peg of the Thai baht came under strong pressure and was abandoned. Our crisis period ends in December 1998 when the currency attacks had ended. The post-crisis period (1304 observations) starts in January 1999 and goes up to December 2003.

### 4.1.1 Pre-Crisis: February 1994–May 1997
Table 3.1 reports the regression results for the pre-crisis period and shows the tight peg around the US dollar. The $\alpha_2$ coefficients in equation (3.1) are all close to unity and reveal the strong efforts by Asian governments to keep the currencies stable against the dollar on a day-to-day basis. The $\alpha_2$ coefficients range from 0.82 for the Singapore dollar up to 1.00 for the Chinese yuan, Hong Kong dollar, and Indonesian rupiah. The correlation coefficients ($R^2$) being close to unity indicate that fluctuations of the East Asian exchange rate against the Swiss franc can be almost fully explained by fluctuations of the dollar against the Swiss franc.

More specifically, the $\alpha_2$ coefficients of the Chinese yuan, the Hong Kong dollar and the Indonesian rupiah are unity. Pre-crisis, Indonesia let its currency crawl smoothly downward at 4 to 5 percent per year, but nevertheless it kept the rupiah virtually fixed to the dollar on a day-to-day basis. China and Hong Kong maintained their fixed pegs to the dollar with no downward crawl. The $\alpha_2$ coefficients of the Korean won, the Philippine peso, and the Taiwan dollar are very close to unity with lower, but still large t-statistics. For the Thai baht and the Malaysian ringgit the $\alpha_2$ coefficients are still close to 0.9 with some small weight on the yen as measured by $\alpha_3$.

Singapore pegged less closely to the dollar. Its $\alpha_2$ was still 0.82 and highly statistically significant but some small weight was given to the yen and mark. Indeed, on a lower frequency basis, before 1997 the Singapore dollar drifted smoothly upward against the US dollar at about 1 to 2 percent per year. Singapore's somewhat different behavior is quite consistent with its being a creditor country with longer–term domestic capital markets. With a less fragile domestic financial system, the authorities were less concerned with pegging to the dollar and could give more weight to other currencies such as the yen.

*Table 3.1    Pegging on a high-frequency basis, pre-crisis (02/01/94– 05/30/97)*

|  | Constant $\alpha_1$ | Dollar $\alpha_2$ | Yen $\alpha_3$ | DM $\alpha_4$ | $R^2$ |
|---|---|---|---|---|---|
| Chinese Yuan | -0.00 | 1.01*** | -0.01 | -0.02 | 0.97 |
|  | (-1.15) | (158.63) | (-1.48) | (-1.70) |  |
| Hong Kong Dollar | 0.00 | 1.00*** | 0.00 | -0.01 | 1.00 |
|  | (0.30) | (454.79) | (0.25) | (-1.36) |  |
| Indonesian Rupiah | 0.00 | 1.00*** | -0.01 | 0.01 | 0.97 |
|  | (3.19) | (144.93) | (-0.92) | (0.85) |  |
| Korean Won | 0.00 | 0.97*** | 0.06*** | 0.01 | 0.93 |
|  | (1.42) | (66.27) | (3.31) | (0.29) |  |
| Malaysian Ringgit | -0.00 | 0.88*** | 0.09*** | 0.01 | 0.90 |
|  | (-1.48) | (54.80) | (5.30) | (0.45) |  |
| Philippine Peso | -0.00 | 0.97*** | 0.02 | -0.01 | 0.86 |
|  | (-0.34) | (43.34) | (0.74) | (-0.45) |  |
| Singapore Dollar | -0.00 | 0.82*** | 0.14*** | 0.08*** | 0.86 |
|  | (-1.32) | (34.37) | (4.83) | (2.97) |  |
| New Taiwan Dollar | 0.00 | 0.98*** | 0.03** | -0.01 | 0.93 |
|  | (0.84) | (57.30) | (1.38) | (-0.54) |  |
| Thai Baht | -0.00 | 0.92*** | 0.08*** | -0.01 | 0.95 |
|  | (-0.61) | (81.25) | (5.17) | (-0.35) |  |

*Source:* Datastream. Daily data. T-Statistics in Parentheses. * significant at the 10% level. ** significant at the 5% level. *** significant at the 1% level. 869 observations. White heteroskedasticity-consistent standard errors and covariance.

In contrast to the high weights of the dollar, Table 3.1 shows that the $\alpha_3$ coefficients for the yen and the $\alpha_4$ coefficients for the mark are small or close to zero. Small weights can be observed for the Japanese yen for Korea, Malaysia, Singapore, Taiwan, and Thailand – but in general the weights are low, ranging from 0.03 (new Taiwan dollar) to 0.14 (Singapore dollar).

### 4.1.2  Crisis: June 1997–December 1998
During this period, attempts to stabilize East Asian currencies against the dollar broke down. Large capital outflows and high volatility in the foreign

exchange markets defeated any official stabilization efforts. As shown in Figure 3.1, only China and Hong Kong continued with unwavering dollar pegs. All other countries abandoned their peg at low as well as high frequencies.

For high-frequency observations, Table 3.2 shows the estimations of the equation (3.1) for the crisis period. For $\alpha_2$ the significantly smaller t-values for all countries except China and Hong Kong represent higher standard errors and thus higher volatility in the exchange rate against the dollar. The goodness-of-fit for these regressions falls completely apart: $R^2$ fell sharply.

*Table 3.2*     *Pegging on a high-frequency basis, crisis (06/01/97–12/31/98)*

| | Constant $\alpha_1$ | Dollar $\alpha_2$ | Yen $\alpha_3$ | DM $\alpha_4$ | $R^2$ |
|---|---|---|---|---|---|
| Chinese Yuan | -0.00 | 0.99*** | 0.00 | 0.01 | 0.99 |
| | (-0.39) | (165.56) | (0.68) | (1.45) | |
| Hong Kong Dollar | 0.00 | 1.00*** | 0.01** | 0.00 | 0.99 |
| | (0.01) | (194.07) | (1.99) | (0.11) | |
| Indonesian Rupiah | 0.00 | 0.48 | 0.64** | -0.16 | 0.03 |
| | (1.12) | (1.01) | (2.36) | (-0.28) | |
| Korean Won | 0.00 | 1.22*** | 0.05*** | 0.05 | 0.13 |
| | (0.62) | (7.05) | (0.59) | (0.58) | |
| Malaysian Ringgit | 0.00 | 0.70*** | 0.33*** | 0.11 | 0.20 |
| | (1.39) | (5.19) | (3.95) | (0.62) | |
| Philippine Peso | 0.00 | 0.75*** | 0.25*** | 0.27 | 0.24 |
| | (1.42) | (5.24) | (4.51) | (1.25) | |
| Singapore Dollar | 0.00 | 0.69*** | 0.33*** | 0.02 | 0.49 |
| | (1.01) | (10.16) | (6.53) | (0.18) | |
| New Taiwan Dollar | 0.00 | 0.87*** | 0.08** | 0.11 | 0.59 |
| | (1.24) | (15.19) | (2.91) | (1.69) | |
| Thai Baht | 0.00 | 0.64*** | 0.32*** | 0.21 | 0.15 |
| | (1.04) | (4.45) | (3.81) | (1.10) | |

*Source:* See Table 3.1., 415 observations.

The decline in $R^2$ is particularly marked for the rupiah, won, ringgit, peso, and baht. Non-crisis Singapore and Taiwan coped with the crisis by lowering the weight of the US dollar and increasing the weight of the Japanese yen, which itself had depreciated sharply. Except for China and Hong Kong, the weight of the yen, i.e., the $\alpha_3$ coefficients, increased during the crisis.

Clearly, by refusing to devalue in the great crisis, China and Hong Kong helped contain the inadvertently beggar-thy-neighbour devaluations in Indonesia, Korea, Malaysia, Philippines, and Thailand. Indeed, Malaysia's pegging of the ringgit in September 1998 – albeit at a depreciated level – also helped contain contagious exchange rate changes in the region.

### 4.1.3 Post-crisis: January 1999–December 2003

After the 1997–98 crisis, however, dollar pegging – at least when measured on a high-frequency, i.e. day-to-day basis – has made a remarkable return. As shown in Table 3.3, the $\alpha_2$ coefficients for all countries again have returned toward the high values of the pre-crisis period. Except for Indonesia and to some extent the Philippines, the goodness-of-fit as measured by $R^2$ for each country's regression equation again becomes tight. The smaller East Asian crisis countries have largely returned to the pre-crisis practise of informal dollar pegging.

*Table 3.3    Pegging on a high-frequency basis, post-crisis (01/01/99–12/31/03)*

|                    | Constant | Dollar     | Yen      | DM       | $R^2$ |
|--------------------|----------|------------|----------|----------|-------|
| Chinese Yuan       | 0.00     | 1.00***    | -0.00    | -0.01    | 0.99  |
|                    | (0.00)   | (228.69)   | (-0.07)  | (-1.36)  |       |
| Hong Kong Dollar   | 0.00     | 1.00***    | 0.00**   | 0.00     | 1.00  |
|                    | (0.13)   | (545.81)   | (2.20)   | (0.49)   |       |
| Indonesian Rupiah  | 0.00     | 0.95***    | 0.21***  | -0.01    | 0.32  |
|                    | (0.15)   | (15.31)    | (4.03)   | (0.00)   |       |
| Korean Won         | -0.00    | 0.85***    | 0.18***  | -0.00    | 0.74  |
|                    | (-0.01)  | (37.44)    | (9.72)   | (-0.01)  |       |
| Malaysian Ringgit  | -0.00    | 1.00***    | 0.00**   | 0.00     | 1.00  |
|                    | (-0.07)  | (979.34)   | (35.98)  | (0.01)   |       |
| Philippine Peso    | 0.00*    | 0.93***    | 0.10***  | -0.01    | 0.64  |
|                    | (1.85)   | (32.41)    | (4.05)   | (-0.45)  |       |
| Singapore Dollar   | 0.00     | 0.75***    | 0.20***  | 0.05***  | 0.80  |
|                    | (0.38)   | (41.66)    | (13.40)  | (1.93)   |       |
| New Taiwan Dollar  | 0.00     | 0.94***    | 0.03*    | 0.02     | 0.92  |
|                    | (0.76)   | (84.61)    | (3.14)   | (0.92)   |       |
| Thai Baht          | 0.00     | 0.78***    | 0.18***  | 0.02**   | 0.77  |
|                    | (0.97)   | (39.30)    | (11.06)  | (0.64)   |       |

*Source:* See Table 3.1., 1304 observations.

True, as argued by Kawai (2002) the Japanese yen seems to have assumed a certain post-crisis role in some currency baskets – particularly those of Indonesia, Thailand, Korea, and Singapore – but the yen weights remain low in comparison to the US dollar. Small values for the goodness–of–fit of the regressions for the Indonesian rupiah and the Philippine peso indicate, however, that both countries have been less successful in stabilizing their currencies after the Asian currency crisis. In particular, Indonesian foreign exchange policy and domestic inflation remain out of control.

Using rolling regressions, the country panels in Figure 3.2 summarize the dollar's weight in each East Asian currency basket during the 1990s. Based on daily data, the rolling 130-day $\alpha_2$ and $\alpha_3$ coefficients are plotted for each of the East Asian countries (except Japan). A window of 130 days corresponds to an observation period of six months (five observations per week). The first window starts on 1 January 1990 and ends on 29 June 1990. The $\alpha_2$ and $\alpha_3$ coefficients are calculated for the first period. Then the window is shifted by one day and the $\alpha_2$ and $\alpha_3$ coefficients are calculated again, up to December 2003. A value of unity stands for a 100 percent weight of the respective currency in the respective currency basket. If the coefficient rises above unity, the estimation process is unstable.

Figure 3.2 shows the time path of the dollar weights in the East Asian currency baskets. China and Hong Kong have a very stable dollar weight of unity for the whole observation period. For the other countries in the pre-crisis period, the dollar weights are also close to unity but slightly more volatile. However, during the 1997–98 crisis, the exchange rate stabilization broke down in Indonesia, Korea, Malaysia, Philippines, and Thailand. In these crisis economies, Figure 3.3 shows sharp declines of their $\alpha_2$ coefficients. Also Singapore lowers the dollar's weight in its currency basket during the crisis.

After the crisis, Figure 3.2 shows that countries have evolved differently. The stabilization process seems still out of control in Indonesia. Malaysia has increased the dollar's weight to 100 percent. In Korea, Philippines, Singapore, Taiwan, and Thailand the trend is somewhat uncertain. For Korea, Thailand, and Singapore the weights of the dollar in the currency baskets seem to decline as we concluded from the Wald tests reported above. For Taiwan and the Philippines the weights are more stable and roughly the same as the in the pre-crisis period.

In general we observe that the post-crisis weights of the dollar and yen in the currency baskets of Korea, Philippines, Taiwan, and Thailand seem more flexible (volatile) than in the pre-crisis period – but that the dollar continues to predominate.

## 4.2   Reducing Daily Exchange Rate Volatility against the Dollar

However, knowing the dollar's $\alpha_2$ coefficients and the yen's $\alpha_3$ coefficients from equation (3.1) is not the whole story on exchange rate volatility. In principle, the dollar could get the highest relative weight (as per Frankel and Wei, 1994) in the currency basket without the absolute day-to-day volatility of any one East Asian currency against the dollar returning to its pre-crisis level.

Thus, a more direct but complementary test is necessary. We measure volatility as the percentage daily change of the national currency against the dollar (first log differences) from January 1990 through December 2003. The y-axes in the different country panels in Figure 3.3 have the same scale of ±8 percent against the dollar for all currencies.

To understand what is high and what is low volatility we need a standard of comparison. Calvo and Reinhart (2002) suggest that the only truly floating exchange rates are those of the inner group of mature industrial countries, such as the United States, Japan, Germany or Switzerland. Because these countries have mature, long-term domestic capital markets, their governments have little incentive for day-to-day exchange rate stabilization. Figure 3.3 compares the daily dollar volatilities of the East Asian countries to those of Germany, Japan, and Switzerland.[4]

As shown in Figure 3.3, the daily volatility of the dollar exchange rates of Germany, Japan, and Switzerland are indeed an order of magnitude higher than those of our East Asian countries in the non-crisis periods. Not only is the daily exchange volatility of these industrial countries very high, but it does not change significantly over time. In contrast, the volatility of the East Asian currencies is generally much lower – but with greater variability over time.

Specifically, the hard pegs of China and Hong Kong exhibit extremely low day-to-day volatility as well as a high stability over time. Discretionary changes in the Chinese yuan in the early 1990s occurred before the introduction of the hard peg in February 1994. Since then, the yuan has been even more stable on a day-to-day basis than has the Hong Kong dollar.

For all the other East Asian economies, we observe a changing pattern of daily volatility over time. Up to 1997–98 , high-frequency volatility was low except in the Philippines, which experienced higher volatility in the first half of the 1990s – although not as high as in the industrial countries. During the Asian crisis turmoil in the capital and currency markets is reflected in much greater day-to-day volatility which is most striking for Indonesia, Korea, Malaysia, Philippines, and Thailand. For the post-crisis period we observe a more heterogeneous pattern. First, Singapore and Taiwan, not as strongly affected by the crisis, returned rather fast to the pre-crisis pattern. Note that Singapore stabilizes its currency on the basis of a more diversified currency basket, and therefore its overall exchange rate volatility is smaller than Figure 3.3 suggests. Second, Malaysia has adopted capital controls and a hard peg to the dollar, so that its exchange rate volatility has declined to zero.

Third, Korea and Thailand have significantly reduced exchange rate volatility, but it seems still to be slightly higher than before the crisis. The larger weight of the yen in the Thai and Korean currency baskets makes a complete return to the pre-crisis level of dollar pegging more difficult. Finally, although Indonesia and the Philippines have been quite successful in reducing the day-to-day volatility of their exchange rates compared to the crisis, volatility is still much higher than before.

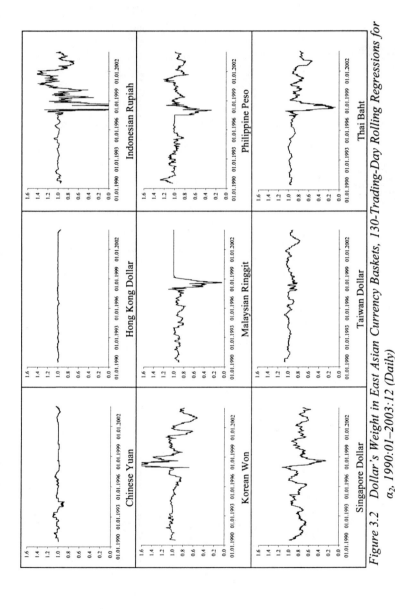

*Figure 3.2   Dollar's Weight in East Asian Currency Baskets, 130-Trading-Day Rolling Regressions for $\alpha_2$, 1990:01–2003:12 (Daily)*

*Source:* IMF: IFS, Central Bank of China. Index 1980:01 = 100. Note different scale for Indonesia.

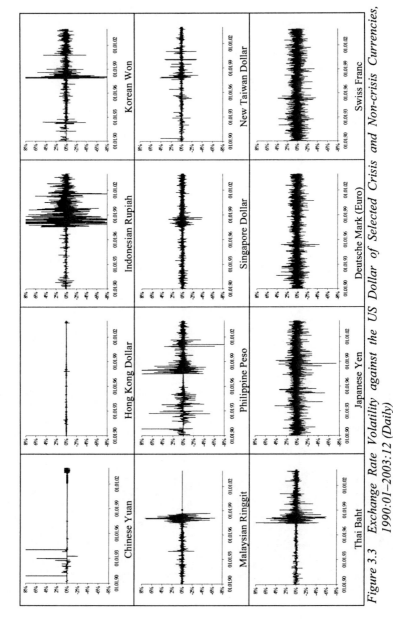

*Figure 3.3  Exchange Rate Volatility against the US Dollar of Selected Crisis and Non-crisis Currencies, 1990:01–2003:12 (Daily)*

*Source:* Datastream. Volatility is daily percentage changes against the dollar.

The evidence given in Figure 3.3 is supported by Table 3.4, which reports the standard deviations of daily exchange rate fluctuations against the dollar. In the pre-crisis period, the standard deviations of the day-to-day exchange rate volatility of all East Asian currencies are much smaller than the standard deviations of the so-called free floaters (Japan, Germany, and Switzerland) which are our comparison set. The standard deviations of the hard pegs (China and Hong Kong) are close to zero during and after the crisis. For Indonesia, Korea, Malaysia, Philippines and Thailand the standard deviations in Table 3.4 increase massively during the crisis period – with Singapore and Taiwan increasing less. In contrast exchange rate variability against the Japanese yen is high, similar to the industrial countries.

Since the crisis, the standard deviations of all affected countries have declined again (Table 3.4). Except for Malaysia, this exchange rate volatility of the crisis economies for the whole post-crisis period (1999–2003) is still larger than before the crisis. However, the volatility was relatively higher at the beginning of the post-crisis period in 1999 than more recently in 2003.

*Table 3.4     Standard Deviations of Daily Exchange Rate Fluctuations against the Dollar*

|  | Pre-crisis | Crisis | Post-crisis | 2003 |
|---|---|---|---|---|
| Chinese Yuan | 0.03 | 0.01 | 0.00 | 0.00 |
| Hong Kong Dollar | 0.02 | 0.03 | 0.00 | 0.00 |
| Indonesian Rupiah | 0.17 | 4.43 | 1.15 | 0.42 |
| Korean Won | 0.22 | 2.35 | 0.44 | 0.51 |
| Malaysian Ringgit | 0.25 | 1.53 | 0.01 | 0.00 |
| Philippine Peso | 0.37 | 1.31 | 0.53 | 0.27 |
| Singapore Dollar | 0.20 | 0.75 | 0.27 | 0.36 |
| New Taiwan Dollar | 0.19 | 0.50 | 0.21 | 0.15 |
| Thai Baht | 0.21 | 1.55 | 0.39 | 0.26 |
| Japanese Yen | 0.67 | 1.00 | 0.64 | 0.53 |
| Deutsche Mark | 0.60 | 0.58 | 0.66 | 0.63 |
| Swiss Franc | 0.69 | 0.66 | 0.71 | 0.72 |

*Source:* Datastream. Percent changes. Pre-crisis = 02/01/94–05/30/97, crisis = 06/01/97–12/31/98, post-crisis = 01/01/99–12/31/03, 2003 = 01/01/03–12/31/03.

To underline this last point, suppose our 'post-crisis' period includes only daily observations in the year 2003. Then the right–hand column in Table 3.4 shows that many East Asian currencies as the Philippine peso, the Taiwan dollar, and to some extent the Thai baht are now less or about equally volatile against the dollar than they were before the crisis. In 2003, only Indonesia and Korea still had a significantly higher standard deviation. All East Asian countries except Indonesia seem to have more or less returned to the pre-crisis level of high-frequency pegging.

## 5   THE CASE AGAINST BASKET EXCHANGE RATE PEGGING

A major reason of the Asian crisis was the deep devaluation of the yen in 1997–98 (McKinnon and Schnabl, 2003). When the smaller East Asian economies peg to the dollar, they become collectively more vulnerable to fluctuations between the dollar and yen. When the yen is high against the dollar, their exports – and inflows of foreign direct investment from Japan – boom. When the yen depreciates, their international competitiveness falls – sometimes precipitously as in 1997–98.

In the aftermath of the Asian crisis many authors including Williamson (2000), Kawai (2002), and Ogawa and Ito (2002) have proposed increasing the weight of the Japanese yen in the East Asian currency baskets. Because Japan and the smaller East Asian economies are closely linked in trade, they contend that a larger weight of the Japanese yen in the currency baskets of the smaller East Asian economies would reduce variance in trade flows. Japan in particular would like to reduce variance in its own international competitiveness from fluctuations in the yen/dollar rate by having its increasingly important East Asian neighbors give more weight to the yen in setting their exchange rates. For instance, Williamson (2000) proposes to give a weight of 33 percent to the dollar, the yen, and the euro respectively.

However we have tried to show that unilateral pegs to the dollar might well be preferred to the currency-basket approach – certainly from the perspective of the smaller East Asian economies. First, because the dollar invoicing of trade throughout the whole East Asian region is so prevalent, collective pegging to the dollar provides a quite strong nominal anchor for the national price levels of the smaller countries – albeit in non-crisis periods. Of course the success of this nominal anchor depends heavily on the stability of the US price level and US monetary policy. But in recent years, US prices have been quite stable while Japan has experienced deflationary pressure. Those advocating basket pegging are more concerned with minimizing the variance in a country's *real* effective exchange rate rather than with stabilizing its domestic *nominal* price level. Indeed, a commitment to stabilize real effective exchange rates leaves the nominal price level indeterminate.

Second, at a more microeconomic level, pegging to just one major international currency helps individual merchants and bankers better hedge their own foreign exchange risks. Because of the missing bond and forward exchange markets in developing countries, governments provide an informal hedge by keeping the domestic currency stable against the dominant currency, i.e., the dollar in East Asia. This then exposes merchants to 'extraneous' fluctuations of the yen against the dollar which, however, they can partially hedge by making use of the well-developed forward market between yen and dollars. If a Korean importer of Japanese products needs to pay 100 yen in 60 days, he can buy yen 60 days forward for dollars – and then trade won for dollars in 60 days at a presumed unchanged (soft peg of the won against the dollar) exchange rate – what we call double hedging.

However, under a basket peg, the spot exchange rate of the dollar against the won in 60 days would be more uncertain. Because the dollar is the natural intervention currency that governments use, the Korean authorities would be obligated to keep changing the won/dollar rate as the dollar fluctuates against the yen and euro. This then would confuse the Korean merchant's hedging strategy – particularly if the weights of the major currencies in the basket were somewhat uncertain, and the timing of official changes in the won/dollar rate in order to track the yen was also uncertain. In effect, people who argue that basket pegging would reduce risk are only looking at movements in spot exchange rates as if merchants could not hedge. That is, they are not accounting for the forward hedging strategies that almost all merchants use.

Finally, picking the appropriate official weights in a currency basket is problematic. A simple trade-weighted basket would not reflect the dollar's overwhelming predominance as a currency of invoice – where external dollar prices of goods and services are sticky and do not vary much with changes in the yen/dollar rate. Nor would it reflect the currency of denomination of outstanding foreign currency debts.

All in all, the best exchange rate strategy for any small East Asian economy may be the simple 'corner solution' of pegging just to the dollar – as is the normal current practice by East Asian governments. However, we do not deny that large fluctuations in the yen/dollar exchange rate create serious problems of risk management for the East Asian dollar peggers (McKinnon and Schnabl, 2003), and even bigger problems for Japan itself. But the straightforward solution to this East Asian exchange rate dilemma is for Japan to peg the yen to the dollar in a convincing fashion – which may require US cooperation, as discussed in McKinnon and Ohno (1997) – rather than beseeching nine or so other East Asian countries to give more weight to the yen by introducing basket pegging.

## 6   CONCLUSION: AN EVENTUAL RETURN TO LOW-FREQUENCY PEGGING?

With the benefit of hindsight, the post-crisis return to high-frequency dollar pegging – Table 3.4 and Figure 3.2 – is hardly surprising. For emerging markets in East Asia and elsewhere suffering from incomplete capital markets (original sin), high-frequency dollar pegging is an important tool for hedging foreign exchange risk and stabilizing exchange rates. But could this clandestine return to high-frequency pegging augur an eventual return to low-frequency pegging as well?

Learning from the vulnerability to yen/dollar depreciation, many East Asian countries seem to be allowing more exchange rate variability at lower frequencies in the post-crisis period. In support of the finding of Hernández and Montiel (2003) Figure 3.1 shows more dollar exchange rate drift after than before the crisis on a month-to-month basis. For Indonesia, Korea, Philippines, Singapore, Taiwan, and Thailand monthly exchange fluctuations are greater than before – although those for China, Hong Kong, and Malaysia remain (close to) zero.

A more formal analysis of low-frequency exchange rate stabilization against the yen is given by Table 3.5, which allows us to compare the standard deviations of monthly exchange rate fluctuations against the dollar and the yen in the pre-crisis and post-crisis period. We observe that for all East Asian countries – except the hard peg countries, China, Hong Kong and Malaysia – the monthly exchange rate variability against the dollar is still significantly higher than in the pre-crisis period (Table 3.5), but much less than in the crisis itself.

An alternative approach for showing exchange rate smoothing at low frequencies in the East Asian post-crisis era is to use the euro's fluctuations against the dollar as the benchmark. As is largely true in practice, we assume that the European Central Bank – behaving as a free floater – leaves the dollar/euro rate to market forces. We partition the data into two sub-periods: 1999–2001 when the dollar appreciated generally against the euro, and 2002 up to December 2003 when the dollar generally depreciated against the euro.

Figure 3.4 plots the cumulative depreciation of the euro and all East Asian currencies for the period of dollar appreciation. All East Asian currencies except the Philippine peso but including the Japanese yen depreciated less than the euro against the dollar. Since the beginning of 2002, when the dollar started depreciating, the picture is reversed: Figure 3.5 shows that all East Asian currencies appreciated considerably less than the euro did. (At the same time, with the exception of Indonesia, the smaller East Asian economies appreciated less than Japan did – thereby also safeguarding their competitiveness against Japan.)

*Table 3.5    Standard Deviations of Monthly Exchange Rate Fluctuations against the Dollar*

|  | Pre-crisis | Crisis | Post-crisis |
|---|---|---|---|
| Chinese Yuan | 0.25 | 0.03 | 0.00 |
| Hong Kong Dollar | 0.08 | 0.07 | 0.04 |
| Indonesian Rupiah | 0.26 | 26.54 | 5.28 |
| Korean Won | 1.01 | 11.53 | 1.96 |
| Malaysian Ringgit | 1.06 | 6.69 | 0.00 |
| Philippine Peso | 1.19 | 5.25 | 1.71 |
| Singapore Dollar | 0.76 | 2.88 | 1.20 |
| New Taiwan Dollar | 1.01 | 2.63 | 1.37 |
| Thai Baht | 0.43 | 8.88 | 1.62 |
| Japanese Yen | 3.66 | 3.64 | 2.43 |
| Deutsche Mark | 2.20 | 2.33 | 2.57 |
| Swiss Franc | 2.62 | 2.60 | 2.55 |

*Source:* IMF: IFS. Percent Changes. Pre-crisis = February 1994 – Mai 1997, crisis = June 1997–, December 1998, post-crisis = January 1999–December 2003.

In resisting this exchange market pressure for currency appreciation, each East Asian central bank intervened heavily to buy dollars. As shown in Figure 3.6 the official foreign reserves in East Asian countries have increased surprisingly fast in China, Hong Kong, Indonesia, Korea, Malaysia, Philippines, Taiwan, Thailand, and particularly Japan. Indeed, in 2003, the Japanese government intervened truly massively: official reserves rose by 186 billion US dollars, which is greater than Japan's trade surplus.

In the crisis countries Indonesia, Korea, and the Philippines foreign exchange reserves have risen far above their pre-crisis levels. In contrast, the official foreign exchange reserves of the benchmark free floater Germany (Euroland) hardly changed. Only Singapore, which devolves most of its foreign reserves to a government-run overseas investment corporation, has kept 'official' reserves close to their pre-crisis level. Far beyond simply rebuilding their pre-crisis levels of exchange reserves, East Asian governments have evidently been intervening massively to prevent their exchange rates from appreciating.

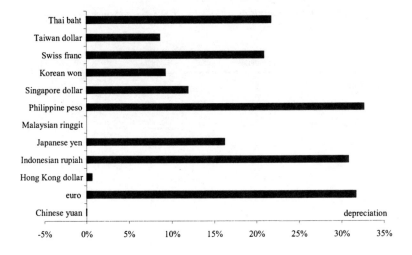

*Figure 3.4    Exchange Rate Changes against the US dollar 01/01/1999–*
*12/31/2001*

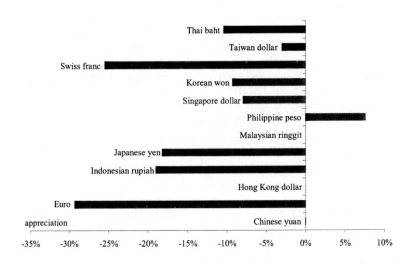

*Figure 3.5    Exchange Rate Changes against the US dollar 01/01/2002–*
*12/31/2003*

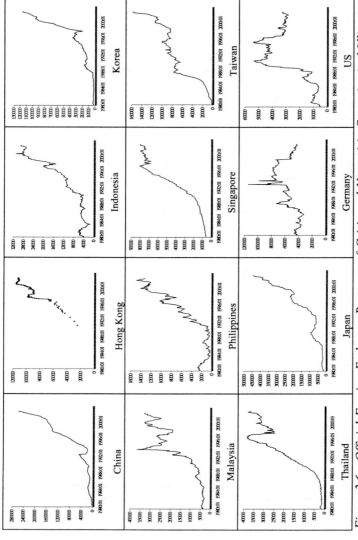

*Figure 3.6  Official Foreign Exchange Reserves of Crisis and Non-crisis Countries in Millions of Dollars, 1980:01–2003:12 (Monthly)*

Source: IMF: IFS. Million Dollars. Note different scales on the y-axis.

In summary, all East Asian countries now seem to be pursuing similar low frequency exchange rate strategies with respect to the dollar, but to different degrees. China, Hong Kong, and Malaysia maintain hard fixes to the dollar. Japan, while adhering in principle to exchange rate flexibility, restricts appreciation pressure by sporadic but quite massive (and possibly unsterilized) foreign exchange interventions.

Over the long run, sustaining exchange rate stability in East Asia at low frequencies will mainly depend on the region's two largest economies – China and Japan. So far, China has taken the lead by firmly keeping its exchange rate stable at 8.28 yuan/dollar since 1994 – despite domestic pressure and foreign advice to depreciate in the 1997–98 crisis, and foreign pressure to appreciate in 2002–2003. Although fluctuations in the yen/dollar rate have been much more of a disturbing influence, particularly the deep depreciation of the yen that aggravated the great East Asian crisis of 1997–98, the post-crisis signs are now favorable. Japan itself, by smoothing out sharp exchange rate fluctuations of the yen against the dollar, seems to have already contributed to greater exchange rate stability in East Asia.

To be sure, more formal 'parity' commitments to peg the yuan and yen to the dollar would encourage the smaller East Asian countries to similarly peg their dollar exchange rates – thus creating a zone of greater monetary and exchange rate stability for the increasingly integrated East Asian economy. However, even if Japan returns to being a dangerous outlier with wide fluctuations in the yen/dollar rate, having the other East Asian countries stabilize their dollar exchange rates collectively seems more rational than the IMF's cumulative institutional wisdom of pushing for greater exchange rate flexibility – with no well-defined constraint on how any one country's rate affects its neighbors.

## NOTES

[1]  Before the 1990s, China's official exchange rate against the dollar was often changed and different rates existed for commercial transactions. Only the official exchange rate is reported in Figure 3.1.

[2]  The difference between the price level for traded and nontraded goods (the Balassa–Samuelson effect) is only significant for Hong Kong and Korea.

[3]  As the leading currency of the European currency system, representing the euro since 01/01/1999.

[4]  These countries are free floaters against the dollar but not necessarily against other currencies. For instance, before January 1999 Germany was a member of the European Monetary System which implied a stabilization of its exchange rate against other EMU currencies. Also Switzerland might tend to reduce exchange rate volatility against the euro.

# REFERENCES

Calvo, Guillermo and Carmen Reinhart (2002), 'Fear of Floating', *Quarterly Journal of Economics*, **117**, 379–408.

Eichengreen, Barry and Ricardo Hausmann (1999), 'Exchange Rates and Financial Fragility', *NBER Working Paper*, No. 7418.

Fischer, Stanley (2001), 'Exchange Rate Regimes: Is the Bipolar View Correct?', *Journal of Economic Perspectives*, **15**, 3–24.

Frankel, Jeffrey and Shang-Jin Wei (1994), 'Yen Bloc or Dollar Bloc? Exchange Rate Policies in East Asian Economies', in Takatoshi Ito and Anne Krueger (eds.), *Macroeconomic Linkages: Savings, Exchange Rates, and Capital Flows*, Chicago: University of Chicago Press, 295–329.

Frankel, Jeffrey (1999), 'No Single Currency Regime is Right for All Countries or at All Times', *NBER Working Paper*, No. 7338.

Hernández, Leonardo and Peter Montiel (2003), 'Post-Crisis Exchange Rate Policy in Five Asian Countries: Filling in the "Hollow Middle"?', *Journal of the Japanese and International Economies*, **17**, 336–69.

Kawai, Masahiro (2002), 'Exchange Rate Arrangements in East Asia: Lessons from the 1997–98 Currency Crisis', *Bank of Japan Institute for Monetary and Economic Studies Discussion Paper*, No. E-17.

Kwan, Chi-Hung, Yen Bloc (2001), *Toward Economic Integration in Asia*, Washington, DC: Brookings Institution.

McKinnon, Ronald and Kenichi Ohno (1997), *Dollar and Yen: Resolving Economic Conflict between the United States and Japan*, Cambridge, Massachusetts: The MIT Press.

McKinnon, Ronald and Gunther Schnabl (2003), 'Synchronized Business Cycles in East Asia: Fluctuations in the Yen–Dollar Exchange Rate', *The World Economy*, **26**, 1067–88.

Ogawa, Eiji and Takatoshi Ito (2002), 'On the Desirability of a Regional Basket Currency Arrangement', *Journal of Japanese and International Economies*, **16**, 317–34.

Sato, Kiyotaka (1999), 'The International Use of the Japanese Yen: the Case of Japan's Trade with East Asia', *The World Economy*, **22**, 547-84.

Schnabl, Gunther (2004), 'De jure versus de facto Exchange Rate Stabilization in Central and Eastern Europe', *Aussenwirtschaft*, **59** (2), 171–90.

Williamson, John (2000), *Exchange Rate Regimes for Emerging Markets: Reviving the Intermediate Option*, Washington, DC: Institute for International Economics.

# 4. Integration and Convergence of Financial Markets in the European Union

## Bala Batavia, Parameswar Nandakumar and Cheick Wagué

### 1 INTRODUCTION

The positive impact of the single market on trade is not a contentious issue, though the estimates of the *quantitative* effects vary. Nor does it seem that the trade volume effects vary to any great extent across the spectrum of the members of the common market. The extent of financial integration is, in contrast, still a debated issue, and there is evidence that some countries have made – relatively – slow progress along this path (see Lemmen and Eijffinger, 1995a). In this chapter, a fresh attempt is made to rank the countries in terms of the extent of financial integration achieved. A distinction is also sought to be made between *regional* and *global* integration, and the convergence achieved after entry into the EMU is weeded apart from the single market effects.

Related work available in the literature is discussed in the next section, with the objective of providing the backdrop to the current study; it is not to be interpreted as a comprehensive survey of the literature. Section 3 supplies the details of the models used for analyzing the financial aspects of the unification process, while Section 4 describes the data used and the empirical results obtained. There is a final, concluding section.

### 2 BACKGROUND AND RELATED LITERATURE

There are a number of approaches to the evaluation of the extent of financial openness and integration in the literature. The distinction between these two concepts – of openness and integration – was perhaps thrown up most vividly by the Asian crisis of the mid–1990s. The perception that financial openness, which could just entail a complete opening up to international capital flows, does not encompass a process of financial reforms – which is needed for true integration – has been gaining ground (see Le, 2000; Batavia et al., 2004). A number of indices have also been developed which give a pointer to the degrees of financial openness and integration achieved in an economy.

The World Bank Index (World Bank, 2000) takes into account the facilitation of cross-border flows by the home country, and is properly considered an index of financial openness. Other indices used for ranking countries in terms of openness include the ratio of FDI inflows and that of portfolio capital inflows to GDP (see Batavia et al., 2004). The ratio of foreign assets held to GDP or exports is sometimes considered an indicator of country-specific risk, with the risk progressively reducing as the ratio increases. However, in general, the components of assets as well as liabilities matter, as again exemplified by the Asian crisis where the affected countries often had a high proportion of short-run debt.

Rankings of countries in terms of financial openness are given in the empirical section. There we also provide comparisons in terms of some measures of financial integration, which are discussed here in this section. Integration would imply internal reforms as well, not the least in the banking sector, and norms of transparency similar to those prevailing in the most advanced markets. These criteria would weigh at least as important in a process of financial integration as that of providing complete convertibility on the capital account.

The foregoing implies that an economy can be financially more integrated with a distant trading partner than with a geographic neighbor. Eichengreen and Pempel (2002) state that this is true of the East Asian economies which are financially more integrated with the industrial nations of the western hemisphere than with each other. They attribute this to the fact that trade liberalization has proceeded further with those geographically distant economies than within East Asia, so that the progress on the financial front is a natural outcome, given the complementary relation between trade and financial flows. We take a leaf out of such reasoning in checking for the degree of financial integration of the EU countries with non-EU markets (primarily the US) as well[1].

There are at least four measures of financial integration mentioned in the literature. These are:

1. covered interest parity (CIP),
2. uncovered interest rate parity,
3. real interest rate parity (RIP), and
4. Feldstein–Horioka Index.

Of the interest rate parity conditions, it is the covered parity condition that is usually met first as integration proceeds, and ought to be met by now for the EU countries. But this may not have been achieved even by, say, the mid-1990s, and therefore the nominal interest rate differential is often used to represent the degree of financial integration – and the intensity of capital controls – in empirical work on the determinants of integration, as in Lemmer and Eijffinger (1995b). The uncovered interest rate parity condition is more difficult to verify as it incorporates a variable that is not directly observable, the speculative exchange rate premium, though proxies are not hard to come by. Most tests of this condition, which use the forward premium as a proxy for the speculative premium, are not confirmative. Marston (1994) does tackle this problem in a way by employing survey data on exchange rate expectations as a direct measure of the speculative exchange rate premium.

The real interest rate parity condition is usually taken to be a test of complete financial integration, encompassing both a test of capital mobility and one of *macroeconomic convergence*. The reasons for this condition not being fulfilled can be numerous, and it should be fair to suggest that financial integration has proceeded further in terms of short-run flows, whereas international substitutability when it comes to long-term bonds, equities and real investments is still lagging behind.

More specifically, the RIP condition also implies that the purchasing power parity (PPP) condition, which is a long-run price convergence condition, is met. In fact, the non-fulfillment of the RIP condition can be considered due to an integration or country risk premium, and a convergence premium, with the former relating to the non-fulfillment of the CIP condition and the latter to that of the PPP condition:

$$RIPV_t = (i_{h,t} - i_{f,t} - F_{p,t}) + (\pi_{h,t} - \pi_{f,t} - F_{p,t}) \qquad (4.1)$$

where *RIPV* is the deviation from the real interest rate parity condition, $i_{h,t}$ is the home nominal interest rate at time $t$, $i_f$ is the nominal foreign interest rate, $F_p$ is the forward exchange rate premium or the expected rate of appreciation, $\pi_h$ is the inflation at home and $\pi_f$ is the inflation abroad. Actual inflation rates proxy for expected rates. The first term in equation (4.1) should have approached zero with integration in the single market, while the macroeconomic convergence premium should be reduced after entry into the EMU. However, we let the figures speak for themselves in the empirical Section 4.

The Feldstein–Horioka Test (1980) (hereafter F–H Test) for financial integration has also been used as extensively as the interest rate parity conditions, and is considered equivalent to the RIP condition, since it deals with investment flows that depend on real interest rates. However, a zero F–H coefficient for the national savings ratio variable as a determinant of investment in a regression, which is deemed to represent complete financial integration, has never been thrown up in empirical estimates. It is something of a paradox that cross-section and time series studies show a rising coefficient, indicating falling integration over time. Such a result emerges in Feldstein (1983) and Dooley et al. (1984) among others. A number of subsequent studies have suggested reasons why national savings and investment levels may be correlated even if real interest rate parity held. One explanation is that large countries (such as Germany) that can influence the level of world real interest rates will tend to have positively correlated savings and investment rates. Another view, that 'endogenous' government policies (say, with respect to the current account) may be the reason for the F–H coefficient being closer to one than zero for most countries has been put forward by Tobin (1983), Summers (1988), Bayoumi (1990) and others. However, this problem could be handled by having a data set over a long period of time (to take care of cyclical effects), and it does seem worthwhile to compare financial integration levels in the EU countries in terms of this well-known coefficient also. However, since we are already incorporating the real interest rate parity test, which is considered equivalent to a test of the F–H condition, we do not include the latter separately.

Another test of financial integration is based on the Euler equation, which characterizes inter-temporal expenditure, and proceeds by correlating consumption levels across countries – since the welfare gains made possible by the globalization of capital markets include the smoothing of the time paths of consumption[2]. Using a related test, Lemmen and Eijffinger (1995b) have ranked the EU countries in the following fashion in terms of progress in financial integration: high integration in Belgium, Germany, the Netherlands and the UK; medium levels of integration in Austria, Denmark, Finland, France, Ireland, Italy, Spain and Sweden, and low levels of integration in Greece and Portugal. In this study we work with more recent data, and provide individual country rankings.

International markets typically provide national agents with a wider range of investment opportunities, and make also possible higher rates of output growth. But a striking result in this stream of analysis is that under certain assumptions (including the absence of transaction costs), domestic consumption is related to world output, and not to domestic output. This can be captured in cross-country correlations of consumption and output, where consumption correlations should be larger than the correlations of outputs. This has given rise to the so-called 'consumption correlation puzzle', with empirical work throwing up consumption correlations smaller than output coefficients (Baxter and Crucini, 1995; Stockman and Tesar, 1995; Obstfeld, 1994). However, it is still possible to rank countries in terms of the level of integration given by the results, and we do proceed with that task in the present study.

Thus, the work on gauging the level of financial integration in the recent decades of reforms and internationalization have encompassed tests on interest rate parity (*nominal* as well as *real*) and the Feldstein–Horioka and the Euler equation tests, not to mention the use of the ratios of financial openness. Usually, the tests on financial integration involve the determination of co-integrating relationships, similar to the work on real integration done with variables such as industrial production. In the present study, rankings on global and regional financial integration are discussed according to almost all of these criteria.

## 3   MODELS FOR ESTIMATION

Equation (4.2) is the covered interest rate parity condition tested for individual EU countries, against the German mark prior to the formation of the monetary union, and against the Euro rates beyond that date:

$$i_{j,t} = \alpha_0 + \beta_0 i_{f,t} + \varepsilon_{0,t} \qquad (4.2)$$

$i_{j,t}$ is the short-run interest rate at period $t$ in the member country, while $i_{f,t}$ is the corresponding rate for the EU area as a whole, proxied by the German rate. The regression provides estimates of the coefficients $\beta_0$, which can be used for country-ranking purposes.

The interest rate parity condition in relation to US short-run rates is also estimated as below, providing information about the degree of global financial integration:

$$i_{j,t} = \alpha_1 + \beta_1 i_{u,t} + \varepsilon_{1,t} \qquad (4.3)$$

In equation (4.3), $i_{u,t}$ is the US short-run (three–month) interest rate on bonds.

As described in the previous section, the integration and the convergence premiums, corresponding to the non-fulfillment of the CIP and PPP conditions respectively, can be obtained. The convergence premium can be calculated as:

$$P_{c,t} = \pi_{h,t} - \pi_{f,t} - F_{p,t} \qquad (4.4)$$

where $\pi_{h,t}$ is inflation in the individual country while $\pi_{f,t}$ is inflation in the EU area as a whole. $F_{p,t}$ is the three–month forward exchange rate premium for the national currency.

The convergence premium represented in equation (4.4) may be expected to reduce or even go to zero as a country enters the EMU, but this has to be empirically verified as stated earlier. It may be possible to proxy this premium in related empirical analyses by the volatility of the exchange rate with the Euro, which is, by definition, zero for an EMU member.

Equation (4.5) below is the real interest rate $r$ parity test for the EU area, while (4.6) tests for the country's real interest rate integration with the dollar area:

$$r_{h,t} = \alpha_2 + \beta_2 r_{f,t} + \varepsilon_{2,t} \tag{4.5}$$

$$r_{h,t} = \alpha_3 + \beta_3 r_{u,t} + \varepsilon_{3,t} \tag{4.6}$$

To make a ranking of financial integration based on consumption and output correlation, we do the following. An aggregate time series of EU consumption is calculated, weighing individual country consumption by the population variable.

The individual country consumption levels are regressed on this aggregated variable. Correlation coefficients are computed for country and aggregate EU consumption levels, and the following equation is estimated for each country:

$$C_{h,t} = \alpha_4 + \beta_4 C_{EU,t} + \varepsilon_{4,t} \tag{4.7}$$

where $C_{h,t}$ is the individual country consumption level, while $C_{EU,t}$ is the aggregate, country-weighted EU consumption level. We also estimate the relation between individual country consumption and output levels (with some resemblance at least to an ordinary consumption function!):

$$C_{h,t} = \alpha_5 + \beta_5 Y_{h,t} + \varepsilon_{5,t} \tag{4.8}$$

In equation (4.8), $Y_{h,t}$ are the individual country output (GDP) levels. The correlation coefficients (see Table 4.6 in Section 4) together with the regression coefficients in (4.7) and (4.8) provide a basis for making inter-country comparisons (in Section 4) of the degree of financial integration achieved.


# 4   DESCRIPTION OF DATA AND EMPIRICAL RESULTS

The specified equations are run with annual data for the period 1978–2002, and with quarterly data for the period 1985–2004. The data source for all the

variables is the publication *International Financial Statistics (IFS)*, published
by the International Monetary Fund, and the linked websites.

Table 4.1 below provides the results of the nominal interest rate parity
tests for individual countries, using German short-run nominal rates. In Table
4.1, significance of the coefficient at 1 percent level, 5 percent and 10 percent
levels are signaled by three, two and one stars respectively. As can be seen
from the table, all the coefficients, except for those of the US, Greece and,
quite surprisingly, that of the Netherlands, are highly significant.

The coefficients for the UK, Portugal, Spain, Denmark, Sweden, Ireland
and Belgium indicate that these countries are on the path to full financial
integration according to the nominal interest rate parity criteria. Finland,
Austria, France and Italy lag behind according to this measurement, while
Greece and the Netherlands exhibit no integration tendencies at all.

It would be interesting to compare the process of financial integration
within Europe with that occurring – for the EU countries – on a global scale.
For this, the results of the estimation using US short-run interest rates as the
independent variable will provide interesting information.

*Table 4.1    Nominal interest rate parity tests*[*]

| Country | Adjusted $R^2$ | t-value | Coefficient | Rho |
|---|---|---|---|---|
| Austria | 0.94 | 4.13** | 0.27 | 0.91 |
| Belgium | 0.95 | 4.99** | 0.47 | 0.88 |
| Denmark | 0.97 | 4.38** | 0.61 | 0.95 |
| Finland | 0.97 | 2.01** | 0.36 | 0.96 |
| France | 0.96 | 3.28** | 0.17 | 0.92 |
| USA | 0.94 | 1.34 | 0.24 | 0.98 |
| Greece | 0.05 | 0.29 | 0.05 | 0.99 |
| Ireland | 0.49 | 2.45** | 0.49 | 0.91 |
| Italy | 0.97 | 2.47** | 0.24 | 0.97 |
| Netherlands | 0.90 | 1.01 | 0.07 | 0.90 |
| Portugal | 0.93 | 5.39*** | 1.12 | 0.93 |
| Spain | 0.98 | 5.10*** | 0.63 | 0.98 |
| Sweden | 0.96 | 2.38** | 0.59 | 0.97 |
| UK | 0.96 | 4.94** | 1.08 | 0.96 |

*Note:* [*]EU (Germany). Short-run Rates Quarterly Data 1985–2004.

In contrast to the results tabulated in Table 4.1, the results in Table 4.2
show that the European core exhibits much less financial integration on a
global scale, as measured by the integration with the North American market.

The coefficient is significant only for the UK, which seems to be more integrated (in the nominal interest rate parity sense) with the USA, than most countries are within the EU area.

*Table 4.2    Nominal interest rate parity**

| Country | Adjusted $R^2$ | t-value | Coefficient | Rho |
|---------|---------------|---------|-------------|-----|
| Austria | 0.92 | -0.56 | -0.03 | 0.94 |
| Belgium | 0.14 | 1.52 | 0.14 | 0.96 |
| Denmark | 0.02 | 0.20 | 0.02 | 0.97 |
| Finland | 0.97 | -0.19 | -0.02 | 0.97 |
| France | 0.04 | 0.97 | 0.04 | 0.94 |
| Germany | 0.97 | 1.28 | 0.10 | 0.99 |
| Greece | 0.99 | -0.71 | -0.10 | 0.99 |
| Ireland | 0.93 | -0.26 | -0.04 | 0.93 |
| Italy | 0.99 | 0.54 | 0.04 | 0.97 |
| Netherlands | 0.81 | 1.04 | 0.05 | 0.89 |
| Portugal | 0.99 | 0.10 | 0.02 | 0.95 |
| Spain | 0.98 | 1.13 | 0.10 | 0.99 |
| Sweden | 0.96 | 0.34 | 0.06 | 0.97 |
| UK | 0.96 | 3.18** | 0.49 | 0.95 |

*Note*:    *Interest Rates, Quarterly Rates 1985–2004.

Let us now see how the country relations fare under the more rigorous test of real interest rate parity. Table 4.3 gives the results of the real interest rate parity test within the EU.

It can be seen that the European core holds up quite robustly even in the case of the demanding real interest rate parity test; Austria, Belgium, France and Italy exhibit coefficients that are significant at the 5 percent level, and close to the values with nominal interest rate parity test. Ireland also throws up a coefficient that is significant and with almost the same value as in Table 4.1. The other European countries, including the UK, do not give out coefficients of integration that are significant.

The results in Table 4.4 indicate real financial integration with the North American market for a few countries, namely Austria, Belgium and the Netherlands. However, we need to view this against the background of the results obtained for nominal interest rate parity; none of these countries exhibited financial integration with the USA under that criteria. This means that inflation differentials could be just offsetting nominal interest rate differentials, so that the separate elements in equation (4.1) are not being satisfied. Thus no definite conclusion can be drawn from Table 4.4 about the extent of real financial integration for Austria, Belgium and the Netherlands.

*Table 4.3    Real interest rate parity tests**

| Country | Adjusted $R^2$ | t-value | Coefficient | Rho |
|---|---|---|---|---|
| Austria | 0.77 | 2.66** | 0.21 | 0.88 |
| Belgium | 0.83 | 2.55** | 0.22 | 0.90 |
| Denmark | 0.95 | 1.23 | 0.13 | 0.95 |
| Finland | 0.93 | 1.55 | 0.19 | 0.93 |
| France | 0.94 | 2.93** | 0.18 | 0.86 |
| USA | 0.90 | 1.88 | 0.17 | 0.94 |
| Greece | 0.94 | -0.21 | -0.05 | 0.93 |
| Ireland | 0.46 | 2.82** | 0.40 | 0.93 |
| Italy | 0.92 | 2.48** | 0.18 | 0.97 |
| Netherlands | 0.80 | 1.86 | 0.25 | 0.28 |
| Portugal | 0.73 | -0.62 | -0.13 | 0.86 |
| Spain | 0.87 | 0.54 | 0.07 | 0.95 |
| Sweden | 0.01 | 0.05 | 0.01 | 0.83 |
| UK | 0.79 | 1.11 | 0.13 | 0.80 |

*Note:*    *German (EU) real interest rates 1985–2004.

The results in Table 4.4 indicate real financial integration with the North American market for a few countries, namely Austria, Belgium, and the Netherlands. However, we need to view this against the background of the results obtained for nominal interest rate parity; none of these countries exhibited financial integration with the USA under that criteria. This means that inflation differentials could be just offsetting nominal interest rate differentials, so that the separate elements in equation (4.1) are not being satisfied. Thus no definite conclusion can be drawn from Table 4.4 about the extent of real financial integration for Austria, Belgium and the Netherlands.

The key results from the nominal and real interest rate parity tests for the EU area, and for the EU–North America linkages may be summed up as follows: The European core group, i.e., Austria–Belgium–Italy–France group, has achieved considerable financial integration in nominal and real terms, within the EU area, but is loosely linked to the North American market. New entrants like Sweden, Finland, Spain, and Ireland are also well integrated to the EU market. Significant integration with the North American market is exhibited only by the UK.

**Consumption Correlation and Euler Test Regressions**
Table 4.5 provides the correlation coefficients between individual country consumption levels and the weighed EU consumption level, and the results of the consumption correlations within the EU are given in Table 4.6.

*Table 4.4    Individual country rates against US rates: Real rates*

| Country | Adjusted $R^2$ | t-value | Coefficient | Rho |
|---------|----------------|---------|-------------|-----|
| Austria | 0.79 | 3.66** | 0.38 | 0.79 |
| Belgium | 0.83 | 2.09** | 0.25 | 0.92 |
| Denmark | 0.90 | -0.11 | -0.16 | 0.96 |
| Finland | 0.87 | -0.05 | -0.01 | 0.93 |
| France | 0.75 | 1.84 | 0.15 | 0.83 |
| Germany | 0.77 | 1.89 | 0.27 | 0.88 |
| Greece | 0.89 | 0.64 | 0.19 | 0.93 |
| Ireland | 0.90 | -1.11 | -0.22 | 0.95 |
| Italy | 0.91 | 1.50 | 0.15 | 0.97 |
| Netherlands | 0.85 | 5.75*** | 0.54 | 0.18 |
| Portugal | 0.73 | -1.0 | -0.30 | 0.86 |
| Spain | 0.87 | 0.04 | 0.01 | 0.96 |
| Sweden | 0.68 | 1.30 | 0.34 | 0.81 |
| UK | 0.82 | 1.43 | 0.82 | 0.87 |

*Table 4.5    Consumption correlations*

| Country | Consumption correlation with EU aggregate consumption |
|---------|-------------------------------------------------------|
| Austria | 0.294 |
| Belgium | 0.462 |
| Denmark | 0.039 |
| Finland | 0.094 |
| France | 0.443 |
| USA | 0.737 |
| Greece | 0.418 |
| Ireland | 0.456 |
| Italy | 0.668 |
| Netherlands | 0.285 |
| Portugal | 0.495 |
| Spain | 0.731 |
| Sweden | 0.504 |
| UK | 0.365 |

*Table 4.6    Consumptions correlation matrix*

|     | A | B | DK | FIN | F | GER | GR | IRE | I | NL | POR | E | S | UK | USA |
|-----|---|---|----|-----|---|-----|----|----|---|----|-----|---|---|----|----|
| A   | 1 | | | | | | | | | | | | | | |
| B   | 0.31 | 1 | | | | | | | | | | | | | |
| DK  | 0.00 | 0.41 | 1 | | | | | | | | | | | | |
| FIN | 0.15 | 0.21 | 0.07 | 1 | | | | | | | | | | | |
| F   | 0.31 | 0.49 | -0.05 | 0.52 | 1 | | | | | | | | | | |
| GER | 0.16 | 0.17 | 0.05 | -0.38 | 0.02 | 1 | | | | | | | | | |
| GR  | 0.11 | 0.33 | -0.21 | 0.23 | 0.26 | 0.05 | 1 | | | | | | | | |
| IRE | 0.14 | 0.41 | 0.13 | 0.17 | 0.37 | 0.03 | 0.14 | 1 | | | | | | | |
| I   | 0.12 | 0.13 | -0.09 | 0.21 | 0.27 | 0.30 | 0.16 | 0.58 | 1 | | | | | | |
| NL  | 0.15 | 0.24 | 0.17 | -0.70 | -0.15 | 0.18 | -0.01 | 0.18 | 0.22 | 1 | | | | | |
| POR | 0.11 | -0.1 | -0.42 | 0.10 | 0.26 | 0.15 | 0.75 | 0.23 | 0.40 | 0.02 | 1 | | | | |
| E   | 0.26 | 0.51 | -0.12 | 0.28 | 0.60 | 0.28 | 0.38 | 0.57 | 0.53 | 0.27 | 0.47 | 1 | | | |
| S   | 0.10 | 0.46 | 0.20 | 0.62 | 0.61 | 0.09 | 0.15 | 0.32 | 0.36 | 0.08 | 0.17 | 0.61 | 1 | | |
| UK  | 0.12 | 0.37 | 0.23 | 0.39 | 0.39 | -0.16 | 0.38 | 0.38 | 0.18 | 0.03 | 0.25 | 0.36 | 0.50 | 1 | |
| USA | 0.03 | 0.40 | 0.43 | 0.25 | 0.17 | -0.26 | 0.15 | 0.33 | - | 0.00 | -0.09 | 0.24 | 0.30 | 0.64 | 1 |

To complement the consumption correlations that were derived, individual country consumption levels were regressed on an aggregate, weighted measure of EU consumption, and also against own GDP volumes as well as weighted European and US GDP volumes. With increasing integration, we may expect that country consumption levels be more related to aggregate European consumption than to the domestic output levels. The results, only the significant ones, are reported in Table 4.7.

US GDP is significant only in explaining consumption in the UK, Ireland and Italy. But home GDP and European consumption are more significant than US GDP as determinants of consumption in Italy. Looking at the correlation table, UK consumption is highly correlated with consumption in the USA, with a medium level of correlation with the USA exhibited also by Ireland, Sweden, Denmark and Finland. Consumption in the four large nations, Germany, France, Italy and Spain are highly correlated with aggregate EU consumption, with Germany and Italy, together with Portugal, Austria and Netherlands exhibiting a very low correlation with US consumption.

The findings from the analysis of consumption correlations and estimates may be summed up as follows: financial integration within the EU has occurred to the greatest extent for the four largest nations and for Belgium, Ireland and Portugal. Next in the degree of integration would come Greece and Sweden, with Sweden also showing a 'medium' degree of financial integration from the analysis of consumption relationships with the USA.

*Table 4.7    Euler regressions*

| Country | Own GDP | EU GDP | US GDP | EU Consumption | Constant | R Squared |
|---|---|---|---|---|---|---|
| Austria | 0.8041 (4.372***) | | NOT SIGNIF | NOT SIGNIF | 0.4834 (1.01) | 0.50 |
| | | 0.512 (1.91*) | | | 1.665 (1.32) | 0.14 |
| Belgium | 1.213 (2.988**) | NOT SIGNIF | NOT SIGNIF | | -1.628 (-1.71) | 0.28 |
| | | | | 0.7155 (2.44**) | -0.356 (-0.41) | 0.213 |
| Denmark | 1.1406 (5.776***) | NOT SIGNIF | NOT SIGNIF | NOT SIGNIF | -0.9525 (-1.944*) | 0.60 |
| Finland | 0.6599 (6.711***) | NOT SIGNIF | NOT SIGNIF | NOT SIGNIF | 0.7913 (1.97*) | 0.672 |
| Germany | 1.6295 (12.47***) | | NOT SIGNIF | | -1.224 (2.554**) | 0.876 |
| | | 1.9275 (2.403**) | | | -1.807 (-0.9) | 0.208 |
| | | | | 2.0965 (5.1***) | -2.5017 (-2.09**) | 0.543 |
| Greece | 1.4902 (2.058**) | | NOT SIGNIF | | -0.2593 (-0.138) | 0.169 |
| | | 2.40 (2.272**) | | | -2.612 (-0.45) | 0.19 |
| | | | | 1.5476 (2.157**) | -0.826 (-0.19) | 0.175 |
| Ireland | 0.8353 (4.072***) | | | | -0.1474 (-1.4) | 0.43 |
| | | 1.771 (2.756**) | | | -0.2954 (0.1795) | 0.257 |
| | | | 1.0803 (2.817**) | | 0.6175 (0.713) | 0.215 |
| | | | | 1.0724 (2.403**) | -0.058 (-0.079) | 0.21 |

*Note:*    * Dependent Variable: Country Consumption.                    *continued overleaf*

*Global Divergence in Trade, Money and Policy*

*Table 4.7 (continued)*

| Country | Own GDP | EU GDP | US GDP | EU Consumption | Constant | R Squared |
|---|---|---|---|---|---|---|
| Italy | 1.4784 (5.636***) | | | | -0.5519 (0.85) | 0.59 |
| | | 1.554 (4.216***) | | | -1.1102 (-1.16) | 0.447 |
| | | | 0.6203 (2.327**) | | 0.6675 (0.7713) | 0.19 |
| | | | | 1.0447 (4.21***) | -0.058 (-0.079) | 0.45 |
| Netherlands | 0.7437 (1.411) | NOT SIGNIF | NOT SIGNIF | NOT SIGNIF | -0.275 (-0.2018) | 0.08 |
| Portugal | 0.8959 (2.105**) | | NOT SIGNIF | | 1.1076 (0.693) | 0.17 |
| | | 1.7563 (2.011**) | | | -0.3147 (-0.63) | 0.16 |
| | | | | 1.484 (2.670**) | 0.1235 (1.65) | 0.25 |
| Spain | 1.0211 (8.2788***) | | NOT SIGNIF | | -0.0861 (-0.228) | 0.76 |
| | | 1.346 (5.203***) | | | -0.5098 (-0.7) | 0.552 |
| | | | | 0.8706 (5.026***) | 0.4121 (0.5158) | 0.534 |
| Sweden | 1.1765 (3.543**) | NOT SIGNIF | NOT SIGNIF | | -0.819 (-1.86) | 0.363 |
| | | | | 0.6618 (2.735**) | 0.2939 (0.403) | 0.254 |
| UK | 1.0054 (6.102***) | NOT SIGNIF | | NOT SIGNIF | 0.1204 (1.29) | 0.635 |
| | | | 0.581 (2.498**) | | 1.205 (1.47) | 0.221 |

The UK, Denmark, Finland and – surprisingly – the Netherlands are very weakly integrated with the EU. The UK is more integrated financially with the US market, with Ireland, Sweden, Denmark and Finland also showing some degree of integration with the USA. So Ireland and Sweden – and to some extent Belgium – are countries which have proceeded far in terms of integration in Europe as well as globally.

When these results from the Euler regressions and consumption correlations are matched with the interest rate parity tests, it is possible to make a tentative ranking of the EU countries in terms of the degree of financial integration regionally as well as globally. The following picture given in Table 4.8 seems to emerge:

*Table 4.8  Degree of financial integration*

| EU | | | World Economy | | | Integration |
|---|---|---|---|---|---|---|
| High Integration | Medium Integration | Low Integration | High Integration | Medium Integration | Low Integration | in EU and Globally |
| A | S | GR | UK | S | GER | S |
| B | | NL | | IRE | E | IRE |
| GER | | UK | | FIN | F | FIN |
| F | | DK | | DK | GR | DK |
| I | | FIN | | | NL | UK |
| E | | | | | A | |
| IRE | | | | | POR | |
| POR | | | | | I | |
| | | | | | B | |

Finally, the convergence premiums for countries within the EMU are given in Table 4.9. Please note that the premiums have been calculated for period averages, and that it is the perceived trend that is of interest, not the actual numbers themselves. Expected exchange rate changes have been proxied by current changes, and the German exchange rate replaces Euro rates for the earlier years.

*Table 4.9    Convergence premiums for EMU countries*

| Country | 1993–95 | 1997–98 | 1999–2000 | 2001–2003 |
|---|---|---|---|---|
| Austria | -0.01 | -0.57 | 0.19 | 0.33 |
| Belgium | -1.01 | -0.40 | 0.57 | 0.29 |
| Finland | -4.27 | 0.81 | 0.99 | -0.31 |
| France | -0.96 | -0.51 | -0.17 | 0.29 |
| Greece | 19.45 | -4.70 | – | 1.90 |
| Ireland | 5.14 | -9.30 | 2.34 | 2.73 |
| Italy | 5.94 | -2.44 | 0.84 | 1.03 |
| Netherlands | -0.69 | 1.10 | 1.10 | 1.77 |
| Portugal | 5.45 | -3.67 | 1.31 | 2.13 |
| Spain | 8.66 | 3.72 | 1.60 | 1.61 |

The main points to be noted from Table 4.9 is that macroeconomic convergence does seem to have taken place as countries moved into the monetary union, this phenomenon being especially marked in the case of the countries (Spain, Greece, Portugal) which are late entrants to the EU. For the older community members like the Netherlands, Austria, Belgium and France, the convergence trend is less sharp.

## 5  CONCLUSIONS

The process of financial integration that has accelerated in Europe does reveal some interesting trends and patterns. Macroeconomic convergence, as reflected in convergence premiums, has been taking place over the last decade, and has been picking up pace more in the new entrants to the EU, such as Spain, Greece and Portugal. But the level or the degree of financial integration does not follow the same pattern.

Interest rate parity tests as well as Euler-type estimates for country consumption levels were conducted to study the degree of financial integration of each EU member within the EU as well as globally – with the US market serving as a proxy for the rest of the world. The picture that emerges is relatively complex, with country rankings in the degree of financial integration achieved hinging upon whether it is regional or global integration that is being focused upon. The large, core EU nations, Germany, France, Spain, Italy and Belgium, are clearly integrated strongly with the aggregate EU market, and very weakly linked globally. Small open economies that are advanced in skill and knowledge levels, such as Sweden, Denmark, Ireland and Finland, are integrated – to a medium extent – regionally as well as globally. The new, relatively less advanced, members, Portugal and Greece, are only integrated regionally, and to a lesser extent than the core members. The UK stands out in that it is integrated strongly to the US market, perhaps to a greater extent than to the EU markets.

It should be of interest to also study the extent of financial integration that has occurred in the latest group of – Eastern European – nations to enter the EU. This could throw some light on their ability to move smoothly into the monetary union; as such an analysis could be a useful complement to the tests usually done on asymmetries and common trends for prospective members.

## NOTES

[1] From the point of view of risk-sharing through international diversification, a larger union with non-heterogeneous members may be better, and it is not really clear that only members with synchronized macroeconomic shocks should participate. An implication for risk-sharing is that globalization *may* be a better strategy than regional groupings, and that is the reason why we check for global as well as regional financial integration.

[2] The correlation of consumption across countries in a global financial environment is easily derived (see Obstfeld and Rogoff, 1996).

## REFERENCES

Batavia, Bala, Parameswar Nandakumar and Cheick Wague (2004), 'Distinguishing Between Financial Openness and True Financial Integration: Results From a Multi-Country Study', *Journal of Economic Asymmetries*, **1** (1), 33-47.

Baxter, Marianne and Mario J. Crucini (1995), 'Business Cycles and the Asset Structure of Foreign Trade', *International Economic Review*, **36**, 821-855.

Bayoumi, Tamim (1990), 'Savings-Investment Correlations & Immobile Capital: Government Policy or Endogenous Behavior?', *IMF Staff Papers*, **37** (2), 360-387.

Dooley, Michael P., Jeffrey A. Frankel and Donald J. Mathieson (1984), 'International Capital Mobility: What Do Savings-Investment Correlations Tell Us?', *IMF Staff Papers*, **34** (3), 503-530.

Eichengreen, Barry and T.J. Pempel (2002), 'Why Has There Been Less Financial Integration in East Asia Than in Europe?', *Mimeo*, Institute of East Asian Studies and the Institute of European Studies.

Feldstein, Martin (1983), 'Domestic Savings and International Capital Movements in the Long Run and Short Run', *European Economic Review*, **21**, 129-151.

Feldstein. Martin and Charles Horioka (1980), 'Domestic Savings and International Capital Flows', *The Economic Journal*, **90**, 314-329.

Lemmen, Jan J.G. and Sylvester C.W. Eiiffinger (1995a), 'Financial Integration in Europe: Evidence from Euler Equation Tests', *Discussion Paper*, No. 32, Tilburg University.

Lemmen, Jan J.G. and Sylvester C.W. Eijffinger (1995b), 'The Fundamental Determinants of Financial Integration in the European Union', *Mimeo*, Department of Economics and Center for Economic Research, Tilburg University.

Marston, Richard C. (1994), *Real Interest Rates in the Group of Five Industrial Countries: A Study of International Financial Integration*, Cambridge, MA: Cambridge University Press.

Obstfeld, Maurice (1994), 'Are Industry Country Consumption Risks Globally Diversified?' in Leiderman, L. and A. Razin (eds), *Capital Mobility: The Impact on Consumption, Investment and Growth*, Cambridge, Cambridge University Press.

Obstfeld, Maurice and Kenneth Rogoff (1996), *Foundations of International Macroeconomics*, Cambridge, MA: MIT Press.

Stockman, Alan C. and Linda L. Tesar (1995), 'Tastes and Technology in a Two Country Model of the Business Cycle: Explaining International Co-movements', *American Economic Review*, **85**, 168-185.

Summers, Lawrence (1988), 'Tax Policy and International Competition', in J. Frenkel (ed.), *International Aspects of Financial Policies*, Chicago: University of Chicago Press.

Tobin, James (1983), 'Domestic Saving and International Capital Movement in the Long Run and the Short Run by M. Feldstein: Comment', *European Economic Review*, **21**, 153-156.

World Bank (2000), 'Financial Openness', in *The Quality of Growth*, World Bank and Oxford University Press.

PART THREE


ASYMMETRIES IN
BANKING SECTORS

# 5. Asymmetries in US Banking: The Role of Black-owned Banks

## Nicholas A. Lash

## 1 INTRODUCTION

The US banking industry is characterized by an asymmetry between the great majority of banks which are non-minority- or white-owned, and those owned by minorities, such as African-Americans, or blacks. The latter, smaller and less capitalized than the typical US banks, exist partially to undertake an important role that is to provide needed, and otherwise insufficiently provided, credit and other banking services to low-income, minority communities.

This chapter reviews the following:

1. the historical evolution of black-owned banks,
2. the current viability of black-owned banks,
3. whether non-minority banks discriminate against minority loan applicants,
4. whether black- and minority-owned banks discriminate against minority loan applicants, and
5. the role of the Community Reinvestment Act in serving minority neighborhoods.

Currently, there are approximately 7900 banks in the United States but only 30 are black-owned (see Table 5.1). Thus, while blacks, or African-Americans, comprise about 12 percent of the US population, black banks amount to only 0.4 percent of the total number of the US's total banks. Moreover, black banks are small in size with an average asset size of $125 million and their size ranges from $12 to $438 million. Moreover, black banks have had a rocky history. Since 1888, at least 218 black banks have been established, but today only 30 remain.

Whether or not the numerical under-representation of black banks poses a problem depends both on the viability of these institutions and also whether

*Table 5.1     Existing Black-owned Banks: 2004*

| Bank Name | Location | Black Ownership Date | Assets (in thousands) |
|---|---|---|---|
| Alamerica Bank | Birmingham, AL | 10/24/02 | 54,546 |
| Commonwealth National Bank | Mobile, AL | 2/19/76 | 46,635 |
| First Tuskegee Bank | Tuskegee, AL | 10/12/91 | 61,166 |
| Citizens Trust Bank | Atlanta, GA | 12/31/59 | 360,418 |
| Capital City Bank & Trust Co | Atlanta, GA | 10/3/94 | 137,250 |
| Carver State Bank | Savannah, GA | 12/31/59 | 24,111 |
| Highland Community Bank | Chicago, IL | 11/5/70 | 104,063 |
| Community Bank of Lawndale | Chicago, IL | 6/20/77 | 45,799 |
| Seaway NB Chicago | Chicago, IL | 1/2/65 | 316,529 |
| Liberty Bank & Trust Co | New Orleans, LA | 11/16/72 | 295,155 |
| United Bank & Trust Co | New Orleans, LA | 9/29/90 | 26,954 |
| Harbor Bank of MD | Baltimore, MD | 9/13/82 | 219,051 |
| Industrial Bank NA | Oxon Hill, MD | 12/31/59 | 302,549 |
| One United Bank | Boston, MA | 8/2/82 | 438,562 |
| First Independence NB Detroit | Detroit, MI | 5/14/70 | 150,320 |
| Douglass National Bank | Kansas City, MO | 9/4/83 | 94,275 |
| Gateway Bank | Saint Louis, MO | 6/18/65 | 33,553 |
| City NB of New Jersey | Newark, NJ | 6/11/73 | 235,858 |
| Mechanics & Farmers Bank | Durham, NC | 12/31/59 | 219,223 |
| Millenia Community Bank | Greenville, NC | 9/22/00 | 24,986 |
| American State Bank | Tulsa, OK | 11/9/70 | 12,144 |
| United Bank of Philadelphia | Philadelphia, PA | 1/5/93 | 74,982 |
| South Carolina Community Bank | Columbia, SC | 3/27/99 | 33,136 |
| Tri-State Bank of Memphis | Memphis, TN | 12/31/59 | 141,276 |
| Memphis First Community Bank | Memphis, TN | 1/20/00 | 27,355 |
| Citizens Savings Bank & Trust Co | Nashville, TN | 12/31/59 | 54,849 |
| Unity National Bank | Houston, TX | 2/1/89 | 55,888 |
| First State Bank | Danville, VA | 12/31/59 | 40,499 |
| North Milwaukee State Bank | Milwaukee, WI | 2/12/71 | 54,885 |
| Legacy Bank | Milwaukee, WI | 11/23/99 | 81,572 |
| **Average Assets (in thousands)** | | | 125,586 |
| **Asset Range (in thousands)** | | | 12,144 to 438,562 |

*Source:* Minority-owned Banks, Federal Reserve, December 31, 2003.

banks that are not black-owned are adequately serving black communities. Serious questions have arisen regarding the adequacy of these services, and in fact date back more than 150 years (Harris, 1992). Moreover, given that black neighborhoods tend to be low-income, and therefore especially in need of growth and development, several questions are in order. These include the following:

1.   are non-minority or white banks doing an adequate job of serving black communities,
2.   do non-minority banks and black banks themselves discriminate against black customers, and
3.   do black banks have a unique and irreplaceable role in fostering the growth and development of their communities?

The purpose of this review is to investigate what policy and research-based answers have been given to the above important questions. Attention also will be devoted to policy measures, other than the promotion of black-owned banks, such as the Community Reinvestment Act to provide banking services to black communities and foster community development.

## 2   THE HISTORICAL EVOLUTION OF BLACK-OWNED BANKS

### 2.1   1851 to 1888: The Origins

In 1851, African-American ministers, business leaders and other interested parties met to devise a strategy for lifting the economic status of African-Americans. An important part of the planning was the recommendation that a mutual savings bank be established both to encourage thrift within the community and also to help fund blacks interested in establishing businesses. The Civil War put such plans on hold. During the latter part of the Civil War, the federal government established military and 'free labor' banks under the aegis of Union generals to serve as depository institutions and encourage thrift for emancipated blacks and black Union soldiers. The first such bank was the Free Labor Bank established in 1864 in New Orleans. In that same year, two other military banks, catering to black Union soldiers were established in Norfolk, Virginia and Beaufort, South Carolina.

### 2.2   Freedmen's Bank

After the end of the Civil War, Congress used unclaimed deposits from the military banks to fund and establish the Freedmen's Savings and Trust Company (Freedmen's Bank) in 1865 to provide depository services for blacks. Headquartered in New York City, it had 34 branches across the country. It was looked upon as a philanthropic venture that would encourage thrift. Although established and managed by white organizers, there were at that time no blacks with banking experience; the bank hired numerous blacks in various capacities. Moreover, black business leaders served in the bank's advisory council and boards of trustees. The bank, however, was soon suffering losses. In March 1874, to shore up confidence in Freedmen's Bank, the highly esteemed civil rights leader and abolitionist, Frederick Douglass became president and invested $10,000 of his own funds in the institution. Soon after taking office however, Douglass discovered to his shock that the bank was insolvent and so, at his insistence, the bank closed its doors in June 1874 only nine years after its inception.

Harris (1992, p. 42) blames Freedman's Bank's rapid demise on incompetent management, speculation and fraud. 'The persons who were responsible for the failure of the institution were irresponsible plunderers typical of a large group of financial speculators who rose to ascendancy in the country's economic life in the post-Civil War period'. Irons (1999) believes that the Bank was doomed to fail from the beginning given that its goals of serving as a philanthropic, venture capital bank was at odds with the principles of sound banking. There had been a widespread belief, which was partially inspired by the pictures of President Lincoln, General Grant and notable others on the covers of depositors' passbooks, that the bank's deposits were guaranteed by the federal government. Unfortunately, no such guarantee existed, and almost $ 3 million in deposits were lost.

## 2.3   The First Phase: 1888-1930s

After the fall of Freedmen's Bank several important forces in the African-American community such as churches, fraternal organizations and burial societies encouraged the creation of black banks. In 1888, the first two black-owned banks were organized. They were the Savings Bank of the Grand Fountain United Order of True Reformers, in Richmond, Virginia, and the Capital Savings Bank in Washington, DC. The two banks were the first of 134 black banks established between 1888 and 1934. These banks included both chartered institutions and private banks that conducted general banking activities. In addition to the banks, numerous industrial loan, building and loan, and credit unions were organized. An important source of deposits to the new banks came from mutual aid societies. The creation of these 134 black banks marked the inception of American black capitalism.

These two banks played an important role in providing banking services, particularly loans, to the black community. Their lending was aimed at black-owned businesses, mutual aid societies and churches. Ammons (1996) believes that such lending was especially important given the unwillingness of other banks to provide banking services to blacks. Absent these banks, it is unclear whether blacks would have been able to finance businesses or home ownership.

Harris (1992) has proposed several reasons, racial and economic, as to why white banks would not provide more banking services to the black community. One obvious cause would be prejudice by white management. Another would be prejudice by white customers who might avoid an institution with a large black clientele. In terms of economic factors, deposits by African-Americans tended to be small and not always cost-effective. Also, the profitability of loans to blacks would be limited by their small scale, illiquidity and high risk particularly in black enterprises such as amusement and recreation. Whatever the reasons, there is a widespread perception that during this period, white- (or non-minority-) owned banks were not adequately meeting the needs of the black community.

## 2.4   Two 'Kings of the Hills'

Two of the most prominent black banks in the pre-Depression period, the Binga Bank and the Douglass National Bank, were established in Chicago. Jess Binga came to Chicago with only $10 in his pocket, but after opening a real estate office in 1893, he became one of the wealthiest and most respected blacks in Chicago. Using his wealth along with that of his wife, he established the Midwest's first black bank in 1908. The Binga Bank, building upon Binga's expertise, emphasized real estate lending. Originally a private bank, it received a state charter in 1921. It soon became one of the most celebrated black business ventures and was considered a model for black business success. The Binga Bank was soon followed by the birth of several other black banks in Chicago and Detroit.

Anthony Overton, formerly both a slave ('for one year and fourteen days') and a judge, joined P.W. Chavers, another wealthy businessman, to establish the Douglass National Bank, the second nationally chartered black bank in the nation and the first in the Midwest. During the booming 1920s, the Douglass Bank provided healthy competition for the Binga Bank and these two South-side Chicago institutions grew and prospered until together they accounted for over one-third of the nation's total deposits in black banks. As Harris (1992, p. xi) puts it, 'The Chicago banking giants were known nationally as the "Kings of the Hills" in Negro Finance. Douglass National was singled out as symbolic of the Negro potential in commercial banking'.

From 1929 to 1933, over one-third of the nation's banks failed. One of the casualties was the Binga Bank, which in 1931 was the first Chicago bank to fail. Jess Binga was arrested and charged with embezzlement and real estate manipulation. He spent three years in prison, and died penniless in 1950.

After three bank runs, Overton's Douglass National also was closed in 1932. Unlike Binga, Overton was able to retain some wealth and a moderately comfortable lifestyle. The demise of the Binga and Douglass National Banks, however, left a long-term void in Midwest black communities. By the end of 1933, of the 134 black banks that had been created nationwide since 1888, only nine remained.

### 2.5   After the Trauma: The Depression to the 1950s

After 1933, black bank growth slowed dramatically with no new banks organized until 1947 and the creation of two new institutions: the Memphis State Bank of Memphis, Tennessee, and the Douglass State Bank of Kansas City, Kansas. Also, from 1922 until 1964, and until the organization of Riverside National Bank of Houston, Texas, there were no black nationally chartered banks in the United States.

During and after the Great Depression, black banks suffered even more than white banks, as they were smaller, had lower rates of loan repayment, and high-risk fixed costs. (Harris, 1992; Thieblot, 1970). An additional problem was the high-risk unemployment of African-Americans in urban areas. During this period, several million blacks migrated from the South to urban areas in the North. This migration contributed to the closing of numerous black banks in the South but did, in some cases, provide business lending opportunities to the surviving black banks in northern urban areas. Yet given the climate of massive bank failures and economic stagnation, surviving banks, black and non-black alike, followed conservative lending and investment approaches which limited the funding available for commerce.

### 2.6   First Growth, Then Decline: 1950s to 2004

The 1954 to 1964 period saw a major expansion of civil rights both through important civil rights legislation and US Supreme Court decisions. Accordingly, the bank regulatory climate became more supportive of minority banking. In 1969 and 1971, President Nixon, in line with his vision of 'Black Capitalism', signed executive orders to promote minority businesses. In accordance, the Commerce and Treasury Departments established the Minority Bank Development Program. Consequently, government agencies have been encouraged to make deposits in banks designated as minority-owned.

As a result of favorable regulation and growing confidence in the ability of the black community to organize their own banks, black banks grew from 11 in 1963, to 29 in 1971 and 47 in 1980 (see Table 5.2). Their average assets almost doubled from $16 million to $30 million. Simultaneously, other minority-owned banks such as those having Mexican, Puerto Rican, Asian- and Native-American ownership, also grew, jumping from eight in 1971 to 48 in 1980. In fact, despite their growth, black banks declined from 80 percent of total minority banks in 1971 to less than half by 1980. Currently, there are 110 minority-owned banks in the United States of which only 30 are black-owned. There also are 37 Asian-American banks, 18 Hispanic, 30 native-American, five women-owned and one multiracial-owned bank. Table 5.3 shows that in terms of average asset size, Hispanic banks are easily largest with $1.547 billion, native-American are smallest, $74.8 million, with black banks being in the middle, $125.6 million.

*Table 5.2    Banks Established by African-Americans*

| Years | US |
|-------|-----|
| 1888-1934 | 134 |
| 1935-1946 | 0 |
| 1947-1969 | 22 |
| 1970-1979 | 34 |
| 1980-1982 | 6 |
| Since 1992 | 7 |
| TOTAL | 218 |

*Sources:* Abram L. Harris (1992), Ammons (1996), and Minority-
owned Banks, Federal Reserve, December 31, 2003.

The 1980s were not kind to US banks. In just ten years from 1982 and 1992, some 1500 US banks failed. This surge in failures represented three-quarters of all bank failures since the inception of the FDIC in 1934. A number of factors contributed to this increase including the rapid rise in interest rates from 1979 to 1982, the collapse in oil, real estate, and other commodity prices, financial institution deregulation, and consequently, increased competition. Black banks were also affected adversely, and their numbers declined from 48 in 1980, to 34 in 1990 and 30 in 2004. Hence black banks account for but 27 percent of 110 minority banks.

## 3   DO BLACK BANKS HAVE A SPECIAL ROLE?

According to the 'essentiality doctrine', if a bank's services are deemed essential to its community, the Federal Deposit Insurance Corporation has the authority to assist that bank to prevent it from failing (Sprague, 1986). This doctrine was first utilized in 1971, to save the Unity Bank of Boston from failure, and a year later, Detroit's Bank of the Commonwealth was bailed out. In both cases, the assistance was granted because the banks were judged essential to serve their black communities. Such policies beg the questions as to whether black banks play an essential role in their communities and also whether such banks are financially viable.

*Table 5.3     Minority-owned Banks*

|  | Number | Average Asset Size (in thousands of $) | Establishment Date of Oldest Institution |
|---|---|---|---|
| African-American | 30 | 125,586 | 1959 |
| Women | 9 | 109,575 | 1978 |
| Hispanic-American | 18 | 1,546,667 | 1969 |
| Asian-American | 37 | 404,746 | 1962 |
| Native-American | 15 | 74,819 | 1971 |
| Multiracial Minority | 1 | 101,700 | 2002 |

*Source:* Minority-owned Banks, December 31, 2003, Federal Reserve.

### 3.1   Black Bank Sources and Uses of Funds

In comparing the financial statements of black banks to the rest of the US banking community, a number of differences come to light. In terms of sources of funds, compared to non-minority banks, black banks rely heavily on small, high-activity deposits. In addition, black banks, of all minority banks, have attracted the greatest amount of government deposits with 11 percent of their funds coming from this source. Lawrence (1997) cites the rapid growth of black banks from 1971 to 1995 as being partially attributable to the Minority Bank Development Program (also known as the Minority Bank Deposit Program). As mentioned previously, this program, announced by the US Treasury Department on October 2, 1970, was designed to encourage the development of minority businesses. In order to increase the amount of bank funds available to local, minority communities, companies and government agencies such as the departments of Defense and Energy, as will as the Internal Revenue Service, were encouraged to make deposits with qualifying depository institutions. In addition, black banks have also attracted the US Treasury's Tax and Loan Accounts, which represent the Treasury's excess cash balances in addition to employer payments for federal taxes due.

It is unclear, however, how much black and other minority banks, benefit from the Minority Bank Development Program. Government deposits are volatile and regulations require that government deposits, more than $100,000, be backed by the pledging of government securities. Price (1994) has found that the marginal cost of US government deposits is higher than that of other bank deposits and so he questions the usefulness of the Minority Bank Development Program to black banks. Given their volatility and cost, Lawrence's (1997) empirical results suggest that higher levels of government deposits may retard bank lending in minority communities. Perhaps not by coincidence, black banks, which as a whole receive two-to-four times more assistance under the Minority Bank Development Program than other minority banks, are the least profitable and viable. Regarding equity capital, Irons (1971), Bates and Bradford (1980), and Lawrence have all found that black banks have over the years had significantly less capital than non-minority banks, and thus have less cushion to absorb losses.

In their uses of funds, black banks have proportionally more liquid assets such as US government securities and sales of federal funds than non-minority banks. This high degree of liquidity has been criticized because it leaves fewer funds available for making loans. Thus, contrary to one of their purposes, that is, to recycle deposits into their communities in the form of loans, black banks may instead serve as conduits by which local deposit funds are exported to other markets through sales of federal funds and purchases of securities. In defense of black banks, however, Bates and Bradford (1980) found that black banks' apparent excess liquidity was attributable to their high loan losses and their reliance on small, high-volatility deposits from low-income households.

Moreover, black banks' relatively high liquidity and consequently low loan-to-asset ratios may be attributed at least partially to their small size as smaller institutions typically have relatively low average loan-to-asset ratios. For example, Clair (1988) found that black banks' loan-to-asset ratios were not significantly different from non-minority banks in the same region. In this study, Clair defined the relevant region for comparing banks to be the same zip code rather than the more conventional usage of the same SMSA. In addition, Price (1992) found that compared to similarly sized non-minority banks, small minority banks actually have higher loan-to-asset ratios.

Dahl (1994), on the other hand, found evidence suggesting that black banks are indeed less aggressive in making loans than non-minority banks. He examined the impact of a change in bank ownership upon lending behavior. That is, he focused upon those banks whose ownership changed either from minority to non-minority or vice versa. His results suggest that loan growth was slower for those banks that changed from non-minority to minority ownership. While Dahl's finding supports the notion that black banks make proportionally less loans than non-minority banks, it should be noted, however, that in his sample of 19 minority banks, only seven of these were black banks.

Of their loan portfolios, a relatively high share is devoted to real estate loans, as is true with most of the nation's small banks, and a relatively low share to consumer and agricultural loans. Bostic/Canner (1998) finds that for mortgages, black, as compared to white, banks originate smaller loans and make loans in areas with higher poverty rates and minority populations. Moreover, black banks' loans have higher loan-to-income ratios. Also, along with Hispanic-owned banks, black banks make two-to-three times more insider loans to officers and directors than does the average bank which could be cause for concern as insider loans have been found to be positively correlated with bank failures (Kummer et al., 1989). All in all, black banks have below-average loan activity but suffer above-average loan losses. Whether or not black bank lending fills an important void in low-income, minority neighborhoods is a controversial topic that will be discussed in a later section.

### 3.2   Bank Profitability and Viability

Since the late 1960s controversy has reigned regarding how much of a role minority and particularly black banks could play in developing their communities. Harris (1992) was quite skeptical about the potential contribution that small, undiversified black banks could make and further criticized them for overcharging their black customers. Brimmer (1971) and Irons (1971) wrote the seminal articles on this topic focusing primarily on the profitability of black banks as a measure of their potential to spur the economic development of the black economy. Brimmer was quite critical of black bank performance pointing to their high operating costs, low efficiency, high loan losses and overall lack of managerial talent. Thus, Brimmer concluded that black banks could not provide a significant vehicle to black economic development and instead were more like 'ornaments'. Black's study (1979) found that, in addition to serving customers with poor banking habits, black banks lack ability in loan management and marketing initiative.

In terms of earnings, black banks' gross operating revenues are higher due to their higher service fees but their profits are lower due to their higher costs and greater loan losses. Irons (1971) attributes the higher costs to high-activity deposits and inexperienced personnel. The higher loan losses may reflect inexperienced management and lending in high-risk areas. Nicholson et al. (1981) also found that black banks suffered higher-than-average loan losses during the 1973–75 recession possibly because of the low incomes of their borrowers. Kwast and Black (1983) compared mature black banks with a matched set of non-minority banks. So as to avoid the problems inherent in start-up institutions, they focused on black banks that had been operating for at least four years and found that the average black bank was smaller, less capitalized and less profitable. They attributed the lower profitability to higher liquidity, higher operating costs on liabilities, and, most importantly, higher loan loss rates which are almost three times the rate at non-minority banks. The major sources of the higher loan loss rates were real estate and commercial and industrial loans. Their low capitalization was partially explained by the fact that so few were listed on the stock exchanges.

Lawrence (1997) analyzed the performance of black, Hispanic and Asian-owned banks, relative to peer, non-minority banks operating in the same locality as defined by zip code. He believed that earlier studies that focused on Standard Metropolitan Statistical Areas (SMSAs) rather than zip codes, took too broad a definition of region. He found that black banks, unlike other minority-owned banks, had lower returns on assets than their peer, non-minority, institutions. One of the challenges facing black banks is that they operate in communities plagued by low-income, high unemployment and high crime rates. Yet, surprisingly, Lawrence found demographic and economic variables to be unimportant as non-minority banks were able to operate in these communities without facing financial distress. Thus, Lawrence (1997, p. 20) concludes, 'This would suggest that the policies and decisions of minority bankers are largely to blame for their poor performances rather than the environment in which they operate'. Given that minority-owned banks, particularly black banks, have had consistently weaker profits than non-minority banks, questions have arisen regarding their viability.

### 3.3 Managerial Deficiencies?

Because of their high loan losses, low profitability and high liquidity numerous analysts such as Brimmer (1971) and Irons (1971) concluded that black banks lacked able management. Given that there were few management opportunities for blacks prior to the 1970s, managerial problems could be attributable to inexperience. In fact, Gardner (1982) found that while black bank managers had the same educational levels as managers of other small banks, they had less experience. Also, Boorman (1973) found that banks with more experienced managers were more profitable primarily because of improved loan management and less risky lending. Gardner (1982) found significant differences among black banks with the most profitable having less loan losses and lower overhead costs. She pointed out that while some minority banks have failed, others have performed well. Thus, she recommended more research of successful black banks to discover what lessons could be learned.

# 4   DO BANKS DISCRIMINATE AGAINST BLACK LOAN APPLICANTS?

## 4.1   Do Non-minority Banks Discriminate Against Black Loan Applicants?

A major justification for the support of black and minority banks, both today and historically, has been the charge that non-minority, or white-owned, banks discriminate against black and minority loan applicants, particularly in low- and moderate-income urban areas. Aside from being immoral and contrary to profit-maximization principles, discrimination is illegal and numerous laws prohibit it. Since passage of the Civil Rights Act of 1964, significant attention has been directed toward possible discrimination in the housing and mortgage credit markets. This has led to additional legislation such as the Fair Housing Act of 1968 (FHA, amended in 1988), the Equal Opportunity Credit Act of 1974 (ECOA), the Home Mortgage Disclosure Act of 1975 (HMDA) and the Community Reinvestment Act of 1977 (CRA). Yet, laws themselves do not ensure the elimination of discrimination that by denying credit to needy low- and moderate-income urban areas could accelerate their decline and contribute to a host of social problems. HMDA data released since 1991 has shown much higher rejection rates for black and Hispanic than white mortgage loan applicants. Given the absence of information regarding applicant risk, it is difficult to draw meaningful conclusions, but the results have spawned numerous studies to investigate if bank mortgage lending discriminates against black loan applicants. Early studies have yielded mixed results varying from no evidence of discrimination (Benston and Horsky, 1979), weak evidence of discrimination (Black et al., 1978) and strong statistical evidence (Munnell et al., 1992, 1996). The inconsistency in these studies may be attributable to variations in statistical techniques, model specifications and samples.

Munnell et al. (1992, 1996) of the Federal Reserve Bank of Boston undertook one of the best known studies and found that black and Hispanic mortgage credit applicants were rejected at a rate 2.7 times that of whites. After constructing a model to take into account creditworthiness, they found that the difference in rejection rates declined significantly but that the rejection rate for blacks and Hispanics still remained 1.6 times higher than that of whites. While the results suggest that many minority applicants were denied on legitimate creditworthy grounds, their remaining high rejection rate, after allowing for the creditworthiness of applicants, suggested that racial discrimination could be affecting mortgage loan decisions. All applicants with clean records were approved regardless of race. In the case of marginal applicants, whose records contained blemishes, lenders would use discretion in determining whom to fund. Munnell et al. (1992, p. 3) concluded 'lenders seem more willing to overlook flaws for white applicants than for minority applicants'. This analysis and conclusion triggered a vigorous debate over model specification, statistical techniques (Yezer et al., (1994) find that single-equation models may suggest evidence of discrimination where none exists), data quality (several applicants had negative net worth and so should not have been part of the sample), and omitted variables. In short, some doubted whether the Boston FED model fully accounted for creditworthiness.

Studies suggesting evidence of racial discrimination, such as that of the Boston FED, cite higher rejection rates for black rather than white loan candidates. Yet, the same banks, presumably overwhelmingly white-owned, rejected white loan applicants at higher rates than Asian-American loan candidates. Moreover, Becker (1993) has reasoned that if lenders discriminate against minority loan candidates and thereby hold them to higher standards, then minorities would have lower default rates. Bigoted lenders would be willing to sacrifice some profit to satisfy their urge to discriminate. The evidence, however, shows the opposite: the average default rate for blacks was significantly higher than for whites. For example, Berkovec et al. (1994) found that blacks default more, not less, frequently than comparable whites in FHA mortgage programs. Hence, Becker (1993), Macey (1995) and others do not accept higher rejections rates as evidence of racial discrimination.

## 4.2 Cultural Affinity and Discrimination

Calomiris et al. (1994), however, suggest that the presence of both higher rejection rates and higher default rates does not necessarily preclude the possibility of discrimination among non-minority banks. The authors posit a hypothesis of 'cultural affinity' that suggests that loan officers could have a preference for, and also more accurately assess the creditworthiness of, applicants with similar backgrounds and histories. In deciding whether or not to make a loan, lenders analyze not only applicants' financial creditworthiness through measures such as credit history and financial leverage, but also assess their character. A reading of a marginal applicant's character could make the difference as to whether or not the loan is granted. In judging character through subjective criteria such as dress, manners, behavior and other characteristics, lenders might be better to able to judge applicants of similar background. For minority applicants, for whom cultural clues are difficult to interpret, non-minority lenders may rely more on quantitative measures, which, though valuable, present an incomplete picture of overall creditworthiness. Consequently, minority loan applicants may face greater rejection rates and yet, after securing loans, may also have higher default rates. Thus, the cultural affinity hypothesis shows that higher default rates among black applicants does not necessarily prove the absence of discrimination among non-minority lenders. This hypothesis, also demonstrates that loan officers, who could be free of bigotry, might still unintentionally discriminate against minority applicants.

Hunter and Walker (1996) undertook a study of the cultural affinity hypothesis and found that for applicants with strong credit records, loan decisions were uninfluenced by applicant race. For applicants with spotty records, however, objective, quantitative measures such as credit history and monthly obligations reduced the probability of acceptance significantly more for black and Hispanic applicants, than they did for white applicants. The authors concluded that this difference, that is, that black and Hispanic loan applicants with weak credit records are held to higher standards than their white peers, is due to cultural affinity and not to 'invidious racial discrimination'.

The authors also offered another possible explanation for higher rejection rates of minority loan applicants. That is, because historically, white loan applications have far outnumbered those of minorities, loan officers have had far greater experience with white applicants. Accordingly, loan officers may have learned which non-objective, and possibly mitigating, factors could improve the probability of repayment by white applicants. For minority applicants, such experience and information has been absent.

Bostic (2003) and also Bostic and Canner (1998) investigated the presence of cultural affinity, but they expanded the concept to include not only lender preferences but also those of applicants. That is, marginal applicants might seek out banks with similar racial or ethnic backgrounds where they believe they would receive a more sympathetic hearing and fairer deal. In fact, their evidence shows that marginal black applicants did seek out black banks thereby supporting the view that cultural affinity influences applicant behavior. In contrast to Hunter and Walker (1996), however, they did not find evidence that cultural affinity influences lender behavior, but to the contrary, found that applicants were treated equally regardless of bank ownership. Unlike Hunter and Walker's single–equation approach, Bostic used a two-stage model that tested for the presence of both lender and applicant cultural affinity. He suggested that the Hunter and Walker study, because it did not adjust for applicant cultural affinity, could possibly suffer from selection bias.

### 4.3   Do Black Banks Discriminate Against Black Loan Applicants?

As we have seen, an important part of the argument in favor of establishing black and other minority banks is that minority loan applicants may be discriminated against either because of cultural affinity or outright bigotry. Moreover, minority banks might be better able to evaluate the risk of minority loan applicants and so might be more willing to lend to minority loan applicants. Yet, Black et al. (1997) found evidence suggesting that black banks were more likely than white banks to reject black applicants for mortgage loans. In a more recent study by the same authors (2001), however, in which the bank loan market was defined more narrowly and presumably more appropriately, which is by zip code rather than SMSA, Black et al. (2001) found that black banks were not statistically more likely to reject black applicants.

In contrast, Bostic (2003) found that minority-owned banks rejected loan applications by blacks at twice the rate (35 percent to 17 percent) of non-minority banks. Minority-owned banks also denied a higher percent (16 percent) of Hispanic-American loan applicants than did non-minority banks (13 percent) while bank ownership appeared to have no effect on prospective Asian-American borrowers. Bostic (2003) and Bostic and Canner (1998), however, found that marginal black applicants would be more likely to seek credit at black-owned institutions. Therefore, the higher rejection rates of black applicants at black banks could be attributable to their processing proportionally more marginal applicants than non-minority banks. Bostic (2003) further found that, after adjusting for application risk, the differences in denial rates among banks were insignificant. He concluded that lender decisions were based on objective measures of risk rather than cultural affinity. Given the mixed evidence cited above, it is difficult to conclude decisively that banks, be they non-minority or minority, discriminate against black loan applicants.

## 4.4   The Community Reinvestment Act (CRA)

The US government has, for decades, been attempting to foster an increase in loans and banking services to lower-income minority neighborhoods. Aside from supporting black and other minority–owned banks, the CRA has aimed to induce all banks, regardless of ownership, to increase their lending commitment to low- and moderate-income areas, particularly those in minority neighborhoods. There has been an accusation that banks and thrifts (savings and loan institutions) engage in a policy of 'redlining', that is, in avoiding lending to specific low-income, urban areas. Consequently, in 1977 the CRA was passed to require banks and thrifts to eliminate discriminatory lending practices and encourage an affirmative role in meeting the credit needs of their local communities, defined as those in which they have a branch office. The act has impacted both minority neighborhoods and minority banks.

Regulatory agencies are charged with monitoring and evaluating bank and thrift compliance with the CRA. Institutions having unsatisfactory CRA ratings risk losing the regulatory approval necessary to establish new branches or engage in new activities. For example, in 1989 the Federal Deposit Insurance Corporation rejected the Continental Bank's application to buy a thrift institution due to inadequate compliance with the CRA. This denial, the first of its kind, signaled to a shocked banking community that federal regulators meant business in enforcing the CRA. The CRA is credited for spurring banks to increase their inner city activities. Apgar and Duda (2003) cite evidence suggesting that CRA-regulated institutions significantly outperform other mortgage borrowers in supplying mortgage loans to lower–income borrowers, especially blacks and Hispanics. Yet, Antonakes' study (2001) of Massachusetts's banks finds that the CRA is ineffective in providing adequate banking services to all communities so that those with low-income and high-minority populations continue to be underserved. Recent regulatory liberalization has allowed banks to make loans outside of their branch locations thereby allowing them to bypass the CRA. Consequently, there have been calls for expanding CRA coverage to more lending institutions.

## 4.5 The Controversy Over the CRA

The CRA has generated substantial controversy. On the one hand, community activists have criticized it for lax enforcement pointing out that over 90 percent of all banks receive satisfactory ratings. They have argued that bank examiners have tended to give banks the benefit of doubt unless blatant discrimination was present. If so, it may be due to the difficulty involved in ascertaining conclusively whether discrimination actually exists.

On the other hand, banks have cited high-risk and low-return considerations in justifying the paucity of their inner city lending. Banks further complain that the act is vague, arbitrary, costly and requires excessive paperwork. They also complain of inconsistent evaluation as evidence suggests that regulatory enforcement differs among regulators, agencies and locations.

Macey and Miller (1993) suggest the CRA encourages the funding of substandard, high-risk, borrowing thereby reducing lender safety. The authors suggest that the potential of increasing bad loans combined with other compliance costs make the CRA the most expensive regulation that banks face. In addition, Lacker (1995) among others has suggested that community revitalization is the primary responsibility of governments, not financial institutions.

Black banks have also criticized the CRA. Some banks have charged that the CRA has impaired their economic performance by increasing competition from non-minority banks for their most creditworthy borrowers in low-income areas. Black banks have further charged that non-minority banks have made loans to low- and moderate-income borrowers at below-market interest rates, at the expense of black banks, so as to improve their CRA ratings.

Another problem for black banks is that, as Cox (1993) points out, a Federal Reserve study found that black and other minority banks have much poorer CRA ratings than white-owned banks thereby suggesting that, contrary to their express purpose, they have poor records of providing credit and banking services to their neighborhoods. Also, even though minority banks make far more mortgage loans to minorities (Bostic/Canner, 1998), they tend to target the wealthiest members of their communities. A possible explanation is that the CRA encourages lending institutions, as mentioned above, to subsidize loans to the poor and minorities. Yet, because of their own financial weaknesses, black and other minority institutions have inadequate resources to provide subsidized loans.

Calomiris et al. (1994) point out that the poor CRA ratings of black and other minority banks cannot be attributable to either bigotry or lack of cultural affinity, but may instead reflect the lower wealth or poorer education of minority applicants. Calomiris et al. (p. 654) conclude, 'This suggests that bank rejection of minority applicants that lead to poor CRA ratings are often due not to discrimination but to poor expected performance of the mortgage'.

## 5   CONCLUSION

Despite numerous studies, the debate that Brimmer (1971) and Irons (1971) initiated three decades ago, whether black banks could serve as vehicles of community development, remains alive today. Among the areas of disagreement are the long-term viability of black banks, the managerial competence at black banks, the degree of discrimination existing against black borrowers, and the efficacy of government-sponsored programs such as the Minority Bank Development Program and the Community Reinvestment Act.

Regarding black bank profitability, there may be improvement as the banks grow into more efficient–sized units and as their managers gain experience. Also, more research is necessary to learn what lessons successful black banks have for other banks. Much attention has been devoted to the issue of discrimination against black and minority applicants. The cultural affinity hypothesis has itself spurred several studies. While the evidence is mixed, it is far from clear that either bigotry or cultural affinity shape the behavior of non-minority lenders. In fact, the case has yet to be made convincingly that either non-minority or black banks discriminate against black loan applicants.

For black banks, the high costs and volatility of government deposits emanating from the Minority Bank Development Program appear to surpass their benefits. As for the CRA, whereas banks, in general, have long complained about the CRA, the most onerous effects may fall upon black banks whose financial limitations constrain their ability to aggressively assist their communities. In fact, given their smallness, both in number and size, along with their lackluster earnings, black banks' potential contribution to community development of low–income, urban areas appears limited.

## REFERENCES

Apgar, William C. and Mark Duda (2003), 'The Twenty–Fifth Anniversary of the Community Reinvestment Act: Past Accomplishments and Future Regulatory Challenges', *FRBNY Economic Policy Review*, June, 169–190.

Ammons, Lila (1996), 'The Evolution of Black–Owned Banks in the United States Between the 1880s and 1990s', *Journal of Black Studies*, **26** (4), 467–489.

Antonakes, Steven L. (2001), 'Assessing the Community Reinvestment Act: Impact on Low Income and High–Risk Minority Communities', *Journal of Business and Economic Studies*, **7** (2), 1–31.

Bates, Timothy and William D. Bradford (1980), 'An Analysis of the Portfolio Behavior of Black–Owned Commercial Banks', *Journal of Finance*, **35**, 753–768.

Becker, Gary S. (1993), 'The Evidence Against Banks Doesn't Prove Bias', *Business Week*, April 19, 18.

Benston, George J. and Dan Horsky (1979), 'Redlining and the Demand for Mortgages in the Central City and Suburbs', *Journal of Bank Research*, **10**, 72–87.

Berkovec, James A., Glenn B. Canner, Stuart A. Gabriel and Timothy H. Hannan (1994), 'Race, Redlining, and Residential Mortgage Loan Performance', *Journal of Real Estate Finance and Economics*, **9**, 263–294.

Black, Harold A. (1979), 'Financial Institutions and Urban Revitalization', *Review of Black Political Economy*, **10** (1), 44–58.

Black, Harold A., M. Cary Collins and Ken B. Cyree (1997), 'Do Black–Owned Banks Discriminate Against Black Borrowers?', *Journal of Financial Services Research*, **11**, 189–204.

Black, Harold A., Breck L. Robinson and Robert L. Schweitzer (2001), 'Comparing Lending Decisions of Minority–Owned and White–Owned Banks: Is There Discrimination in Mortgage Lending?', *Review of Financial Economics*, **10**, 23–39.

Black, Harold A., Robert Schweitzer and L. Mandell (1978), 'Discrimination in Mortgage Lending', *American Economic Review*, **68**, 234–241.

Boorman, John T. (1973), *New Minority–Owned Commercial Banks: A Comparative Analysis*, Washington, DC: Federal Deposit Insurance Corporation.

Bostic, Raphael W. (2003), 'A Test of Cultural Affinity in Home Mortgage Lending', *Journal of Financial Services Research*, **23**, 89–112.

Bostic, Raphael W. and Glenn B. Canner (1998), 'Do Minority–Owned Banks Treat Minorities Better? An Empirical Test of the Cultural Affinity Hypothesis', *Proceedings of the 34th Annual Conference on Bank Structure and Competition*, 113–133.

Brimmer, Andrew F. (1971), 'The Black Banks: An Assessment of Performance and Prospects', *Journal of Finance*, **26**, 379–405.

Calomiris, Charles W., Charles M. Kahn and Stanley D. Longhofer (1994), 'Housing–Finance Intervention and Private Incentives: Helping Minorities and the Poor', *Journal of Money, Credit, and Banking*, **26**, 634–678.

Clair, Robert T. (1988), 'The Performance of Black–Owned banks in Their Primary Market Areas', *Federal Reserve Bank of Dallas: Economic Review*, November, 11–20.

Cox, Robert B. (1993), 'Minority Banks Seen Lagging in CRA Arena', *American Banker*, August 30, 1.

Dahl, Drew (1994), 'Black Banks and Community Development: Is There a Reluctance to Lend?', *Journal of Banking and Finance*, **20**, 1289–1301.

Gardner, Mona J. (1982), 'Black–Owned Commercial Banks: A New Look at Their Performance and Management', *Review of Black Political Economy*, **12** (1), 91–101.

Harris, Abram L. (1992), *The Negro as Capitalist: A Study of Banking and Business Among American Negroes*, Chicago, IL: Urban Research Press.

Hunter, William C. and Mary Beth Walker (1996), 'The Cultural Affinity Hypothesis and Mortgage Lending Decisions', *Journal of Real Estate Finance and Economics*, **13** (1), 57–70.

Irons, Edward (1971), 'The Black Banks: An Assessment of Performance and Prospects', *Journal of Finance*, **26**, 407–425.

Irons, Edward (1999), 'Banking, Minority, 1865–1996', in Juliette K. Walker (ed.), *Encyclopedia of African American Business History*, Westport, CT: Greenwood Press, 59–64.

Kummer, Donald R., Nasser Arshadi and Edward C. Lawrence (1989), 'Incentive Problems in Bank Insider Borrowing', *Journal of Financial Services Research*, **3**, 17–31.

Kwast, Myron L. and Harold Black (1983), 'An Analysis of the Behavior of Mature Black–Owned Commercial Banks', *Journal of Economics and Business*, **35**, 41–54.

Lacker, Jeffrey M. (1995), 'Neighborhoods and Banking', *Federal Reserve Bank of Richmond Economic Quarterly*, **81** (2), 13–39.

Lawrence, Edward C. (1997), 'The Viability of Minority–Owned Banks', *The Quarterly Review of Economics and Finance*, **37**, 1–21.

Macey, Jonathon R. (1995), 'The Lowdown on Lending Discrimination', *The Wall Street Journal*, August 9, A8.

Macey, Jonathon R. and Geoffrey P. Miller (1993), 'The Community Reinvestment Act: An Economic Analysis', *The Virginia Law Review*, **79** (2), 291–348.

Munnell, Alicia H., Lynn E. Browne, James McEneaney and Geoffrey M.B. Tootell (1992), 'Mortgage Lending in Boston: Interpreting HMDA Data', *Working Paper*, No. 9–27, Federal Reserve Bank of Boston.

Munnell, Alicia H., Lynn E. Browne, James McEneaney and Geoffrey M.B. Tootell (1996), 'Mortgage Lending in Boston: Interpreting HMDA Data', *American Economic Review*, **86**, 25–53.

Nicholson, Norman, Milton Esbitt and Kent Currie (1981), 'Performance of Minority Banks in a Recession: The 1973–75 Experience', *Baylor Business Studies*, **12** (3), 57–68.

Price, Gregory N. (1990), 'Minority–Owned Banks: History and Trends', *Federal Reserve Bank of Cleveland: Economic Commentary*, July 1.

Price, Gregory N. (1994), 'The Cost of Government Deposits for Black–Owned Commercial Banks', *Review of Black Political Economy*, **23** (1), 9–24.

Sprague, Irvine H. (1986), *Bailout: An Insider's Account of Bank Failures and Rescues*, New York: Basic Books, Inc.

Thieblot, A. (1970), *The Negro in the Banking Industry: Report No. 9*, Philadelphia: University of Pennsylvania, Wharton School of Finance and Commerce, Department of Industry.

Travis, Dempsey J. (1992), 'Prologue', in A. Harris, *The Negro as Capitalist: A Study of Banking and Business Among American Negroes*, Chicago, IL: Urban Research Press, ix–xxiii.

Yezer, A.M., R.F. Phillips and R.P. Trost (1994), 'Bias in Estimates of Discrimination and Default in Mortgage Lending: The Effects of Simultaneity and Self–Selection', *Journal of Real Estate Finance and Economics*, **29**, 197–215.

# 6. The Extranjerización of the Mexican Banking Sector: Expectations and Results

## Carlos A. Rozo

### 1 INTRODUCTION

Banking is one of the most important sectors in an economy since it concentrates on resources needed to finance and promote productive activities and, in consequence, economic growth. It must be in this perspective that Stiglitz (1998) affirms, 'the financial system can be compared with the brain of the economy'. By its intermediation scarce capital is assigned to alternative uses creating thus a link between stability and macroeconomic growth. In this manner banks promote an efficient allocation of financial resources.

The central question of this work is: How have Mexican banks fulfilled these postulates considering that it is one of the sectors of the domestic economy that had most transformations in the last two decades of widespread financial and economic stress. In 1982 the banking system was nationalized, but this situation lasted less than one decade since in the biennium 1990–1992 banks were returned to the private sector. At the end of the 1980s legal reforms were approved and implemented to allow and to promote diversification of credit by means of capital and money market mechanisms. Later on began the opening of the sector to foreign capital by allowing the acquisition of up to 30% of the capital stock of small banks, commercial and investment.

In the mid-1990s the worst financial crisis Mexico experienced occurred as a consequence of the devaluation of the peso in December 1994. This event accelerated liberalization and the transferring of the large commercial banks to foreign capital.[1] These transformations in the ownership structure of the Mexican financial system, not only of its banking sector, had as a central and motivating axis the deregulation and innovation implicit in the dynamics of globalization, which gives full validity to the principles of 'financial

111

liberalization' promoted since the 1980s by the institutions of the Washington Consensus.

The proposed question leads us to inquire on the implications, positive and negative, that bank extranjerización may have for the Mexican economy. The objective is to determine if the entrance of external capital to the banking sector has been effective in promoting growth in domestic saving and in the financing of economic growth, or on the contrary, if foreign capital by not being able to solve problems of the past has made denationalization of credit mechanisms an innocuous and counteractive solution. To put the role played by extranjerización of the banking sectors in the dynamics of economic reform in the right perspective, it is postulated as a hypothesis that the extranjerización process has contributed to a more efficient operation of banks which has resulted in an increased profitability and improvements in the efficiency of the allocation of financial resources.

In consequence, this chapter carries out an analysis of the trajectory of the banking sector in a medium–term vision, from 1982 to 2003, and of the impact that foreign capital has had on this trajectory, especially as expressed by credit behaviour. In this perspective, initially the theoretical debate about the causes and the consequences of foreign investment in banks is presented followed by an examination of the changes in the structure of the Mexican banking sector after its extranjerización. Next, an evaluation of the operation of the sector is made by means of the methods of financial intermediation and an approximation to the CAMEL approach. To this end a comparative analysis is done on the behaviour and the results of the banking sector during three different periods of time: one before the process of extranjerización, a second one of light extranjerización and a final period of strong extranjerización. Finally, pertinent conclusions are presented.

## 2   THE THEORETICAL DEBATE

The causes and consequences of the entrance of foreign investment in the banking sector are topics on which an intense debate exists. This debate, however, has centered on what happens in the industrial countries. Several causes are given for the international expansion of the banks, either by means of fusions or by acquisitions (Deutsche Bundesbank, 2002). Among them stand out:

1.   the search for new clients or the interest to follow their clients abroad;
2.   the possibility to increase administrative efficiency and, in consequence, to reduce operational costs;

3.  the diversification of risk as a central factor in the dynamics of globalization, and
4.  increments in profitability with the purpose of strengthening market power.

The debate on what this investment means for developing countries is still at an initial phase. In fact, the phenomenon is relatively recent if it is considered that entrance of foreign banks to Mexico, and in general to Latin America, accelerated and only became a factor of first magnitude in the second half of the 1990s. Arguments exist in defence of the benefits that openness to foreign banks can bring but arguments are also given about their possible negative effects. The evidence on one or the other is less overwhelming and also rather scarce.

The central argument in defence of the entrance of foreign banks in emerging markets is that these collaborate to improve the health of the national banking system by strengthening the level of capitalization because of the obligation of the buyers to inject new capital. There is also the possibility to provide larger access to capital flows and to offer more liquidity to the economy.

The entrance of healthy banks equally mitigates information effects and reduces transaction costs thus strengthening the balance sheet. This is a consequence of the transfer of abilities, know-how and technologies, the improvements in risk administration and internal controls that affect auditing standards positively, accounting and results dissemination, the administration of credit risk, and the quality of supervision. These are factors that equally promote more competition and force local banks to work with higher standards of efficiency (Crystal et al., 2002; Claessens et al., 1998).

Naturally, a more efficient banking system should improve saving and investment rates. Technological development, as a consequence, becomes a force to impel stronger economic growth. These effects have to do with a greater supply of foreign currencies that contribute to strengthen the domestic currency, to increase foreign reserves and favour the acquisition of imports.

These possible implications have to do with the form in which foreign capital is related to the national economy. Two ways to gain local market control can be to assume local administration control or by way of supervision. The thesis that sustains the different approaches is that remote monitoring of how a business is administered is guided by principles different to those that are practised when the monitoring is direct. It is a principle in the banking business that when credits are given in the local market, having acces to local information is vital and therefore it would be preferable to have a local administrator. When credit allocation has an international bias localism is less important and the decisions to give credit are less correlated with national realities. The analysis in these operational options is necessary in order to evaluate the effect that financial foreign investment can have in improving administrative efficiency and, therefore, the performance of the economy.

Another basic element in the analysis of foreign investment in the banking sector is its impact on the operation of the central bank. The implications that foreign ownership of banks can have on monetary policy, and more directly on the transmission mechanisms of this policy, is basic for the stability of the financial sector. Of particular interest in this respect should be forced acquisitions by non-residents when these are big. Banks that invest abroad are usually big, profitable and with a lot of experience. Therefore one could think that mergers and acquisitions of small banks contribute to the efficiency of the banking sector. But, it is also likely that they impose conditions for the conduct of monetary policy that are not necessarily optimal. In fact, the possibility of negative effects is also recognized. The most outstanding of these can be the loss of control over the national system of payments which depends on the changes to domestic legislation. Among these elements is the authority of regulating institutions to impose sanctions when it is necessary. On top of it are the decisions to grant credit in time and with the appropriate priorities. This is a dilemma for the strategies of banks which affects the national economy when corporate decisions privilege some activities more than others. It concerns decisions about credit allocation, the charge for services or the selection of personnel and directors. This is a situation in which corporate strategies limit the capacity of decisions at the local level for local purchases.

Empirical studies show results that not necessarily sustain all these postulates, especially when one examines the difference between what happens in industrial and developing countries. It is sustained that in the United States foreign banks tend to be less efficient than local ones (Chang et al., 1998; DeYoung and Nolle, 1996; Hasan and Hunter, 1996) while in developing countries foreign banks are more efficient and contribute to make local ones more efficient (Barajas et al., 2000; Claessens et al., 2000). It is also argued that this investment can help the convergence dynamics among the less and the more developed countries.

Studies for the case of Mexico seem to confirm the posture about the benefits brought by foreign banks (Dages et al., 2000; Clarke et al., 2003). However, the critical fact that still demands explanation is that during the period of 1996 to 2002, total bank credit as a proportion of GDP fell significantly. The immediate implication is that as banks' control passed to foreign capital less credit was allocated to the national economy. This fact by itself forces a detailed analysis of the process of extranjerización of the Mexican banking sector since privatization of banks at the beginning of the

1990s and its later extranjerización at the end of that decade were conceived as a way to consolidate a sector capable of facilitating the financing that development requires.

## 3   THE STRUCTURE OF THE EXTRANJERIZACIÓN

At the end of 2003 the biggest bank institutions in the country were controlled by foreign banks with 38.5% of bank assets under Spanish banks' control (BBVA with 25.6% and Santander with 12.9%), 22.3% under control of a US bank (Citibank), 9.3% under control of a British bank (HSBC) and 5% under Canadian control (Scotia Bank). In sum, five large foreign banks controlled 75.1% of bank assets in a very short period of time. Add to that the 15 foreign representations that exist in the country, among those the Bank of Boston, Bank of America, J.P. Morgan, Deutsche Bank, and ING Bank, that accumulate 6.7% of total assets adding up to 81.7% of the total assets of the 32 banks in operation although they only contributed 77% of total credit but collected 92% of total earnings (see Tables 6.1 and 6.2). In consequence, none of the 18 banks privatized a decade earlier during Carlos Salinas of Gortari's government belonged to their original owners. This has been a very quick process of extranjerización when taking into account that at the beginning of the privatization process in 1991 only one foreign bank operated in Mexico with a special concession since 1921 (Citibank). An additional fact appreciated in Table 6.2 is that only two banks accumulate three–quarters of the assets still under Mexican ownership: Banorte with 11.4% and Imbursa with 3.3%. The other ten banks compete for the remaining 3% of total assets.

*Table 6.1    Market share by type of ownership*

|  | Net worth (Pesos, m.) | % | Credit portfolio (Pesos, m.) | % | Profits (Pesos, m.) | % |
|---|---|---|---|---|---|---|
| Total | 1,785,772.25 | 99.9 | 962,370.21 | 99.8 | 21,685.43 | 99.6 |
| Foreign–owned banks | 1,471,714.50 | 82.3 | 747,424.20 | 77.5 | 20,092.10 | 92.3 |
| National–owned banks | 316,717.30 | 17.7 | 217,142.30 | 22.5 | 1,686.40 | 7.8 |

*Source:* Elaboration by author with data from Comisión Nacional Bancaria y de Valores (CNBV), Boletin de Banca Multiple, September 2003.

Between 1991 and 1992, commercial credit institutions that had been under state control since September 1982 were returned to private owners. The bigger participation of foreign capital is correlated with the difficulties that appeared soon in these banks due to mismanagement in credit risk handling and bad supervision.

*Table 6.2     Individual banks' market share by type of ownership*

|  | Net worth | % | Credit portfolio | % | Net profits | % |
|---|---|---|---|---|---|---|
| Total | 1785772.25 | 99.86 | 962370.21 | 99.79 | 21685.43 | 99.6 |
| **Foreign–owned banks** | | | | | | |
| BBVA BANCOMER | 458482.93 | 25.64 | 247674.34 | 25.68 | 4381.57 | 20.1 |
| BANAMEX | 399406.75 | 22.33 | 183321.03 | 19.01 | 7521.48 | 34.5 |
| HSBC | 166043.2 | 9.28 | 111707.64 | 11.58 | 1168.69 | 5.37 |
| SANTANDER MEXICANO | 115517.42 | 6.46 | 68481.87 | 7.1 | 1744.75 | 8.01 |
| SERFIN | 114286.91 | 6.39 | 52136.12 | 5.41 | 2832.79 | 13.0 |
| SCOTIABANK INVERLAT | 88890.77 | 4.97 | 59037.66 | 6.12 | 1321.54 | 6.07 |
| ING BANK | 27327.83 | 1.53 | 2626.41 | 0.27 | 418.17 | 1.92 |
| BANK OF AMERICA | 22054.24 | 1.23 | 166.56 | 0.02 | -136.6 | -0.63 |
| J.P. MORGAN | 18598.38 | 1.04 | 0 | 0 | 178.41 | 0.82 |
| DEL BAJIO | 10730.05 | 0.6 | 8622.81 | 0.89 | 60.68 | 0.28 |
| CREDIT SUISSE | 10491.96 | 0.59 | 0 | 0 | 7.6 | 0.03 |
| DEUTSCHE BANK | 9852.81 | 0.55 | 0 | 0 | -74.73 | -0.34 |
| BBV BANCOMER SERVICIOS | 6562.79 | 0.37 | 0 | 0 | 719.44 | 3.3 |
| BANK OF BOSTON | 5953.15 | 0.33 | 2485.43 | 0.26 | -0.25 | 0 |
| GE CAPITAL BANK | 5490.88 | 0.31 | 4211.17 | 0.44 | -111.1 | -0.51 |
| COMERICA BANK | 3927.15 | 0.22 | 2881.79 | 0.3 | 7.68 | 0.04 |
| A. EXPRESS | 2659.52 | 0.15 | 2196.29 | 0.23 | 93.07 | 0.43 |
| TOKIO MITSUBISHI | 2100.12 | 0.12 | 1552.08 | 0.16 | 40.93 | 0.19 |
| ABN AMRO BANK | 1865.71 | 0.1 | 97.54 | 0.01 | -19.03 | -0.09 |
| BANK ONE | 1139.09 | 0.06 | 225.45 | 0.02 | -7.27 | -0.03 |
| DRESDNER BANK | 332.81 | 0.02 | 0 | 0 | -55.76 | -0.26 |
| Subtotal | 1471714.47 | 82.29 | 747424.19 | 77.5 | 20092.06 | 92.3 |
| **National-owned banks** | | | | | | |
| BANORTE | 203382.86 | 11.37 | 150210.34 | 15.57 | 727.57 | 3.34 |
| INBURSA | 58828.59 | 3.29 | 37963.02 | 3.94 | -104.94 | -0.48 |
| IXE | 11044.27 | 0.62 | 3536.9 | 0.37 | 49.63 | 0.23 |
| AFIRME | 8347.63 | 0.47 | 4340.34 | 0.45 | 52.9 | 0.24 |
| BANCO AZTECA | 7446.55 | 0.42 | 4365.19 | 0.45 | 42.78 | 0.2 |
| INTERACCIONES | 6037.41 | 0.34 | 2944.43 | 0.31 | 24.05 | 0.11 |
| INVEX | 5884.1 | 0.33 | 4084.87 | 0.42 | 17.32 | 0.08 |
| BANREGIO | 5331.92 | 0.3 | 4329.1 | 0.45 | 134.94 | 0.62 |
| MIFEL | 4066.34 | 0.23 | 2865.74 | 0.3 | 49.55 | 0.23 |
| CENTRO | 4006.63 | 0.22 | 1099.75 | 0.11 | 667.51 | 3.06 |
| BANSI | 2341 | 0.13 | 1402.63 | 0.15 | 25.13 | 0.12 |
| Subtotal | 316717.3 | 17.72 | 217142.31 | 22.52 | 1686.44 | 7.75 |

*Source:* Elaborated by author with data from CNBV, Boletin de Banca Múltiple, September 2003.

Consequently, several of them were intervened by government but it was the foreign exchange crisis of December 1994 that pushed banks that were in a precarious financial situation to a complete deterioration of their operational conditions. In 1995 Congress modified legislation relative to the restriction that foreign capital could not control more than 49% of net worth of Mexican banks. In the cases of Banamex, Bancomer and Serfin, the biggest banks in the country, total control was not allowed. Congress modified this exclusion in December 1998.

The effect of this process on the structure of credit markets is a higher degree of concentration. Thus, the Herfindahl index in September 2003 was $H = 0.15$ while in December 1997 it was $H = 0.13$. The story is similar with the C index of concentration. C4 had a value of 65.7% in December 1997 that grew to 68.6% by September 2003 while the C6 ratio changed its values from 74.6% to 81.5% in the same interval. The central factor that differentiates these two moments in time is the degree of control by foreign capital.

# 4   METHODOLOGICAL OBSERVATIONS

## 4.1   Methodology

The study of banks' behaviour should help to evaluate whether the strategies of foreign capital have contributed to strengthen the Mexican financial system and to improve its development in the long run more than in the short run. To this end, in this chapter we carried out an analysis at an aggregated level for the entire banking system. It requires working with average values that naturally differ for each particular bank but given the high grade of market concentration in the six bigger banks relative differences can be minimized. Two methods are applied in the analysis. The first of them is found in the work of King and Levine (1993a, b), Levine (1997) while the other follows the analysis carried out by Dages et al. (2000) and Grier (2001).

The first approach emphasizes the estimation of indicators that measure the degree of financial intermediation reached by the system and, consequently, they are a general measurement of the level of financial development. The second approach focuses on estimating and evaluating different ratios of the balance sheet and the behaviour of banks that serve to show the operational strength of the system. This is an analysis of the CAMEL type that examines capital adequacy, asset quality, management, earnings and liquidity. These indicators are suggestive of the financial conditions and performance quality of banks.

## 4.2   The Periodización

The emphasis in this chapter is in the comparative analysis of financial ratios before and through the extranjerización process which makes it necessary to define periods in the development of the system. With a quarterly database[3] from 1992 to 2002 three periods have been chosen and differentiated by levels of foreign ownership of banks. The initial period from 1992 to 1995 is classified as national capital given the low level of foreign capital; it is also a period of transition given that banks stop being public entities to become private firms. The other two periods are distinguished for the presence of foreign capital. 1996 to 1998 is taken as a second period with light level of extranjerización and starting in 1999 the period is defined as strong extranjerización.

## 5   THE FALL OF CREDIT

The long-term tendency of real bank credit and of its proportion in relationship to GDP is very clear in Figure 6.1. From 1969 on it grew more or less uninterruptedly up to 1994 when it reached its maximum level of 548,808 million pesos, which meant a growth from 17.9% to 41.8% as a proportion of GDP. From then on, the absolute level of real credit starts to fall up to its minimum of 251 billion pesos in 2001 although it grows to 258 billion pesos in 2002. In one decade the level of real credit experienced a boisterous fall of 52%. As a proportion of the GDP it went down to 15.7% in 2001 with a slight turnaround to 16% in 2002. Consequently, credit levels in 2002 were equivalent to those at the end of the 1970s. In this long-term context we examine what happened with credit growth in the three periods proposed in this study.

In average quarterly nominal terms bank credit grew from 444 billion pesos in the period 1992–1995 to 919 billion pesos in the last period but in real terms it decreases from 393 to 265 million pesos (Table 6.3). This is consistent with the average quarterly rates of growth of -1.41% in the most recent period after being 2.38% in the transition period. These results are complemented by data of the Bank of Mexico that show that bank financing as a proportion of the total financing has constantly diminished from 61.2% in the fourth quarter of 1994 to 35.6% in the third quarter of 2003. Volatility of lending, on the contrary, moves in a positive direction as indicated by standard deviations (Table 6.3). It decreases significantly from the initial to the final period as much in nominal as in real terms, but it deserves to be mentioned that volatility is bigger in real than in nominal terms. The normalized standard deviations, an indicator of the average volatility for a unit of loan growth, confirm this tendency towards more stability. Of course, it is no gain that stability in credit allocation goes hand in hand with smaller credit flows.

This fall in the allocation of credit is paradoxical since it happened in spite of the legal reforms that were considered necessary to impel the transformation of the financial system in order to motivate savings. At present, only 10% of Mexicans have access to credit while 70% of the population has no contact with the financial system whereas the biggest companies concentrate nearly 90% of available credit, one of the highest levels of financial concentration in the world.

Together with the reduction in bank credit an additional factor to consider is the significant change in credit allocation (Table 6.4). A larger proportion of credit goes to consumption while the proportion to productive activities has decreased. Credit allocation for consumption increased from 2.8% in the first quarter of 1997 to 7.9% at the end of 2002 while credit to the mortgage sector rose from 5% to 12.5% although it even went up to 17% at the end of 1998.

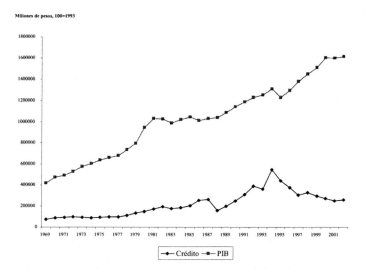

Millones de pesos, 100=1993

*Figure 6.1    Tendencies in levels of GDP and bank credit portfolio*

As a result, starting in 1995 borrowers had to find alternative sources of finance. Mexican companies had to find other financial sources for their growth, such as credits from suppliers, which implied taking bigger risks and higher costs. Traditional methods to guarantee payment like credit letters, credit deposits and other payment guarantees have affected a company's competitiveness due to higher costs.

It is positive that consumers have a bigger participation in credit allocation but when their improvement happens at the expense of credit to the productive sector the net gain is uncertain. For example, credit to non-financial firms sank from 40% in 1996 to 32.5% at the end of 2002. Another activity that has grown significantly, although it receives a low proportion of the total amount is credit among financial institutions that grew to 2.7% at the end of 2002 after accounting for just 0.4% in 1996.

*Table 6.3     Average growth rates of bank credit*

|  | Nominal (Pesos, m.) | % | Real (Pesos, m.) | % |
|---|---|---|---|---|
| 1T92 – 4T95 |  |  |  |  |
| Average | 444,097.90 | 6.73 | 393.20 | 2.38 |
| Standard deviation | 115,018.90 | 8.97 | 54.80 | 10.29 |
| Normalized SD | 0.25 | 1.33 | 0.13 | 4.29 |
| 1T96 – 4T98 |  |  |  |  |
| Average | 738,170.60 | 2.53 | 323.30 | -1.79 |
| Standard deviation | 71,296.70 | 4.68 | 28.40 | 4.74 |
| Normalized SD | 0.09 | 1.84 | 0.087 | -2.90 |
| 1T99 – 4T02 |  |  |  |  |
| Average | 919,594.10 | 0.73 | 264.90 | -1.41 |
| Standard deviation | 29,435.40 | 2.01 | 16.70 | 2.74 |
| Normalized SD | 0.03 | 2.75 | 0.063 | -1.92 |

*Source:* Author's estimation.

*Table 6.4     Distribution of credit by line of business*

|  | Con/ Tot | Mortgage/ Tot | Firms/ Tot | Fin/ Tot | Gov/ Tot | Foba/ Tot | PrivS/ Tot | PubS/ Tot |
|---|---|---|---|---|---|---|---|---|
| 1997–98 | 3.3 | 13.9 | 39.0 | 1.2 | 6.0 | 31.2 | 57.4 | 37.1 |
| 1999–02 | 4.9 | 14.2 | 32.2 | 1.7 | 14.7 | 32.3 | 53.0 | 47.0 |

*Source:* Author's estimation.

Highly paradoxical is growth of bank credit to the government sector with a share of 20.7% of total credit by the end of 2002. But there are also the bank resources to the FOBAPROA that grew from 29.6% at the end of 1996 to 39.4% in the first quarter of 2000 although it decreased quickly to 23.7%

by the end of 2002. When adding these two items, bank credit in official hands sums up to 45% of total credit. It seems like a return to the 1980s, highly criticized then when the nationalized banking system was used to finance the public sector.

A persistent falling tendency in credit volume and a distribution that does not favour the productive sector contradicts the previous theoretical reasoning. Without credit creation no liquidity is pumped into the economy and neither is there new economic activity without new purchasing power. It is not a good performance of the dynamics of extranjerización although this behaviour is perfectly in accordance with the practice of specialization in retail banking. According to *The Economist* it occurs because 'Retail banking is less subject to the ups and downs of the business cycle than wholesale or investment banking. The profitability of retail has in turn encouraged banks to invest more in their retail operations. The past few years have reminded banks that retail is less risky than the more glamorous bits of banking' (2004, p. 4).

# 6  EVALUATION OF THE BANK OPERATION

## 6.1  Development of the financial intermediation

To measure levels of financial intermediation King and Levine propose four indicators.[4] The first two measure the magnitude of financial intermediation while the other two measure the allocation of credit. PROFUNDIZACIÓN measures the size of the formal financial system while BANKS measures the services provided by banks by examining the relative importance of bank deposits with respect to total deposits of the private sector plus those of the public sector. Increasing values of these indicators correspond to more services provided by these institutions. Of the other two indicators IPCRÉDITO measures the proportion of credit that goes to private companies belonging to the non-financial sector as a proportion of credit going to public and private entities. In consequence, the growth of this ratio manifests a redistribution of credit from the public towards the private sector whereas a reduction shows the opposite. IPCRÉDITOY measures the level of credit dedicated to private companies of the non-financial sector as a proportion of GDP. Its growth exemplifies a bigger attention to the private sector in the assignment of credit.

The tendency of each of these indicators, displayed in Figure 6.2, makes it evident that in the first quarter of 1995 there is an abrupt break in the levels of three of them. Naturally, this was a consequence of the exchange crisis of December 1994. The exception to this behaviour is PROFUNDIZACIÓN that maintains a relatively constant and stable behaviour along the entire period although it experiences modifications of magnitude in each one of the three periods of study (Table 6.5). Its average level in the period of transition is the highest at 27% but decreases to 21% in the period of strong extranjerización which points to a loss of relevance of the financial sector. The entrance of foreign capital does not seem to have contributed to augment the relative importance of the sector within the Mexican economy. Additionally, this indicator's volatility expressed by the standard deviation grows from one period to the other. Thus, a loss of influence of banks within the financial sector is accompanied by instability.

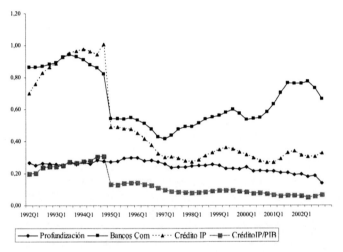

*Figure 6.2    Mexico: tendencies of indicators of financial development*

The tendency of the other three indicators shows an abrupt reduction in the first quarter of 1995 with varying behaviour subsequently. BANKS tends to grow after the fall of 1995; after falling from 80% to 49% it increases to 65% in the last period. This result points to an increasing presence of banks inside the financial sector. This success, however, is not manifested in the allocation of credit to the productive sector (IPCRÉDITO) since the smaller level in the second period continues to fall (although just a little) in the third period. Furthermore, the last two indicators point to a distribution of credit that does not favour the productive sector.

*Table 6.5     Indicators of financial development*

|                     | Profundización | Banks | IPCrédito | IPCréditoY |
|---------------------|----------------|-------|-----------|------------|
| **1992–1995**       |                |       |           |            |
| Average             | 0.27           | 0.80  | 0.79      | 0.23       |
| Standard deviation  | 0.01           | 0.15  | 0.19      | 0.06       |
| **1996–1998**       |                |       |           |            |
| Average             | 0.26           | 0.49  | 0.33      | 0.10       |
| Standard deviation  | 0.02           | 0.04  | 0.05      | 0.02       |
| **1999–2002**       |                |       |           |            |
| Average             | 0.21           | 0.65  | 0.32      | 0.07       |
| Standard deviation  | 0.03           | 0.09  | 0.03      | 0.01       |

*Source:* Author's estimation.

On the whole, these indicators of financial development do not lead to a positive evaluation of foreign capital in the consolidation of the Mexican banking industry if we accept the postulate of King and Levine that 'if financial sector interactions with the private sector are more indicative of the provision of productivity enhancing financial services than financial sector interactions with the public sector, higher values of PRIVATE [IPCRÉDITO] and PRIV/Y [IPCRÉDITOY] should indicate greater financial development' (1993a, p. 529).

The average coefficients that King and Levine obtained for a sample of 77 countries for the period 1960–989 have similar levels to those that we found for Mexico in the period of transition. This confirms the validity of our results. In sum, the comparison of these indicators gives sufficient evidence of deterioration in bank intermediation in Mexico despite the entrance of foreign capital.

## 6.2   Analysis Type CAMEL

The framework of reference for this analysis is the degree of stability of bank loans and the readiness of supply of funds. It is necessary to recognize that uncertainty or volatility, inconvenience per se, is negative for the narrow and negative correlation that it has with growth. In this context, the expectation is that the pattern of loans could have variations given the differences that can exist in the reasons and the objectives of banks as well as in the balance sheet health and the diversification of sources of funds. These elements can have significant effects on interest rate sensibility to the supply of loans and on the expansion or contraction of loan supply. In fact, in the debate about the uncertainty or volatility of credit it is argued that interest rate sensibility of loans can be bigger for banks with closer ties to international capital markets given the bigger range of profitable investment opportunities. Of course, banks with foreign capital are more likely to have these ties that make larger modifications in the behaviour of loan supplies feasible. Then, the existence of distinct behaviour for each one of the periods of analysis depends on the reasons for which banks lend. If loans have transaction-based motives an improvement in economic conditions offers opportunities to which banks respond as a way of accommodation to changing conditions of demand. If loans respond to lending motives credit can still expand under negative aggregate demand conditions. In fact, under positive economic conditions clients could pay their credits off and therefore supply would decrease.

In this case, the quality of the balance sheet determines the behaviour of banks. If banks under foreign capital control are intent on correcting their balance sheets then a positive economic environment is not enough to have an expansion of credit since banks use the opportunity to improve their operational conditions. If banks prefer to take advantage of profitable investment opportunities they could be taking even bigger risks.

The stability of credit is equally a function of the source of borrowed funds. Dependence on local demand deposits or on cyclically sensitive funds would give a pattern of highly volatile credit to local conditions which does not necessarily happen if the affiliates of foreign banks appeal to their main houses in which economic conditions can be different than local ones. This source of resources, naturally, makes the local economy more dependent on the conditions abroad.

### 6.2.1   Quality of the credit portfolio

Poor quality of credit portfolio is a fundamental cause of bank failure due to its negative effects on credit risk. Figure 6.3 shows the improvement that Mexican banks experienced in portfolio quality in the last decade. The non-performing loan ratio (NLR), non-performing loans in relation to total loans, grew to 22.1% by 1995 but decreased to 4.6% by the last quarter of 2002. Consequently, the average quarterly level of this ratio per period decreased from 18.9% in the first period to 12.3% in the second and to 6.7% in the last period. The tendency is similar when this coefficient is calculated with relation to total assets: 12.9%, 8.6% and 4.3% for each one of the periods.

This tendency makes one in every ten loan users a dilatory debtor while in 1995 seven in ten fell in this category. Comparatively this is a very positive situation if it is considered that Chile with one of the healthiest banking sectors on the continent has a ratio very similar to that of Mexico while Brazil stands at three for each ten clients and Argentina is in the most precarious situation where seven of every ten are dilatory debtors. This level and this tendency in the NLR strengthen the argument that banks have been oriented to balance sheet reparation.

A problem in the defence of the previous argument is that the provisions that banks should make against bad loans to achieve improvements in its NLR have not behaved as they are supposed to (see Table 6.6). In the first period the quarterly average of this item was 5.6 billion real pesos with a reduction in the following period to 4.7 billion and a further fall to 1.5 billion pesos in the last period. The coefficient of provisions to NLR grows from 7.5% to 11.1% between the first and the second period but decreases to 8.4% for the third period. Something different happens when we consider preventive estimates for credit risks that banks began accumulating in 1997. Although its average annual level falls from the second to the third period from 22.4 billion to 19.4 billion pesos, the coefficient increases from 63% to 114% which could be taken as the substitution of one source of preventive funds for another. Overall, these countertendencies are not suggestive of perfect efficient financial intermediation and higher precaution to reallocate funds.

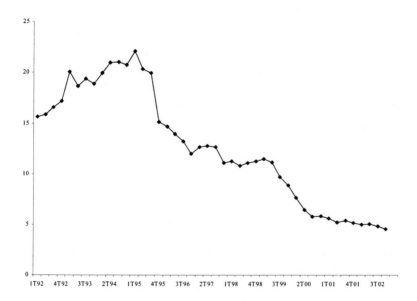

*Figure 6.3   Non-performing loan ratio*

*Table 6.6 Provisions against risk*

|  | Provisions[a] | Estimations[b] | Prov/NonPerLoan % | Estim/NonPerLoan % |
|---|---|---|---|---|
| 1T92 – 4T95 |  |  |  |  |
| Average | 5.4 |  | 7.5 |  |
| Standard deviation | 4.0 |  | 5.9 |  |
| 1T96 – 4T98 |  |  |  |  |
| Average | 4.7 | 22.4 | 11.1 | 63.0 |
| Standard deviation | 4.1 | 0.6 | 9.2 | 3.6 |
| 1T99 – 4T02 |  |  |  |  |
| Average | 1.5 | 19.4 | 8.4 | 114.1 |
| Standard deviation | 0.9 | 4.4 | 3.7 | 19.8 |

In order to explain the fall of the NLR, we argue the existence of other factors that have greatly contributed to this result. Among those we highlight:

1. The creation of the Bureau of Credit.
2. The substantive reduction in the proportion of consumption loans that decreased to 30% in 2002 from 75% in 1993.
3. The smaller flexibility in payment plans. In 1995 the average time of liquidation of credit calls was 24 months while in 2003 it was 14.
4. The reduction of interest rates and larger incentives for trustworthy clients.
5. Better control and monitoring mechanisms, internally as well as externally.

### 5.2.2   Capitalization Level

Another positive change in bank performance that contributes to the quality of credit is the improvement in the capitalization grade as can be seen in the two capitalization coefficients calculated by the Bank of Mexico. One is related to the risk incurred by credit emission and the other relates to total risk of the banking sector (Figure 6.4). Their evolution makes it evident that the banking system has improved its capitalization level during the period of study.

At the end of the process of privatization capitalization of total risk was hardly 7%, below the level required by the Basle's Accord of 1988. Two years later this level was in-line with international requirements with quarterly levels above 10%. Since then this coefficient grew though not in a homogeneous path over time. Its maximum value of 16.22% was reached in the last quarter of 1999 but it fell to 15.3% by the third quarter of 2003.

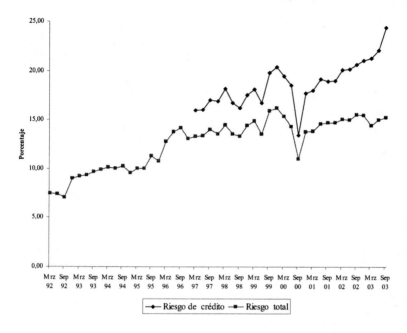

*Figure 6.4    Capitalization ratios*

The average quarterly level for total risk grew as the process of bank extranjerización advanced. In the initial period this level did not reach 10% but it reached 13.7% in the second period and for the third period it grew to 14.7%. Its highest level of stability, expressed by the standard deviation, is in the intermediate period. Although volatility grew in the last period it was much smaller than in the first period. Credit risk capitalization manifests a similar trajectory.

In sum, it can be argued that foreign ownership of banks has contributed to higher levels of capitalization and that their tendency validates the hypothesis that the main objective of foreign bankers has been that of cleaning their balance sheets.

Strengthening banks capitalization as a central task of the new owners is confirmed when examining the significant changes in the shares of paid and earned capital as proportions of net worth. While earned capital falls, paid capital grows. As indicated in Figure 6.5 paid capital's participation rises from a quarterly average of 17% in the initial period to 68% in the period of light extranjerización and to 81% during strong extranjerización. Earned capital moves in the opposite direction.

*Table 6.7     Average capitalization ratios*

|  | **Credit risk** | **Total risk** | **Differential** |
|---|---|---|---|
| 1T92 – 4T95 |  |  |  |
| Average |  | 9.46 |  |
| Standard deviation |  | 2.55 |  |
| 1T96 – 4T98 |  |  |  |
| Average | 16.83 | 13.67 | 3.06 |
| Standard deviation | 0.72 | 0.51 |  |
| 1T99 – 4T02 |  |  |  |
| Average | 18.82 | 14.64 | 4.19 |
| Standard deviation | 1.78 | 1.19 |  |

*Source:* Author's estimation.

In this way, one of the fundamental purposes of openness to foreign banks, facilitating capitalization of banks, was fulfilled. Consequently, as net capital grows in relation to higher risk assets banks offer a higher grade of depositors' protection.

### 6.2.3   Profitability profile

Accepting that profitability is the supreme indicator of success of any firm the tendency during the decade of study contradicts some of the previous results. Initially, there is a falling development with the drop from the 8.6 billion real pesos in the last quarter of 1993 to a loss of 3.5 billion in the last quarter of 1996. Later on there are short cycles with a clear growth up to the 4.3 billion real pesos in the last quarter of 2002 (Figure 6.6). The final result is that net average earnings per period falls abruptly from the first to the second period, 3.75 billion to 0.09 billion pesos but recovers significantly in the final period to an average of 2.62 billion pesos. The higher degree of stability in this indicator is significant but paradoxical since profits improved when credit liquidity fell.

Traditional indicators of yields on capital (ROE), on assets (ROA) as well as on profit margins show similar tendencies although their strengths vary. Margins experience the largest recovery when passing from 2.7% to 41.7% that duplicates the average level of 18.6% of the initial period though with a higher volatility in recent periods. ROA, considered as the best indicator to evaluate bank administration, increases from 0.1% to 0.62%, a level very close to that in the initial period but still below 1% considered as quality level (Grier, 2002). ROE renders similar results. It increases from 0.19% to 6.62% though it remains below the average level of the initial period and far from quality level, considered to be between 10% and 15%. It is worth noticing

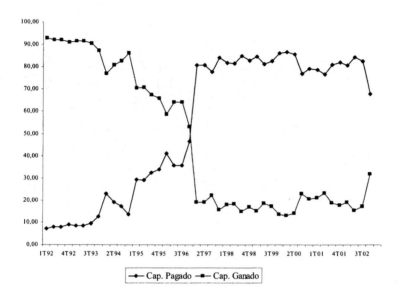

*Figure 6.5    Paid capital and earned capital shares*

*Figure 6.6    Net real profits*

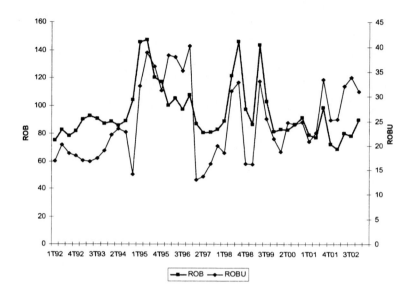

*Figure 6.7    Credit profitability (ROB) versus non-bank business profitability (ROBU)*

that in the initial period this indicator was closer to quality value; likewise, stability of these last indicators is larger at the end than it was at the beginning of the study period.

The other indicators presented also confirm the positive tendency of profitability in the last period. Additionally they are evidence of the structural transformation from traditional banking business, receiving short–term deposits to grant long–term loans, towards financial markets' business.

The banks' yield coefficient (ROB) relates net utility to financial margin as an indicator of profitability of bank business while the coefficient of market yield (ROBU) relates net utility to the activities for which banks charge commissions and fees. It is assumed as an indicator of profitability of financial or non-bank business. These two indicators confirm the recovery of profitability in the most recent period but their time evolution (Figure 6.7) shows that more recently, since the third quarter of 2001, the levels of ROBU are above those of ROB, and with a spread that grows. This confirms the greater relevance of non-bank activities in earning levels.

The importance of revenues of the non-bank business is what is captured by the last indicator, ROBS. In the first period financial business revenues were on average 22% of those of the banking business but for the most recent period they have risen to a quarterly average of 30%, as a result of the constant increase from 15% in the initial quarter of 1997 to 43% in the third quarter of 2002 (Figure 6.8). Thus, bank earnings result increasingly from the financial business at the expense of the banking business, with the biggest jump in this direction during the phase of strong extranjerización.

The importance of FOBAPROA notes interests on profitability cannot be minimized, since they jumped from 29.6% at the beginning of 1997 to 39.4% at the beginning of 2000 although it fell to 23.7% by the end of 2002. Not without reason it can be argued that the success in the financial business of banks is the cause of better profitability indicators.

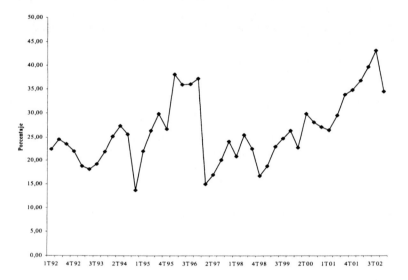

*Figure 6.8    Commissions and fees over financial margin (ROBS)*

The primary factor of profit growth is the high cost of financing for loan takers to whom drops in interest rates and low costs of the resources have not been permeated. The cost of financing was high given that the spread between active and passive rates was not reduced in spite of the fall in the interbank equilibrium interest rate (TIIE) that decreased to a fourth of its value from 34.2% to 8.4% between 4 January 1999 and 31 December 2002. Thus, banks' intermediation margin, the difference between the deposit and the loans rates averages 15 percentage points in the first semester of 2003. Certainly, this is the lowest range since banks were privatized but it is high for international standards if it is considered that in the United States this range is not higher than 5.5 points and in Canada not higher than 6.5 points (Romero, 1998; Guillen, 2002). However, in Chile this spread was 22 percentage points and in Brazil it shot to 73 points (Rodríguez, 2003, p. 3A).

The ideal situation is to arrive at industrial countries' levels but it implies that radical changes are needed in factors affecting this margin like implicit risk in the grant of loans, weights of administrative costs, uncertainty in the levels of interest rates and the discretionary handling of commissions.

The fact is: banks pay low and charge dear. For example, bank notes pay less than 2% while debit cards barely reach 0.6%. So benefits to savers are at historical minimum levels while payments made for services is high which corresponds to the high fees and commissions banks charge (Banxico, 2004). Credit cards go on average at around 38%, plus annuities, monthly interests, a 10% plus surcharge for disposition of cash in ATMS, and charges for delay payments. A forced conclusion is that to charge high fees is an explanatory factor for the tendency towards retail banking and an instrument towards healthy balance sheets.

### 6.2.4   Operative efficiency

Earnings growing faster by financial rather than by banking business have little to do with efficiency in the operation of banks. Of the three indicators in Table 6.8 two question that banks' operational efficiency improved significantly by openness to foreign capital. The coefficient of operating cost to operating income, the more relevant indicator, shows improvement in the last period but its average level remains higher than that of the initial period. It is a positive but unsatisfactory result. Additionally its volatility stays high.

*Table 6.8    Indicators of operational efficiency*

|                     | Cost/Income | Cost/Net worth | Cost/Assets |
|---------------------|:-----------:|:--------------:|:-----------:|
| 1T92 – 4T95         |             |                |             |
| Average             | 74.9        | 44.0           | 6.1         |
| Standard deviation  | 6.2         | 20.6           | 0.6         |
| 1T96 – 4T98         |             |                |             |
| Average             | 107.0       | 28.1           | 7.8         |
| Standard deviation  | 19.2        | 15.9           | 1.0         |
| 1T99 – 4T02         |             |                |             |
| Average             | 83.1        | 13.3           | 9.3         |
| Standard deviation  | 16.1        | 2.3            | 1.0         |

*Source:* Author's estimation.

The relationship of costs to assets is even less satisfactory since its average level increases period after period to a final increase of more than 50%. Volatility also rises. The third coefficient that relates costs with net worth is the only one that presents a positive behaviour by the constant reduction of its yearly average as for its higher degree of stability which matches appropriately with banks' priority of improving the capitalization level. These results tend to support the argument that without economic growth the reduction of costs of financial intermediation is very unlikely (Harrison et al., 1999; Greenwood and Smith, 1997).

## 7.  FACTORS DETERMINING THE LOW LEVEL OF CREDIT

The monetary and financial crisis of 1994–1995 that caused stressing conditions for the operation of the Mexican economy appears as the underlying cause of the collapse of credit. Factors inherent to the operation of companies were affected such as the level of programmed investment and managerial, administrative and financial practices. The aggregate result of these factors is twofold. They constitute a force that pushed down demand for credit and at the same time hindered the evaluation of credit applicants' payment capacity. Additionally, there are macroeconomic factors that negatively affect microeconomic dynamics and augment demand deficiencies. Among them is the absence of structural reforms in the fiscal, labour and energy fields.

The other side of this coin is the readiness of supply conditions for loanable funds. Central in this respect is the level of domestic savings which has experienced a high grade of volatility as manifested in the increment of yearly averages, as a proportion of GDP, ranging from 16.5% to 22.3% between the first and the second periods and falling to 19.3% in the last one. A complementary factor that inhibits credit is the very high percentage of banks' assets kept in financial instruments as futures, reports, etc.

Now, let us examine what happened to supply of funds by how bank deposits have evolved. By 1994 total bank deposits grew to an equivalent of 47.2% of the GDP but afterwards they fell to a level of 22% in 2002. In consequence, the average yearly level of 40.6% of GDP in the transition period decreased to 33.1% in the period of light extranjerización to a further fall to 23.9% in that of strong extranjerización. This happened because real deposits decreased from 61.9 to 35.8 billion pesos. This indicates that the entrance of foreign banks could not revert the falling tendency in deposits propitiated by the devaluation of 1994. It can also be a sign of greater sensibility by foreign banks to market signs as a result of their greater dependence on international markets (Dages et al., 2000).

This reduction in deposits is caused by several factors. One is the low yield savers received on time deposits and checking accounts which made them shift their assets into financial market instruments. This has opened the way to competition between banks and other financial institutions that offer better yields. Another factor is the bigger use that company treasuries make of accounting practices off the balance sheet in order to improve profitability. The elimination of deposit insurance introduces another negative element since taking a bigger risk without compensation in profitability motivates to find other investment options.

*Table 6.9      Sources of loanable funds**

|  | Saving deposits | Demand deposits | Time deposits | Bank bonds | Interbank loans | Obligations | Repurchases |
|---|---|---|---|---|---|---|---|
| 1992–95 | 0.28 | 16.71 | 40.54 | 4.57 | 15.79 | 2.09 | 20.02 |
| 1996–98 | 2.51 | 16.72 | 45.13 | 5.01 | 21.98 | 2.85 | 6.00 |
| 1999–02 | 6.33 | 25.68 | 49.20 | 1.53 | 18.33 | 1.81 | 0.16 |

*Note:* *As percentage of total deposits.
*Source:* Author's estimation.

The change in sources of funds is another factor affecting deposits. Table 6.9 points to an increment in the proportion captured by different deposit channels while decreasing those of other sources; in particular it highlights the elimination of repurchase agreements. Bank bonds as well as interbank lending that increased in the intermediate period decreased in the final one. These changes in the sources of funds have made resources more liquid as well as cheaper and thus constitute a negative incentive for growth.

## 8   CONCLUSIONS

The result of the extranjerización process is that by the end of 2003 about 82% of net worth of banks in Mexico were under foreign capital control in a highly concentrated market in which only six banks, five foreign–owned, control 81% of total net worth.

Foreign control of banks has contributed to an improvement in the health of the banking system by strengthening the capitalization level. Nonetheless, this has not contributed to improvements in the national saving rate nor in the volume of loanable resources. Extranjerización, then, has not induced a larger relative presence of the banking sector in the national economy nor a larger allocation of credit to the productive sector. This result does not agree with the standard of a good operating banking system whose function is to facilitate the investment resources a country requires for growth. It is not a good behaviour of extranjerización dynamics since credit availability has not even grown at levels previous to extranjerización.

These results validate the argument that the initial objective of foreign banks has been heavily focused on balance sheet repair. The level and the tendency in non-performing loans strengthen this argument. However, the dependence in local demand deposits and in cyclically sensitive funds has given a pattern of credit highly vulnerable to local conditions.

Consequently, we are forced to accept that there have been other factors beyond banks strategies that contributed to the positive result in broad indicators of banks' health as can be the creation of the bureau of credit, the reduction in the proportion of consumption loans, the smallest flexibility in payment plans, better control and monitoring mechanisms and the reduction in interest rates and in inflation levels as a result of monetary policy.

Nevertheless, extranjerización has significantly contributed to the recovery of banks' profitability although not reaching the high levels of earnings of the early 1990s. Earnings, however, come more from the financial business than from the bank business which seems to have reduced pressure to improve the operational efficiency of banks. It may mean that without economic growth it is unlikely to reduce the costs of financial intermediation.

On the whole, the evidence points to refute the hypothesis that the extranjerización process has impacted significantly banks' efficiency and profitability in order to improve the allocation of resources.

In sum, the higher liquidity of assets and the null expansion of loans, portfolios point definitively towards a defensive strategy of banks which put more attention to balance sheet repair by way of restructuring operations than by market expansion. Equally important is to recognize that banks moved along with the trend of the economy since they cannot mobilize resources that do not exist. Mexicans do not save because the low pace of economic growth does not allow it. Up to now, the only expectation is that the balance sheet repair strategy becomes the foundation for future growth.

## NOTES

[1] In this chapter the process through which domestic banks are transferred to foreign ones is called 'bank extranjerización'.

[2] The institution created for this purpose was the Fondo Bancario de Protección al Ahorro (FOBAPROA).

[3] A large part of this database was facilitated by Juan Manuel Ugarte of the Comisión Nacional Bancaria y de Valores for which we express our gratitude. However, a good part of the series had to be codified by the author to be able to have a compatible time series. Constant changes in accounting by the Commission made this procedure necessary.

[4] Following the methodology proposed by King and Levine (1993a, b) the information for the calculation of these indicators is taken from International Financial Statistics of the IMF.

## REFERENCES

Barajas, Adolfo, Roberto Steiner and Natalia Salazar (2000), 'Foreign Investment in Colombia's Financial Sector', in Stijn Claessens and Marion Jansen (eds), *The Internationalisation of Financial Services: Issues and Lessons from Developing Countries*, Boston: Kluwer Academic.

Chang, C. Edward, Iftekhar Hasan and William C. Hunter, 1998 'Efficiency of Multinational Banks: An Empirical Investigation', *Applied Financial Economics*, **8** (6), 1–8.

Claessens, Stijn, Asli Demirguc–Kunt and Harry Huizinga (1998), 'How Does Foreign Entry Affect the Domestic Banking Market', *World Bank Policy Research Working Paper*, No. 1918.

Claessens, Stijn, Asli Demirguc–Kunt and Harry Huizinga (2000), 'The Role of Foreign Banks in Domestic Banking Systems', in Stijn Claessens and Marion Jansen (eds), *The Internationalization of Financial Services: Issues and Lessons from Developing Countries*, Boston: Kluwer Academic.

Clarke, George, Robert Cull, María Soledad Martínez Peria and Susana M. Sanchez (2003), 'Foreign Bank Entry: Experience, Implications for Developing Countries, and Calendar for Further Research', *The World Bank Research Observer*, Spring, 25–59.

Crystal, Jennifer S., Gerard Dages and Linda S. Goldberg (2002), 'Has Foreign Bank Entry Led to Sounder Banks in Latin America?', *Current Issues in Economics and Finance*, **8** (1), 1–6.

Dages, Gerard, Linda Goldberg and Daniel Kinney (2000), 'Foreign and Domestic Bank Participation in Emerging Markets: Lessons from Mexico and Argentina', *FRBNY Economic Policy Review*, September, 17–36.

Deutsche Bundesbank (2002), 'Foreign Investment in the Real and Financial Sector', *Monthly Report*, June, 75–80.

DeYoung, Robert and Daniel E. Nolle (1996), 'Foreign Owned Banks in the United States: Earning Market Share or Buying it?', *Journal of Money, Credit and Banking*, **28** (4), 622–36.

Greenwood, Jeremy and Bruce D. Smith (1997), 'Financial Development and the Development of Financial Markets', *Journal of Economic Dynamics and Control*, 21, 145–181.

Grier, Waymond A. (2001), *Credit Analysis of Financial Institutions*, London: Euromoney Books.

Guillen, Héctor (2002), 'Evolución del Régimen Macrofinanciero en México', *Comercio Exterior*, Julio, 564–74.

Harrison, Paul, Oren Sussman and Joseph Zeira (1999), 'Finance and Growth: Theory and New Evidence', *FEDS Working Paper*, No. 35.

Hasan, Iftehar and William Hunter (1996), 'Efficiency of Japanese Multinationals Banks in the United States', in Andrew H. Chen (ed.), *Research in Finance*, 14, Greenwich, CT: JAI Press.

King, Robert G. and Ross Levine (1993a), 'Finance, Entrepreneurship, and Growth: Theory and Evidence', *Journal of Monetary Economics*, 32 (3), 513–42.

King, Robert G. and Ross Levine (1993b), 'Finance and Growth: Schumpeter Might Be Right', *The Quarterly Journal of Economics*, 108, 717–37.

Levine, Ross (1997), 'Financial Development and Economic Growth: Views and Calendar', *Journal of Economic Literature*, 35, 688–726.

Rodríguez, Eleazar (2003), 'Las Bajas Tasas Aún no se Traducen en Beneficios Para los Usuarios del Crédito Bancario", *El Financiero*, 25 de septiembre.

Romero, H. Carlos (1998), 'Competencia y Regulación en el Sector Bancario de México Después de la Privatización, 1992–1996', *Economía: Teoría y Práctica*, 9, 5–22.

Stiglitz, Joseph (1998), 'The Role of the State in Financial Markets', *Proceedings of the World Bank Annual Conference on Development Economics*, 19-52.

*The Economist*, 'Trust me, I'm a banker. A survey of international banking', 17 April 2004.

PART FOUR


MONETARY POLICY
ISSUES

# 7. Asymmetries in Transatlantic Monetary Policy Relationship? ECB versus FED

**Ansgar Belke and Daniel Gros**

## 1 INTRODUCTION

In this chapter we address the question of whether the ECB has systematically followed the US Federal Reserve in setting interest rates. It is difficult to document 'conventional wisdom' because it seems so obvious to everybody that few bother to actually provide evidence for it. One of the few instances in which it is possible to document the widespread expectation that the ECB follows the FED is related in Garcia-Cervero (2002). In a Reuters poll of economists taken in November 2002, the proportion of those expecting a cut by the ECB almost doubled (from 21 to 43 percent) the day after the FED cut rates on 5 November. Later on, these analysts were proved to be wrong, but were they wrong at changing their mind in the first place?

While many seem to be convinced that the ECB does follow the FED, few seem to ask the obvious question: What could be the rationale for the ECB to follow the FED? The simplest explanation would be that moves by the FED provide the ECB with an important signal (about the state of the US economy and financial markets). One implication of this explanation would be that the ECB should follow the FED almost immediately because it would not have any reason to delay its move once the signal has been given. One could thus account for the episode related above (e.g., Begg et al., 2002, p. 42). The problem with this argument is that it implies that the FED should also follow the ECB because the euro area is of a similar size as the US economy. However, nobody seems to suggest that the FED might also follow the ECB.

Another explanation might be that the US cycle precedes that of the euro area so that the ECB might appear to follow the FED, but in reality it just reacts to the evolution of the euro area's cycle, which happens to lag that of the US. The problem with this explanation is that leads and lags in macroeconomic variables like output and employment are usually measured in months or quarters (Begg et al., (2002) estimate the lag at 3–5 months), whereas the ECB is usually assumed to follow the FED within a much shorter time frame. (See the example reported above.) Moreover, the business cycle effect should be accounted for by the autoregressive element that is present in standard causality tests. Finally, recent research clearly demonstrated that the impact of the US business cycle has become significantly weaker throughout the nineties as compared to the seventies and eighties. This is mainly due to the emergence of multinational firms which can afford to stick to longer-term strategies independent of business cycle troughs (Schroeder et al., 2002). Hence, this approach is not well-suited as an explanation for the 'leader–follower' pattern.

Perhaps the most popular explanation why the ECB might follow the FED is that the ECB is simply slow and inefficient. This explanation would roughly run as follows: The world's financial markets were buffeted over the last years by the emergence and then the bursting of an asset price bubble. The leadership of the FED (Mr. Greenspan in particular) is simply smarter and was quicker to spot the problems. By contrast, so the story seems to go, the ECB is a new institution that still has to find its way, and its decision–making body is too large to reach quick decisions, especially given that it usually tries to forge a consensus before moving (Belke and Gros, 2002a; Wyplosz, 2001).

Another explanation could be grounded in a fundamental difference between the US and the euro zone economies: namely that the US economy is more flexible. This has important implications especially in times of heightened uncertainty. This can be seen most easily through the concept of the 'option value of waiting'. This concept formalizes a common–sense decision rule: if a decision involves some sunk costs, or any other element of irreversibility, it makes sense to postpone the decision until the uncertainty has been resolved. The temptation to postpone investment decisions is particularly strong when sunk costs are high and when the uncertainty is likely to be resolved in the near future. One can imagine in particular enterprises that have to consider normal investment projects, i.e. projects that would be slightly profitable under current circumstances and even more profitable in case the uncertainty is resolved in a positive sense, but would lead to losses if the uncertainty is resolved in a negative sense. In this case the enterprise would lose little (in terms of foregone profits) if it waited with the decision. Once the uncertainty has been resolved it would still have the option to proceed if the outcome is positive.[1]

The concept of the 'option value of waiting' applies also to the ECB. If, during times of unusual uncertainty, it cuts rates today it risks having to reverse its decision soon. The ECB should thus cut today only if it is convinced that such a cut would make sense even if the uncertainty is resolved in a positive way. In this sense, monetary policy is not a game of 'follow the leader', but of setting the right policy in the light of domestic inflation and growth prospects.

The models of decision-making under uncertainty also have a second implication. All decisions involve some transaction costs – whether they are about investment, or about hiring and firing. The last mentioned are especially important in Europe. This implies that businesses facing only a small change in prices may not respond immediately. There is always a band of inaction – a price range within which it does not pay to change course. The size of this band of inaction increases as uncertainty increases. And, given the structural rigidities in the euro zone economy, uncertainties probably affect decision-making in Europe more than they do in the US. As transaction costs (which are effectively sunk costs) are more important in Euroland than in the US it follows that for the ECB the option value of waiting for more information should be higher and might thus explain why the ECB is slower to react to signals than the FED.

The problem with this explanation, however, is that it should hold only for periods when volatility is temporarily higher than usual because the option value argument is valid only if the uncertainty is resolved (diminished) after a certain period. The option value of the waiting argument should thus apply only when financial markets are 'excessively' turbulent. We find some evidence for this hypothesis in the sense that we find that it is mainly after September 2001 that the FED seems to influence the ECB (and not vice versa).

The remainder of this chapter applies a battery of quantitative and qualitative techniques to validate the hypothesis that the ECB systematically follows the US Federal Reserve. This hypothesis can also be put as a question: Does the probability of an interest rate move by the ECB increase after the FED has moved (but not the other way round)? In other words, we check whether the behaviour of the analysts in the poll mentioned at the beginning can be backed up by a careful statistical analysis of the data. We proceed as follows: we first examine in section 2 some prima facie evidence and then proceed in section 3 to a more detailed econometric analysis using Granger causality methods and cointegration and weak exogeneity tests. To ensure robustness we use several different indicators and time periods and a variety of lag structures. In section 4 we then look closer at the EMU period and find that there is a clear structural break around September 2001. Section 5 concludes.

## 2   ECB AND FED INTEREST RATE SETTING – FIRST PRIMA FACIE EVIDENCE

A simple way to answer the question whether the ECB follows the FED might be to look at the behaviour of the official rates set by the ECB and the FED. However, these rates do not move frequently enough to allow the use of standard statistical methods without great caution. Hence one has to find indicators from financial markets, for example short–term interest rates, which complement the analysis and make it more robust. Although central banks do not directly set the most widely watched indicator of short-term monetary conditions, namely the one–month interest rate, they can nevertheless determine pretty much its evolution. If the ECB had systematically followed the evolution in the US (moves by the FED as well as changes in US financial markets), one would expect to find that changes in US interest rates tend to lead changes in euro area short–term rates. At first sight this seems to have been the case if one looks at the short life span of the euro. Figure 7.1 plots the central bank (ECB_REFIN and FED_FUNDS) and the one–month money market interest rate series (EURO_1M and USD_1M) for the euro zone and for the US since the start of EMU. We plot both levels and first differences. As expected, the one–month rates closely move around to the central bank rates. Hence, we feel free to use money market rates to test whether the ECB follows the FED.

This figure suggests at first sight that the US was leading the euro area by around one–quarter both when interest rates were going up, from the trough in early 1999 and when they started falling in early 2001. Many observers concluded from this apparent relationship that the ECB mimicked the FED in its monetary decisions. However, this popular belief was not corroborated by simple statistical analyses with data for monthly realizations of three–month interest rates up to 2001 (Belke et al., 2002; Belke and Gros, 2002b; Gros et al., 2002). This early period was followed by a phase in which the FED lowered its interest rate with an unprecedented speed while the ECB was more hesitant in this respect. The surprise cut by the Federal Reserve of 50bp on 3 January 2001 is often cited as a telling example of the leader–follower relationship because after this move by the Federal Reserve the ECB found itself under increasing and incredibly strong pressure to cut its own rates as well.[2] The last period which can be identified by visual inspection is characterized by the fact that the ECB follows the direction of the FED steps but not by the same magnitude leading by mid-2001 to a positive gap in the interest rate levels between the euro zone and the US (in reversal of the development at the start of EMU). The sample period thus contains two periods with different interest rate differentials.

Interestingly enough these two periods of different interest differentials also broadly cover two different periods on the foreign exchange markets in the sense that until 2001 the euro declined from a temporary peak reached

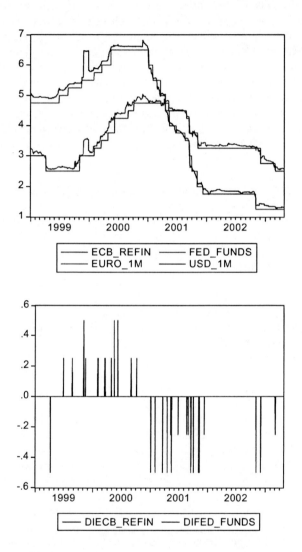

*Figure 7.1 Central bank rates and one-month interest rates in the euro zone and the US (1 January 1999 to 25 April 2003)*

when EMU started, but this was then followed by a period of dollar weakness. The period of dollar strength was associated with higher US interest rates and the period of dollar weakness was associated with lower US interest rates. This is what one would expect in general. But, as usual, it is difficult to disentangle cause and effect. Did changes in (policy) interest rates drive the exchange rate, or did exogenous shocks to the foreign exchange market affect the business cycle on both sides of the Atlantic and hence caused changes in interest rates? We do not want to be drawn in a discussion of this general issue and note just that if exchange rates movement were the exogenous factor one would expect a negative relationship between euro area and US interest rates: a weaker dollar should, ceteris paribus, make it more likely that the Federal Reserve will raise rates, whereas the ECB should become more inclined to cut rates. We did not observe any negative correlation of this kind in the data (whether on a contemporaneous or lagged basis).

We complement the description of these stylized facts by a more institutional view of the monetary policy decision–making process. In Table 7.1 we display a chronology of FED and ECB interest rates movements since 1999 by only referring to meeting dates where at least one of the central banks changed its rate. We assign a change of the interest rate to the day when it is agreed upon since we assume that it is priced into expectations from this day on. Note that the FED has always led the turning points in the interest rate cycle both in June 1999 and in January 2001. In order to address the relationship between interest rate movements among the two central banks we first need to consider how often they take interest rate decisions. Then we comment upon such decisions.

The ECB used to discuss monetary policy at each of its fortnightly meetings. Then on 8 November 2001, this was changed and the ECB decided to discuss monetary policy only once every four weeks (Perez-Quiros and Sicilia 2002, p. 8). This brought the ECB's rhythm closer to that of the FED, which meets every six weeks. If it were not for the possibility of inter-meeting moves the one–month rate should thus open a window of two weeks after a FED meeting during which no change should be expected. But the FED has made three inter-meetings' cuts while the ECB made only one in the aftermath of the terrorist attacks in the US. Indeed this constituted an extraordinary situation resulting in the only co-ordinated inter-meeting when the three central banks, ECB, FED and the Bank of England, cut by 50bp within three days.[3]

There are two further instances (in January 2001, the first easing of the cycle and in November 2001) when the FED made inter-meetings' cuts not triggered by extraordinary events. The ECB does not seem to have this 'urgency' to react to economic information. However, the FED and the ECB

Asymmetries in Transatlantic Monetary Policy Relationship?

have moved within a week on four occasions (apart from the inter-meeting cuts in September 2001) in February 2000, in May 2001 and finally in

*Table 7.1*  *Chronology of central bank rate changes by the Eurosystem and the FED*[*]

| Date | Level | | Change | |
|---|---|---|---|---|
| | FED | ECB | FED | ECB |
| 1 Jan 1999 | – | 3.00 | – | 0 |
| 8 Apr 1999 | – | 2.50 | – | -50 |
| 30 Jun 1999 | 5.00 | – | 25 | – |
| 24 Aug 1999 | 5.25 | – | 25 | – |
| 4 Nov 1999 | – | 3.00 | – | 50 |
| 16 Nov 1999 | 5.50 | – | 25 | – |
| 2 Feb 2000 | 5.75 | – | 25 | – |
| 3 Feb 2000 | – | 3.25 | – | 25 |
| 16 Mar 2000 | – | 3.50 | – | 25 |
| 21 Mar 2000 | 6.00 | – | 25 | – |
| 27 Apr 2000 | | 3.75 | – | 25 |
| 16 May 2000 | 6.50 | – | 50 | – |
| 8 Jun 2000 | – | 4.25 | – | 50 |
| 31 Aug 2000 | – | 4.50 | – | 25 |
| 5 Oct 2000 | – | 4.75 | – | 25 |
| 3 Jan 2001 | 6.00 | – | -50 | – |
| 31 Jan 2001 | 5.50 | – | -50 | – |
| 20 Mar 2001 | 5.00 | – | -50 | – |
| 18 Apr 2001 | 4.50 | – | -50 | – |
| 10 May 2001 | – | 4.50 | – | -25 |
| 14 May 2001 | 4.00 | – | -50 | – |
| 27 Jun 2001 | 3.75 | – | -25 | – |
| 21 Aug 2001 | 3.50 | – | -25 | – |
| 30 Aug 2001 | – | 4.25 | – | -25 |
| 17 Sep 2001 | 3.00 | 3.75 | -50 | -50 |
| 2 Oct 2001 | 2.50 | – | -50 | – |
| 6 Nov 2001 | 2.00 | – | -50 | – |
| 8 Nov 2001 | – | 3.25 | – | -50 |
| 11 Dec 2001 | 1.75 | – | -25 | – |
| 6 Nov 2002 | 1.25 | – | -50 | – |
| 5 Dec 2002 | – | 2.75 | – | -50 |
| 6 Mar 2003 | – | 2.50 | – | -25 |

*Note:*  [*]For the US, the FED funds rate (http://www.federalreserve.gov/fomc/fundsrate.htm2), and for the euro zone the ECB refi rate (http://www.ecb.int/index.html) is tabulated.

November 2001. Hence, we could tentatively conclude that the FED leads the ECB.[4] Note, however, that the FED could be leading the ECB due to pure cyclical considerations (international transmission of the cycle). It is a well-known fact that the business cycle in the US has led Euroland's in the period under consideration by about 1–2 quarters and thus it makes perfect sense that the FED is the first one to change direction on interest rates movements.[5] A statement of an influential member of the ECB Board, Issing, on BBC News one day after the FED's quarter-point cut of interest rates on 27 June 2001, is illuminating in this respect. Asked whether the ECB would follow the FED's lead, he said: 'The FED did what was necessary for the US and we will do what is necessary for Europe'[6]. This statement would suggest that any leader–follower relationship would be purely accidental. It has to be seen, however, in the context of the 'objective functions' or mandates of the two institutions. It is widely perceived that the Federal Reserve pays relatively more attention to growth than the ECB. This is another piece of perceived wisdom that is hard to document since estimates of standard Taylor rule functions fit both the US and the euro area data and the estimates do not yield significant differences in the relative weights attached to inflation and the output gap. We do not want to take a stance on this issue, but it is clear that if the hypothesis that the ECB pays more attention to inflation were true one would expect the ECB to be more cautious in following the FED during an easing cycle.

But the key question we want to address is rather whether, even without any news on the evolution of the euro area economy, a FED decision to cut rates increases the probability of a cut by the ECB (see for instance the Reuters poll mentioned in the introduction). With our high–frequency data (daily and weekly) we can differentiate between time lags caused by different positions along the economic cycle from those which are related to other issues (e.g. the alleged inability of the ECB to react quickly to financial market developments because of the need to reach a consensus in the Governing Council).

If the leader–follower relationship were purely a function of the business cycle lag one would expect that the ECB would follow the FED with a corresponding lag, i.e. 3-6 months later. If the ECB were just slower to react to financial market shocks one would expect it to be able reach a new consensus in its Governing Council about one or two meetings after the FED (where there is only one decision–maker who counts: Chairman Greenspan), implying a lag of about 1–2 months. Finally, in the crude perception of financial markets that the ECB just does not know what to do and just follows immediately the FED, one would expect a lag of less than a month in terms of policy rates, which should translate in a (partial) immediate reaction in the one–month rates used by us.

The procedure used in this chapter to ascertain the existence of a leader-follower relationship essentially is a Granger causality (GC) test procedure. These tests can show whether past values of a certain variable (e.g. US interest rates) influence another variable (e.g. euro interest rates) after one has taken into account the patterns that might link the second variable (euro rates) to its own past. If this is not the case, we speak of Granger non-causality (Greene, 2003). However, Granger causality measures precedence and information content but does not by itself indicate causality in the more common use of the term.

A battery of statistical tests is run covering the entire sample period (1989 to 2003) to test the leader–follower hypothesis also for the Bundesbank and the FED as well as only the euro period. The latter period is even split further into sub-samples to test for robustness of our results.[7] Overall, this gave the result that US interest rates do not influence euro interest rates in the sense of a one-way causation. The US interest rate of the previous time periods did not have a statistically significant one-way influence on the current euro interest rate when all other factors were taken into account. This suggests that the visual impression of a US leadership over the entire period might be misleading for most of the periods analysed by us.

## 3  EMPIRICAL ANALYSIS

This section outlines our statistical approach in more detail. As explained in the first chapter, the administratively set central bank interest rates as well as the one–month money market rates of the US and the euro area were used as both rates are widely watched indicators of the monetary policy stance. In order to cope with the relatively short sample available for the EMU period we also include up to nine years before the start of EMU in our analysis, implicitly testing the validity of the leader–follower hypothesis for the ECB's predecessor, the German Bundesbank, as well. We clearly separate between the Deutsche Mark era and the euro era in our empirical analysis. Our prior was that the results should not be very different between these two sub-periods, the reason being that the goal in monetary policy was almost the same for the Bundesbank than it is for the ECB. However, as will become clear below our prior was not at all confirmed.

The data for the central bank rates, the targeted federal funds rate (funds rate) and the ECB interest rate for main refinancing operations (refi rate), comprise the sample 1999 to 2003, and are taken from the homepages of the ECB and the Federal Reserve. The data for the weekly and daily realizations of the one–month LIBOR euro and dollar interest rates are taken from Datastream Primark. Our pre-EMU rates are synthetic euro rates. We have used the following samples: for central bank rates: 1 January 1999 to 25 April 2003, for weekly realizations of one–month rates: from 6 January, 1989, to 25 April 2003, for daily realizations of one–month rates: 8 May 1989 to 8 May 2003.[8]

### 3.1 Preliminaries

The first step in the empirical work concerned the choice of the statistical procedure. The simplest available procedure was chosen to ascertain the existence of a leader–follower relationship, i.e., the so-called Granger causality tests (and related approaches). In order to make sure that our results do not depend on the particular test period chosen, we ran a battery of statistical tests for a number of periods, e.g. covering the entire euro period (1999 until 2003) and different periods from the end of 1989 onwards. What are the appropriate interest rates in our context? Optimally, we should investigate the instrument of the central bank for monetary policy. Both the ECB and the FED operate in the money market, but at slightly different maturities. They cannot influence longer–term interest rates directly (Borio, 2001), their direct influence is limited to the overnight money market rate in the case of the US and the rate for fortnightly operations in the case of the ECB.[9] The monthly rates we use are, of course, influenced by the expectations about the future path of the shorter rates controlled by the central banks.[10]

A priori, if one uses market interest rate data, it becomes inherently difficult to distinguish policy–makers' intentions from demand disturbances in financial markets (Bergin and Jordá, 2004). However, Figure 7.1 has clearly shown that central bank rates and market rates move closely together. Moreover, using market rates has the advantage that one captures, even if imperfectly, probabilities of future moves of the central bank rates. If one uses only the latter one has only the realizations, not the expectations, which determine market rates which are in turn the rates that influence the economy.

For these reasons we decided to define the interest rate variables as follows:

1.  daily realizations of Central bank rates (targeted FED funds rate and ECB refi rate),
2.  weekly realizations of one–month money market rates, and
3.  daily realizations of one–month money market rates.

Ad (1): The Federal Reserve announces an objective for the federal funds rate, the federal funds target. Hence, it makes sense to use the latter variable as the operating target in our estimations. Hamilton and Jordá (2000) argue that the target data for the federal funds rate accurately reflect the monetary policy stance since they reflect policy considerations instead of demand innovations. ECB decisions concern the setting of the main refinancing operations. So the operating target is the refi rate. With an eye on their impact on the markets, we feel legitimized to include changes in the central bank rates starting with the day of the meeting they were decided upon, i.e. in some cases earlier than their date of de-facto effectiveness.[11]

Ad (2): We preferred one–month rates to three–month rates (as used in Belke and Gros, 2002b and Gros et al., 2002) because it is rather difficult to measure reaction lags of less than three months based on three–month rates. With daily rates we have the maximum of information, but most news on a daily basis come presumably from financial markets. We used LIBOR rates because they are highly comparable since they refer to the same market and to the same time zone, etc.

Ad (3): Here we also used LIBOR rates, but weekly realizations to eliminate (at the price of a smaller sample) some of the noise that might come from short–term disturbances in money markets. With weekly realizations the average number of observations available to detect a leader–follower pattern would be 1–2 if the ECB had followed the FED tightly.

Before the regressions were run, however, an important empirical caveat had to be taken into account. Since the level series seem to contain a unit root[12] and Granger causality tests tend to give misleading results if the variables considered contain unit roots, it was first tested whether the interest rates were actually stationary during the time period considered. The results of the unit root tests are available on request and suggest that the series have to be differenced once (to get the change in interest rates between two periods) in order to make them stationary.

## 3.2  Granger Causality?

The next step was to use Granger causality (GC) analysis to establish whether there is a leader–follower relationship between the changes in the relevant Euro and US interest rates. We conduct separate GC analyses for all of the relevant variables.

First, we used central bank rates. In order to test for the existence of some policy link between the FED decisions on the one hand and the ECB on the other, we perform Granger causality tests among the two intervention rates. This means that we are dealing with daily observations of series that move with discrete jumps (the refi rate for the ECB and the fund rate for the FED). This is somewhat of an extreme exercise because this sort of test is designed for smooth variables instead of variables that jump from one value to another. Note, however, that targets are typically modified in discrete increments rather than continuously. Hence, the very nature of what we want to capture is discrete and represents a structural break in the series. Moreover, the changes in targets are spaced irregularly in time (Hamilton and Jordá, 2000). We could argue that by using this data set we are forcing the series to maximize its co-movements. If we do not find empirical evidence with this data set, it is doubtful that we would find it either with a more 'conventional' data set. The smoother the series (take for instance the monthly three–month LIBOR money market rates we used in Belke and Gros, 2002b and Gros et al., 2002) the more difficult to capture any reaction to abrupt rates changes and the more contaminated this series would be with irrelevant information (Garcia-Cervero, 2002).

Second, we compromised on one–month market rates with an eye on Figure 7.1 which clearly demonstrates that the time pattern of the latter is not too different from that of the central bank rates. Hence, we conducted Granger causality tests for weekly realizations of one–month money market rates and daily realizations of one–month money market rates.

The main results of the Granger causality tests are tabulated in Figures 7.2 to 7.4 and Tables 7.2 and 7.3. We have used the same samples like in our unit root tests to run GC tests. However, we decided to use different numbers of lags. Note that the daily data refer to weekdays and thus a month is about 21 observations rather than 30. In order to limit the loss of degrees of freedom (and limit the analysis to a time span that does not exceed the reaction lag of even the slowest central bank), we do not test for more than five months of history (about 110 working days), and, for simplicity, report results only at the standard 5 percent significance level.

One should also be well aware that the results often depend greatly on the lag structure. For central bank rates we used lags from 1 to 110, for weekly realizations of the one–month rates we applied 1, 2, 3, 4, 9 and 13 ('since interest rate decisions are often met closely to each other a lower lag is more probable') and for daily realizations of these rates 1, 5 (one week), 10, 21, 42 (two months). This procedure enabled us to take into account that the periodicity of the lag is not a priori fixed by theory. For robustness reasons and with an eye on our hypothesis of a possible break in the relation around the start of EMU (and the turn of the year 2000–01), different sample periods were used in a fashion coherent with our unit root tests. By investigating (a) the whole sample of available data from the end of the eighties on until 'today', (b) the limited sample from the end of the eighties on until the end of 1998 and (c) the sample consisting of the EMU period, we clearly separate between the Deutsche Mark era and the euro era in our empirical analysis. Our prior is that the results should not be so much affected – the reason being that the goal in monetary policy was almost the same for the Deutsche Bundesbank than it is for the ECB. However, the behaviour of the

Bundesbank might have also been influenced by the anticipation of EMU. We will discuss this issue later on by asking whether the ECB systematically follows the US Federal Reserve to a larger or smaller extent than the Bundesbank.

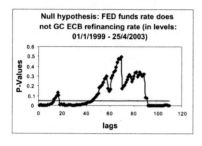 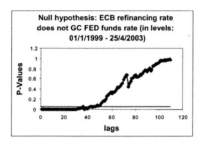

*a) For central bank rates (daily realisations, in levels)*

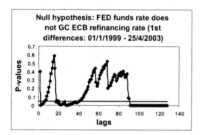 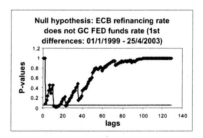

*b) For central bank rates (daily realizations, in differences)*

*Figure 7.2   Results of Granger causality tests (P-values dependent on lag length)*

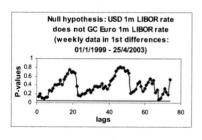 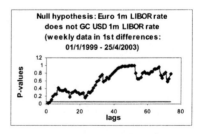

*Figure 7.3   P-values for Granger causality tests of weekly realizations of the one-month LIBOR rates*

The whole range of GC results for levels and first differences of the central bank rates and first differences of the market rates is summarized below. In some cases, we plot the sequence of probability values dependent on the lag structure jointly with the 5 percent significance level as illustrative examples. We regard the hypothesis that the ECB followed the FED as a one-way causality which is corroborated exactly if the p-values are below 5 percent for the GC test with the null hypothesis 'The US rate does not GC the euro rate', but at the same time the p-values are above 5 percent for the GC test with the null hypothesis 'The euro rate does not GC the US rate'.

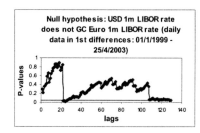 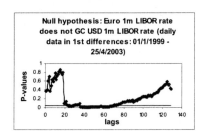

*Figure 7.4    P-values for Granger causality tests of daily realizations of the one-month LIBOR rates*

*Table 7.2    Results of Granger causality tests by sample period and lag length (first differences of weekly realizations of the one-month LIBOR rates)[*]*

| Lag length in weeks | Full sample* | | Pre-EMU* | | EMU* | |
|---|---|---|---|---|---|---|
| | US does not GC EU | EU does not GC US | US does not GC EU | EU does not GC US | US does not GC EU | EU does not GC US |
| 1 | – | – | – | – | – | 0.011 |
| 2 | – | – | – | – | – | 0.045 |
| 3 | – | – | – | – | – | – |
| 4 | – | – | – | – | – | – |
| 9 | – | 0.008 | – | 0.000 | – | – |
| 13 | – | 0.022 | – | 0.002 | – | – |

*Note:*    *Full sample: 06/01/89–25/4/2003, pre-EMU period: 06/01/89–25/12/1998, EMU period: 01/1/1999–25/4/2003.

Ad (1): Results for central bank rates: In a first step, we summarize the results of the GC analysis for the levels of the central bank rates. There is strong and consistent evidence that the FED GC (Granger causes) the ECB, when we limit the analysis to lags up to around 40 days. The relationship holds at virtually all relevant lags within this sample (left graph of Figure 7.2a). Interestingly there is also evidence that at the same time the ECB Granger causes the FED (right graph of Figure 7.2a); but this unwinds as soon as we extend the study to more than 40 working days lags (possibly due to the few breaks). When we extend the number of lags to lags of at least around 90 working days (about 4.5 months) we find again evidence that the FED GC the ECB; this time the relation again holds for all relevant lags. At the same time the hypothesis that the FED does not follow the ECB cannot be rejected at the usual significance level of 5 percent. Hence, we find evidence that the ECB follows the FED in a one-way direction. However, this holds only with long lags. We interpret this as evidence in favour of relevance of cyclical considerations instead of policy interaction. However, given the special time series behaviour of the official central bank rates we do not put a lot of weight on these results.

*Table 7.3*   *Results of Granger causality tests by sample period and lag length (first differences of daily realizations of the one–month LIBOR rates)**

| Lag length in working days | Full sample* | | Pre-EMU* | | EMU* | |
|---|---|---|---|---|---|---|
| | US does not GC EU | EU does not GC US | US does not GC EU | EU does not GC US | US does not GC EU | EU does not GC US |
| 1 | – | 0.021 | – | 0.015 | – | – |
| 5 | – | 0.004 | – | 0.008 | – | – |
| 10 | 0.008 | 0.001 | 0.005 | 0.001 | – | – |
| 21 | 0.001 | 0.000 | 0.002 | 0.001 | – | – |
| 42 | 0.000 | 0.000 | 0.000 | 0.000 | – | 0.004 |

*Note:*   *Full sample: 08/05/89–08/05/2003, pre-EMU period: 08/05/89–31/12/1998, EMU period: 01/1/1999–08/05/2003.

As a second step and as a complementary check, we performed an additional exercise to see whether the main results still hold, this time with the first differences of the central bank interest rates rather than interest rates' levels. Note that now we test whether daily changes in the fund rate GC daily changes in the ECB refinancing rate. The risk is that, due to the high proportion of zeros (since rates do not often change on a daily basis) results get distorted, especially if we include a few lags. In order to minimize this risk we include as many lags as needed so as to guarantee at least one observation different from zero in the history of each variable. Here, we need about 20 working days of history in order to find evidence that the FED GC the ECB, which holds from 20 to 40 and from 90 to more than 120 daily lags and disappears in between. We cannot find any GC running between the FED and the ECB for short lags (10 to 15 day lags), but for these lags there is evidence that the FED GC the ECB. For extremely short lags, the FED seems to impact the ECB in a one-way direction. Hence, it is seems to be possible to find some causality, but we again would warn against putting too much emphasis on these results.

Ad (2): Results for weekly realizations of the one–month rates: In Table 7.2, a surprising pattern emerges. At the usual 0.05 significance level there is no case in which we have to reject the null hypothesis that the US does not influence the euro area. But we also find that in 6 out of the 18 cases considered we have to reject the hypothesis that the euro area interest rates do not influence US rates. This is the case for short lags (1–2 weeks) during the EMU period and for longer lags (9 or 13 weeks) for both the full sample and the pre-EMU period.

Ad (3): Results for daily realizations of the one–month rates: The evidence in Table 7.3 is less one–sided against the hypothesis that the ECB follows the FED. In six cases we find evidence that the FED Granger causes the ECB. However, in all of these cases it is also found at the same time that the US rate is simultaneously determined by the euro interest rate. Hence this cannot be interpreted as evidence for a leader–follower relationship either.[13] As for the weekly data, however, we find several (in this case five) cases in which one has to reject decisively the hypothesis that the ECB does not influence the FED (or more precisely that euro area (pre-EMU: DM or synthetic euro) interest rates do not influence dollar rates).

Do the results deliver an answer to the question whether the Euro area systematically followed the US Federal Reserve? When we look at Tables 7.3 and 7.4 we would be tempted to turn the question around: has the FED systematically followed Euro area developments? And has the euro area influence on the FED been stronger or weaker before EMU? While great caution must be exercised in interpreting these results with fixed lag lengths it is clear that they do not give any support to the null hypothesis that the ECB follows the FED in an asymmetric way (nor seems the Bundesbank have done this during the pre-EMU period). If we limit our analysis to the euro period, the hypothesis of the FED being a follower dominates clearly that of the US being the leader and the euro zone being the follower.

We treat these results with some caution because we are – at least with respect to the correct treatment of the central bank interest rate series – on the 'frontier' of standard time series analysis. We are not surprised that we find a strong structural break between the pre- and post-EMU period. While the ECB has taken over most of the trappings of the Bundesbank (emphasis on price stability, use of monetary indicator, etc.) its behaviour should be different because it is responsible for a much larger and somewhat less open economy (Belke and Gros, 2002a). Moreover, our pre-EMU rates are synthetic euro rates. Hence they contain over 40 percent DEM rates (plus satellites like NL and AUS), but also LIT and FF rates, which at times diverged from DEM rates. While it is generally assumed that the DEM dominated the other currencies, there has been some discussion to what extent the Deutsche Bundesbank did really dominate the EMS. For instance, Fratianni and von Hagen (1990) found that Germany had a limited leadership role among European countries before the start of EMU. Hence it is not surprising that we find a clear–cut structural break between the pre-EMU and the EMU period in terms of the relationship between short-term interest rates.

### 3.3   Testing for Cointegration and for Weak Exogeneity of the US Interest Rate

In this section, we address two questions within the Johansen framework of a cointegrating VAR analysis (Johansen, 1991, 1995). Is there a stochastic co-movement between the US and the euro interest rate? And: If there is a co-movement, is it driven by the US interest rate? Hence, we check for cointegration between the US and the euro interest rates and for weak exogeneity of the US interest rate in the cointegrating VAR before we move to further conclusions. In the preceding chapter, we argued that due to the non-stationary character of the time series, we had to conduct our GC analysis in first differences for the one-month LIBOR rates. This clearly need not be the case if the US and the euro zone time series are cointegrated. In this case, we can additionally use level information in order to identify the nature of the relationship of the two series in the data-generating process.

The results of the cointegration tests between the US and the euro zone interest rates are displayed in Tables 7.4 and 7.5. Due to their administrative nature we refrain from a cointegration analysis of the time series for central bank rate time series. Hence, we only analyse the weekly and daily realizations of the one–month LIBOR rates. If we could reject the null hypothesis of no cointegration vector on the 5 percent level based both on the Johansen 'Maximum eigenvalue' and the 'Trace test', we denote this – if not indicated otherwise – with a 'yes' in column 2 of Tables 7.4 and 7.5.[14] In addition, we test for weak exogeneity of the US interest rate by using an LR test of binding restrictions within the Johansen cointegration test framework (Greene, 2003, pp. 192–193). Conditional on the existence of only one

*Global Divergence in Trade, Money and Policy*

cointegrating relation, the LR test does not reject our imposed binding restriction of weak exogeneity if the realization of the p-value of the LR test statistics is above conventional values. The relevant p-value is tabulated in Tables 7.4 and 7.5, column 4.

*Table 7.4*     *Tests for cointegration and for weak exogeneity for weekly realizations of the one–month LIBOR rates)*

| Lag length in weeks | Full sample[a] | | Pre-EMU[a] | | EMU[a] | |
|---|---|---|---|---|---|---|
| | Cointe-gration IUS IEU (yes or no)[b] | Weak exogeneity of IUS (yes or no)[c] | Cointe-gration IUS IEU (yes or no)[b] | Weak exogeneity of IUS (yes or no)[c] | Cointe-gration IUS IEU (yes or no)[b] | Weak exogeneity of IUS (yes or no)[c] |
| 1 | No | Yes (0.81) | No | No (0.01) | No[d] | No (0.01) |
| 2 | No | Yes (0.97) | No | No (0.01) | No[d] | No (0.00) |
| 3 | No | Yes (0.78) | No | No (0.02) | No[d] | No (0.00) |
| 4 | No | Yes (0.83) | No | No (0.03) | No[d] | No (0.00) |
| 9 | No | Yes (0.56) | Yes | No (0.01) | Yes | No (0.00) |
| 13 | No | Yes (0.25) | Yes | No (0.01) | Yes | No (0.00) |

*Notes:*  [a]Full sample: 08/05/89–08/05/2003, pre-EMU period: 08/05/89–31/12/1998, and EMU period: 01/1/1999–08/05/2003
[b]at 5% level, trace and max-eigenvalue test.
[c]Probability of LR statistic in parenthesis.
[d]none of the series with a unit root, stationary VAR in levels.

According to Hendry (1993), the hypothesis of weak exogeneity cannot be rejected for these regressors if they can be characterized as a pure random walk independent of the stationary cointegration/error-correction term EC(-1). Hence, we restrict the coefficient of EC(-1) to be zero in the ECM representation of the US interest rate and test for the significance of this restriction. Weak exogeneity is already well-known as a necessary condition for an asymptotically efficient estimation of an ECM. An empirical test of this additional exogeneity premise becomes necessary since the ECM we have in mind if the ECB (Bundesbank) really followed the FED represents a restricted model in the sense that it is regarded as an 'autonomous' relation, i.e. it is restricted to one single dependent variable, namely the change in the Euro interest rate. If the hypothesis of weak exogeneity cannot be rejected, the estimation of a fully defined dynamically interdependent system of equations can be avoided. At the same time, estimation can be conducted with more degrees of freedom. Weak exogeneity guarantees that the parameters of the ECM can be estimated without loss of information on the basis of the so-called conditional distribution (Banerjee et al., 1993, p. 18; Fischer and Peytrignet, 1991, p. 483). This ECM is often called a conditional model, since a one-way causation from the regressors like for instance the US interest rate to the endogenous variable euro zone interest rate is assumed. While a test of weak exogeneity represents by itself a necessary step towards the estimation of an ECM, it is of even more use in our context. If the US interest rate could be characterized as weakly exogenous the direction of the causation would be identified as running from the US to the euro zone. Let us now display the results of the cointegration and the weak exogeneity tests (Tables 7.4 and 7.5).

*Table 7.5   Tests for cointegration and for weak exogeneity (for daily realizations of the one-month LIBOR rates)*

| Lag length in working days | Full sample[a] | | Pre-EMU[a] | | EMU[a] | |
|---|---|---|---|---|---|---|
| | Cointegration IUS IEU (yes or no)[b] | Weak exogeneity of IUS (yes or no)[c] | Cointegration IUS IEU (yes or no)[b] | Weak exogeneity of IUS (yes or no)[c] | Cointegration IUS IEU (yes or no)[b] | Weak exogeneity of IUS (yes or no)[c] |
| 1 | Yes | Yes (0.14) | Yes[d] | No (0.00) | No[e] | No (0.00) |
| 5 | Yes | Yes (0.37) | Yes[d] | No (0.01) | No | No (0.01) |
| 10 | Yes | Yes (0.66) | Yes | No (0.01) | No | No (0.01) |
| 21 | Yes[d] | Yes (0.42) | Yes[d] | No (0.04) | No[e] | No (0.00) |
| 42 | Yes[d] | Yes (0.53) | Yes | Yes (0.58) | Yes | No (0.00) |

*Notes:*   [a]Full sample: 08/05/89–08/05/2003, pre-EMU period: 08/05/89–31/12/1998, and EMU period: 01/1/1999–08/05/2003
[b]at 5% level, trace and max-eigenvalue test.
[c]Probability of LR statistic in parenthesis.
[d]for both 5 and 1 percent
[e]none of the series with a unit root, stationary VAR in levels.

For weekly data there are only a few indications of cointegration between the euro and the US interest rates, if we include the Bundesbank years. Only in case of long lags (9 and 13 weeks) both series appear to be cointegrated. If we limit our analysis to the euro period, we often have to conclude that none of the series has a unit root, and a stationary VAR may be specified in terms of the levels of all of the interest rate series. Again, only in case of 9-week and 13-week lags there is evidence of cointegration. For the EMU period, there is no evidence of weak exogeneity of the US interest rate at all. Even in the case of long lags (9 and 13 weeks) with clear evidence of cointegration, the euro and the US interest rates seemed to have moved together without any signs of the US rate being the driving force behind this co-movement. Both for the total period and for the DM period, there is no evidence for cointegration and, hence, no need for us to consider cases of weak exogeneity for these samples.

In case of daily data and the long sample from 1989 to 2003, the evidence for cointegration becomes stronger, the larger the number of lags is (again evidence in favour of 'cyclicality' and against 'policy coordination'). In addition, the US interest rate cannot be rejected to be weakly exogenous. Hence, one might conclude that in this case the hypothesis 'The ECB follows the FED' is corroborated empirically. However, one should be careful with this interpretation since this test does not take into account the structural break induced by the introduction of the euro. For daily data and the other two samples under investigation, there is no evidence of weak exogeneity of the US interest rate. In some cases the cointegration tests indicate that none of the series has a unit root and a stationary VAR may be specified in terms of the levels of both the euro and the US interest rate, although the individual unit root tests conveyed the impression that some of the series are integrated of order one.[15]

## 4   DOES THE RELATIONSHIP CHANGE OVER TIME?

Our main finding so far has been that for the EMU period one does not find an asymmetric and one–way influence of the FED on the ECB. However, just as there was a clear structural break around the start of EMU there might have been another break within the EMU period. Our main candidate for a structural break is September (to be more precise 11 September) 2001, because this started a period of unprecedented political and financial market instability. Our second candidate is in the run-up to the first one, namely the turn-of-year 2000/01 with the uncertainty about an unravelling of the financial equilibrium in the US economy. As explained in the introduction we consider that this (combined) increase in uncertainty should lead to an asymmetry in monetary policy because the increase in uncertainty increases the 'option value of waiting' for policy makers much more in the Euro area, whose economic system is much less flexible than that of the US.

### 4.1   The Role of 11 September 2001: Evidence Based on GC Tests

In order to test this kind of reasoning, we expend some efforts to search for breaks in the relationship between US and euro interest rates around 11 September 2003 via the Granger causality test procedure. For this purpose, we again split up the EMU sample in two sub-periods. This time, the first sub-sample ranges from 1999 until 11 September 2001 and the second comprises the dates from 12 September 2001 until 'today'. We conducted the tests for Granger causality for the same three variables than before: the central bank rates (levels and differences), the weekly (only differences) and

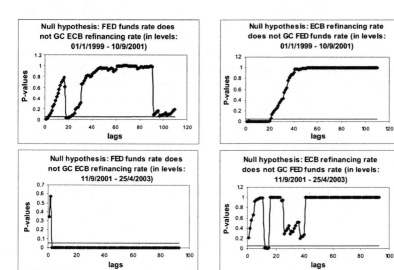

*a) For levels*

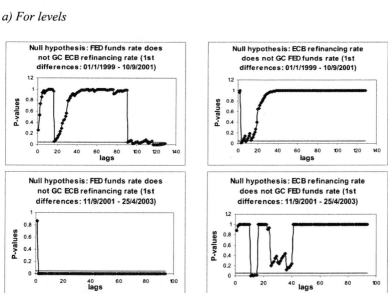

*b) For first differences*

*Figure 7.5    P-values for Granger causality tests of central bank rates (sample split at 11 September 2001)*

*Global Divergence in Trade, Money and Policy*

the daily realizations (only differences) of the one–month money market rate. The results are displayed graphically in Figures 7.5 to 7.7. Like before, we plot the sequence of probability values dependent on the lag structure jointly with the 5 percent significance level. We again feel legitimized to accept the hypothesis of the ECB following the FED as a one-way causality exactly if the p-values are below 5 percent for the null hypothesis 'the US rate does not GC the euro rate', but at the same time the p-values are above 5 percent for the null hypothesis 'the euro rate does not GC the US rate'. In other words, we expect the FED to GC the ECB, but at the same time the ECB not to GC the FED. This time we focus on the difference in results across the sub-samples before and after 11 September.

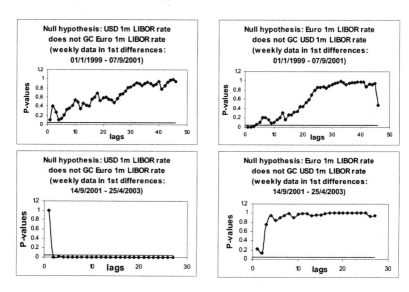

*Figure 7.6    P-values for Granger causality tests of weekly realizations of the one-month LIBOR rates for first differences (sample split at 11 September 2001)*

The results of our sample-split tests are striking. While there is no evidence that the ECB followed the FED before the 11 September, it seems as if the ECB has done so afterwards. After 11 September, the FED Granger causes the ECB, but at the same time the ECB does not Granger cause the FED. Hence, changes in the euro interest rate appear to follow changes in the US rate by one-way causation. A leader–follower pattern according to the option value of waiting emerges. Moreover, the difference between the levels of the interest rates still remains high (see Figure 7.1). Hence, the option

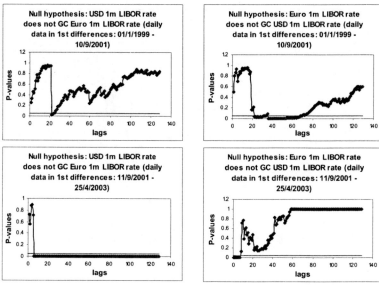

*Figure 7.7    P-values for Granger causality tests of daily realizations of the one–month LIBOR rates for first differences (sample split at 11 September 2001)*

value of waiting with interest decisions also manifests itself in this level difference. All in all, our findings are consistent with the pattern that 11 September 2001, raised the uncertainty for monetary policy making in addition to the generally observed rising uncertainty near turning points of the cycle.[16]

In the introduction, we indicated that we need an uncertainty threshold to trigger on the option argument. Testing for the existence of causality while controlling for the degree of uncertainty might constitute an interesting exercise. Equally, evidence of an 'asymmetric leader–follower' relationship seems to emerge in a period of extraordinary uncertainty. After that, is it business as usual? We briefly check this hypothesis indirectly, and track two market indicators of uncertainty in the stock markets, one for the US (VIX) and one for the euro area (VDAX). VIX is the North American S&P Volatility Index (see Figure 7.8). The VDAX is an index which measures the variation of German stock futures (three months ahead). The source is Datastream Primark.

This figure suggests that EMU coincided with a major increase in uncertainty. Volatility is on average much lower during most of the 1990s.

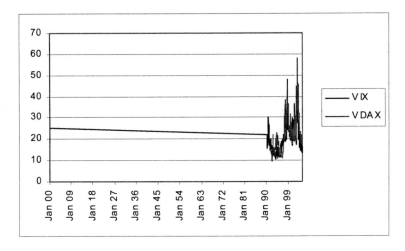

*Figure 7.8    Stock market volatility in the US and in the Euro Area (VIX and VDAX)*

*Source:* Datastream Primark.

Around 1998 one observes a major increase in volatility (probably connected with the series of emerging market crises, rather than EMU). Volatility not only increases, it also becomes more volatile, with a particularly strong increase in the last period used by us, which goes from the end of 2001 until early 2003. This makes our results appear plausible. Moreover, during this period uncertainty is consistently higher for the euro area than for the US which strengthens our main argument that the option value of waiting should be higher for the ECB than for the US since labor and goods market rigidities are higher in the euro area than in the US.

### 4.2    Breaks Around the Turn-of-year 2000/01? Evidence Based on GC Tests

One might still argue that interest rates in Europe tended to be influenced by what had happened on the other side of the Atlantic but that this had changed during 2001. In  that year the  FED cut interest rates at an unprecedented speed (and by an unprecedented magnitude) because it feared an unravelling of the financial equilibrium in the US. The ECB took a more relaxed stance on this point as the euro area economy did not show any of the (potential) disequilibria of the US economy (current account, consumer financial position, overinvestment). For the ECB interest rate setting, this might have induced uncertainty and an option value of waiting. Hence, one might be tempted to conclude that over the whole sample the relationship between the US and the euro interest rate was contemporaneous, while a leader–follower relationship with the FED as the leader becomes significant if only two sub-samples of the EMU period (namely until December 2000) are considered. In order to test whether this kind of reasoning is correct, we take some effort to search for breaks in the relationship between US and euro interest rates around the turn–of–year 2000/01.

For this purpose, we again split up the EMU sample in two sub-periods. This time, the first sub-sample ranges from 1999 until the end-of-year 2000 and the second comprises the dates from 2001 until 'today'. We conducted the tests for Granger causality for the same three variables than before: the central bank rates (levels and differences), the weekly (only differences) and the daily realizations (only differences) of the one–month rate. A representative selection of the results is displayed graphically in Figures 7.9 and 7.10.

Like before, we plot the sequence of probability values dependent on the lag structure jointly with the 5 percent significance level. We again regard the

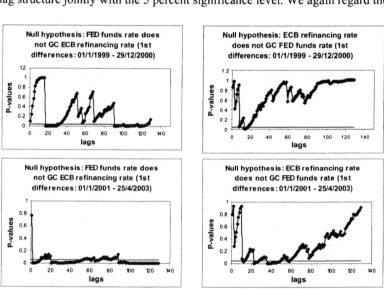

*Figure 7.9    P-values for Granger causality tests of central bank rates (sample split at turn-of-year 2000/01)*

hypothesis of the ECB following the FED as a one-way causality as corroborated if the p-values are below 5 percent for the null hypothesis 'the US rate does not GC the euro rate', but at the same time the p-values are above 5 percent for the null hypothesis 'the euro rate does not GC the US rate'. However, this time we focus on the difference in results across the sub-samples before and after the turn-of-year 2000/01. We only display the results for the first differences of the central bank rates and of the weekly realizations of the one–month LIBOR rates (Figures 7.9 and 7.10).[17]

With respect to the results for weekly data the main impression is that before the suspected break there is a two-way causation between the US interest rate and the euro interest rate for short lags (from 4 to 10 weeks). After this potential break, this mutual impact of US and euro interest rates can be established only for longer lags (from 23 weeks on). Moreover, for very short lags there is even evidence for the ECB leading the FED. However, for the central bank rates, the evidence for the leader–follower hypothesis after the break is much stronger. All in all and although evidence appears to a certain extent weaker, already the turn-of-year 2000/01 (combined with September 2001) represents the starting point for higher general uncertainty which is strong enough to induce for the ECB an option value of waiting with interest rate decisions.[18]

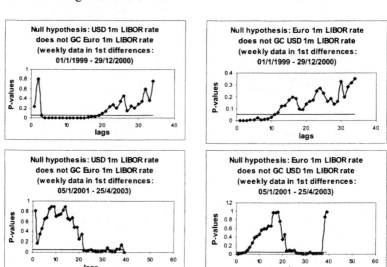

*Figure 7.10    P-values for Granger causality tests of weekly realizations of one–month LIBOR rates for first differences (sample split at turn-of-year 2000/01)*

## 5 CONCLUSIONS

So does the ECB follow the FED?[19] Our answer would be: no, except for the period after the turn-of-year 2000/01 and, more significantly, September 2001. To be more precise, we find that the relationship between the interest rate decisions of the FED and the ECB changes over time. Most of the time it is symmetric. Only after September 2001 do we find a preponderance of the evidence hinting at a significant influence of the US on the euro area, but little in the other direction. However, a note of caution applies here. Since the merger of European national central banks almost certainly resulted in a change of the parameters of the central bank reaction function, the length of the time period which has elapsed since the start of EMU respectively since 11 September is only beginning to be sufficient for our empirical tests. Hence, one should find even more investigations of this highly relevant topic in the future.

What could account for this finding? One hypothesis mentioned in the introduction is that the cyclical position of Euroland lags that of the US, implying that the leader–follower relationship might be spurious. However, the US business cycle has led the euro area one for quite some time now, but we find that the FED leads the ECB only during the most recent period. The emergence of an asymmetric leader–follower relationship renders less likely the popular explanation that the ECB is just slow because it is a new institution that has to find its way in unfamiliar territory. If this had been the case, one would have expected to find evidence for the hypothesis that the FED leads the ECB mainly during the early EMU period, not more recently.

It is always difficult to determine the deeper reasons for correlations over time. But the fact that the asymmetric leader–follower relationship appears only after a major shock which increases global uncertainty suggests to us that the deeper reason why the ECB appears to follow the FED is simply that the euro area economy is less flexible. This makes it optimal also for the ECB to take into account the 'option value of waiting' and react later to shocks. This implies that even if both economies are hit mainly by common shocks (Peiró, 2002) one would find econometrically that the FED seems to be leading the ECB. From this perspective, common shocks imply that the US interest cycle leads the EU if the US is more flexible and also contracts more quickly in response to negative shocks. In contrast to Begg et al. (2002), we do not argue that such rigidities may require monetary policy to play a bigger role. Instead, waiting with interest rate changes becomes valuable if there is a large degree of uncertainty.

We see three directions for further research in this area. First, due to particular pitfalls of applying Granger causality tests to the issue of policy co–ordination autoregressive conditional hazard specifications could be used which allows one to produce dynamic forecasts of the probability of a change in the interest rate target (Hamilton and Jordá, 2000; Bergin and Jordá, 2004). Methods of survival analysis can be applied to test whether a change in the targeted fund rate puts the ECB under pressure to change its refi rates in the same direction, supposing an increasing 'risk'; in other words a rising hazard rate. The duration between a decision of the FED and a possible reaction of the ECB will be defined as 'survival time' (time on risk). This variable will further be assumed to depend not only on time but also on the reaction function of the ECB that mainly contains the preference for low inflation.

Second, as indicated by our cointegration results one could use VARs in levels or single-equation error-correction models: In cases where our tests in Table 7.5 indicate cointegration and weak exogeneity. Tests of weak exogeneity of the US interest rate should be conducted in order to test the hypothesis, that this single vector has to be implemented only in the ECM formulated for the European interest rate. Only if weak exogeneity cannot be rejected and the coefficient estimate of the lagged change in the US interest rate reveals a positive sign, the ECM can in a strict sense be interpreted as a function expressing that the ECB (Bundesbank) has followed the FED.

Third, one could test for the hypothesis that the FED seems to influence the ECB but not vice versa, based on a joint estimation of Taylor-type reaction functions of the two central banks. The hypothesis could be tested by incorporating the decision variable of one central bank into the other central bank's reaction function (Ulrich, 2003).[20] However, the shortage of the observation period so far has largely prevented estimates of reliable Taylor functions for the ECB. Before any reliable results will emerge, significant problems of calibrating parameters versus estimating pre-EMU aggregate data will have to be solved in a satisfying way. Moreover, the specification of the reaction functions is still open to debate. Theoretically, a related question would be to ask how the FED would have reacted if it were responsible for the euro area economy after 11 September (see, e.g., Begg et al. 2002, Wyplosz 2001). Would the FED also have been governed by the option value of waiting and thus lowered interest rates less than it did for the US? This leads one to another transatlantic difference the ECB and the FED have somewhat different mandates (narrow mandate to maintain price stability in the medium run versus broad mandate to promote stable prices and maximum employment).

Starting in late 2003, global financial markets have entered a much calmer period. During this period the leader–follower relationship observed in the immediate aftermath of September 2001 seems to have disappeared as the Federal Reserve has started to increase systematically interest rates in small steps whereas the ECB has not changed its rates for over two years. However, it is too early to proclaim the definite 'independence' of the ECB from the

FED since too little time has passed and a data from a low volatility period makes it always difficult to refute any starting hypothesis.

## NOTES

[1] See Belke and Gros (2002b). For a more formalized treatment of monetary policy effectiveness under uncertainty based on the real option approach see Belke and Goecke (2003).

[2] Wyplosz (2001, p. 1) reports clear anecdotic evidence of the demand by the markets, the media and even by Finance Ministers to cut rates during this period.

[3] The ECB has been criticized for making reactive, rather than proactive, monetary policy decisions in the wake of 11 September. Perhaps, the ECB and other central banks would have waited longer before assessing the outcome of the terrorist strikes, and formulating and timing policy responses without the lead of the FED. However, the decision by the ECB to follow the FED's lead represents a shift to a more pre-emptive policy stance. In cutting interest rates without a clear indication of the likely economic impact of events in the US and the impact on oil prices, the ECB took a risk that cheaper money in Euroland may induce greater price pressures over the medium term that could threaten its 2 percent inflation target. However, according to our option value argument (Gros and Belke, 2003), the ECB was correct in its assessment of the risks to EU growth, and the decision to cut its interest rate has contributed to enhancing the ECB's credibility as a global monetary authority.

[4] In the spring of 1999, the ECB somewhat belatedly reacted to fears of deflation triggered by the LTCM crisis as another exceptional event in our sample.

[5] Begg et al. (2002, p. 42) and Breuss (2002, p. 13) see a time lag between FED and ECB interest rate decisions. They attribute the reason for the FED's moving first to the US cycle leading the euro zone's.

[6] See BBC News (2001).

[7] We used first differences, i.e. changes in interest rates, when the level series seemed to contain a unit root.

[8] Daily data refer to working days only. Weekends and holidays were eliminated.

[9] The ECB also provides some funds at longer maturities (three months).

[10] See Ulrich (2003, p. 7) and Wyplosz (2001). Perez-Quiros and Sicilia (2002) argue that policy announcements made in Council meetings should not trigger any reaction of asset prices in case of full predictability, since market participants have already correctly anticipated these policy decisions on the day when the central bank rate is changed. However, in a world of uncertainty, collective decisions on monetary policy and lack of transparency, effective communication and active guidance to the markets, predictability and the anticipation of the exact timing of interest rate changes might not be fully attainable. This justifies the use of the refi and the targeted funds rate in our case.

[11] For instance, the Governing Council of the ECB decided to lower the minimum bid rate on the main refinancing operations by 0.25 percentage points to 2.50 percent, starting from the operation to be settled on 12 March 2003. In this case, we assigned the change already to 6 March 2003.

[12] The level series does not fluctuate around a constant mean and its variance is not constant and finite.

[13] Overall, our new results confirm those contained in the studies by Belke and Gros (2002b) and Gros et al. (2000) which were based on an investigation of monthly realizations of the three-month LIBOR interest rates and a smaller sample: In no case does one have to reject the null hypothesis that the US interest rate does not 'Granger cause' the euro interest rate and at the same time not reject the null hypothesis that the euro interest rate does not Granger cause the US rate.

[14]  In our cointegration tests we allow for a deterministic trend in the data, i.e. an intercept (and no trend) in the cointegrating equation and in the test VAR. Additional tests assuming that the levels of the interest rates do not have deterministic trends (as is often supposed for interest rates) showed that the results do not change much. However, since the trend is important as a sample property and the relevant interest rates revealed a certain trend within the chosen sample (see Figure 7.1) we do not display these results here.

[15]  An alternative interpretation would be that this apparent contradiction to the results of our unit root tests may be the result of low power of the cointegration tests conducted which is perhaps due to a too small sample size or a specification error. If the latter is the case, this would be evidence for a more complicated relationship between euro and US interest rates than implied by a simple follower-leadership hypothesis tested in this chapter.

[16]  For a general discussion of interest rate decisions in an uncertain environment see Begg et al. (2002).

[17]  The tests for the remaining variables display a similar pattern and are available on request.

[18]  Begg et al. (2002) report in their MECB 4 update that since September 2001, the economic environment has become dramatically more uncertain. In this respect, they refer to, e.g. the sharp drop in stock markets, the large swings in HICP inflation largely unconnected with food or energy prices.

[19]  The ECB has, understandably, not taken any position on this issue. But a recent ECB Working Document (Ehrmann and Fratzscher, 2002) analyses one part of this issue, namely the extent to which the US influences the euro area. The conclusions are interesting: 'There are in particular some US macroeconomic announcements to which European markets react significantly, especially in times of increased uncertainty, like the initial period of EMU or the 2001 recession' and, 'throughout a learning process, the importance given to US news has declined'. As will become clearer below our own results are consistent with the first quote, but go in the opposite direction of the second quote.

[20]  In the light of the results of this chapter, the significance of the funds rate in the ECB's reaction function according to Ulrich (2003) can be characterized as a spurious correlation. Monetary policy is empirically rejected to be a game of 'follow my leader', but of setting the right policy under uncertainty in the light of domestic inflation and growth prospects.

## REFERENCES

Banerjee, Anindya, Juan J. Dolado, John W. Galbraith and David Hendry (1993), *Co-integration, Error Correction, and the Econometric Analysis of Non-stationary Data*, Oxford: Oxford University Press.

BBC News (2001), 'Europe Defies Calls for Rate Cut, BBC News Business', Web: http://news.bbc.co.uk/1/hi/business/1412137.stm, access 2 May 2003.

Begg, David, Fabio Canova, Paul de Grauwe, Antonio Fatás and Philip R. Lane (2002) *Surviving the Slowdown – Monitoring the European Central Bank*, Washington, DC: Brookings Institution.

Belke, Ansgar, and Matthias Goecke (2003), 'Monetary Policy (In-) Effectiveness Under Uncertainty – Some Normative Implications for European Monetary Policy', *University of Hohenheim Department of Economics Discussion Paper*, No. 223/2004.

Belke, Ansgar and Daniel Gros (2002a), 'Designing EU–US Monetary Relations: The Impact of Exchange Rate Variability on Labor Markets on Both Sides of the Atlantic', *World Economy*, **25**, 789–813.

Belke, Ansgar and Daniel Gros (2002b), 'Does the ECB Follow the FED?', *University of Hohenheim Department of Economics Discussion Paper*, No. 211/2002.

Belke, Ansgar, Wim Koesters, Martin Leschke and Thorsten Polleit (2002), 'International Coordination of Monetary Policies – Challenges, Concepts and Consequences, *ECB–Observer – Analyses of the Monetary Policy of the European System of Central Banks*, **4**.

Bergin, Paul R. and Oscar Jordá (2004), 'Measuring Monetary Policy Interdependence', *Journal of International Money and Finance*, **23** (5), 761–83.

Breuss, Fritz (2002), 'Is ECB's Monetary Policy Optimal Already?', *Paper Presented at the International Conference on Policy Modelling*, July 4–6, Brussels.

Ehrmann, Michael and Fratzscher, Marcel (2002), 'Interdependence Between the Euro Area and the US: What Role for EMU?', *ECB Working Paper*, No. 200.

Fischer, Andreas M. and Michael Peytrignet (1991), 'The Lucas Critique in the Light of Swiss Monetary Policy', *Oxford Bulletin of Economics and Statistics*, **53**, 481–93.

Fratianni, Michele und Jurgen von Hagen (1990), 'German Dominance in the EMS: Evidence from Interest Rates', *Journal of International Money and Finance*, **9** (4), 358–75.

Garcia–Cervero, Susana (2002), 'Is the FED Really Leading the Way?', *Deutsche Bank Europe Weekly*, 22 November, 8–10.

Greene, William H. (2003), *Econometric Analysis*, New Jersey: Pearson Education.

Gros, Daniel and Ansgar Belke (2003): 'If the ECB Cuts Rates It Should Do So Boldly', *Financial Times International*, Comment & Analysis, 2 March, 13.

Gros, Daniel, Klaus Durrer, Jan Jimeno, Carlo Monticelli, Roberto Perotti und Francesco Daveri (2002), 'Fiscal and Monetary Policy for a Low–speed Europe', *4th Annual Report of the CEPS Macroeconomic Policy Group*, Brussels: CEPR Studies.

Hamilton, James D. and Oscar Jordá (2000), 'A Model for the Federal Funds Rate Target', *NBER Working Paper*, No. 7847.

Hendry, David F. (1993), 'The Roles of Economic Theory and Econometrics in Time Series Economics', *Paper presented at the 1993 Meeting of the European Econometric Society*, Oxford, mimeo.

Johansen, Soren (1991), 'Estimation and Hypothesis Testing of Cointegration Vectors in Gaussian Vectorautoregressive Models', *Econometrica*, **59**, 1551–1580.

Johansen, Soren (1995), *Likelihood-based Inference in Cointegrated Vector Autoregressive Models*, Oxford: Oxford University Press.

Peiró, Amado (2002), 'Macroeconomic Synchronization between G3 Countries', *German Economic Review*, **3** (2), 137–53.

Perez-Quiros, Gabriel and Jorge Sicilia (2002), 'Is the European Central Bank (and the United States Federal Reserve) Predictable?', *ECB Working Paper*, No. 192.

Schroeder, Michael et al. (2002), 'Neue Übertragungsmechanismen in einer globalisierten Weltwirtschaft – Deutschland und Europa im internationalen Verbund', *Gutachten für das Bundesministerium für Wirtschaft und Technologie*, Centre for European Economic Research (ZEW), Mannheim, documented in Frankfurter Allgemeine Zeitung, 7 June: Der Einfluss der amerikanischen Konjunktur wird schwächer.

Ulrich, Katrin (2003), 'A Comparison Between the FED and the ECB: Taylor Rules', *ZEW Discussion Paper*, No. 03–19.

Wyplosz, Charles (2001), 'The FED and the ECB', *Briefing Note to the Committee for Economic and Monetary Affairs of the European Parliament*, 12 September, Brussels.

# 8. Rethinking Monetary Stabilization in the Presence of an Asset Bubble: Should the Response be Symmetric or Asymmetric?

## Marc Hayford and A.G. Malliaris

## 1 INTRODUCTION

The US stock market boom in the 1990s and the subsequent bust in 2000 generated a debate among central bankers and academics about the appropriate response of monetary policy to the stock market. During the stock market boom of the 1990s, policy makers were uncertain whether the boom reflected a profitable change in fundamentals or a stock market bubble. During this period, Federal Reserve Chairman Alan Greenspan articulated competing hypotheses. He started first in 1996 with his famous notion of 'irrational exuberance' where he floated the idea that maybe investors' excessive optimistic purchases of stock shares was causing stock prices to rise faster than warranted by economic fundamentals, thus generating a stock price bubble.

Later in the decade, Greenspan articulated an alternative hypothesis, that of 'the new economy', where new information technologies had permanently increased labor productivity and more relevant for stocks, profit growth, thus justifying higher stock prices. In the late 1990s, without any hard evidence to prove or disprove these two competing views of the stock market boom, the FED faced a policy dilemma: to take action against the stock boom or to ignore it. In retrospect, the FED chose to essentially ignore or perhaps accommodate the stock market boom while it was growing (Hayford and Malliaris, 2001, 2004, 2005). Both Alan Greenspan (2002) and FED Governor Ben Bernanke (2002) have defended the FED's accommodation of the asset bubble by arguing that there is no low-risk, low-cost incremental monetary tightening that can reliably deflate a bubble. As Greenspan (2002) states: 'If the bursting of an asset bubble creates economic dislocation, then preventing bubbles might seem an attractive goal. But whether incipient bubbles can be detected in real time and whether, once detected, they can be defused without inadvertently precipitating still greater adverse consequences for the economy remain in doubt'.

Once the stock market burst in early 2000 and economic growth slowed in late 2000, the FED began lowering the Federal funds rate on 3 January 2001, in an attempt to reduce the economic impact of declining asset wealth.

In light of the FED's experience of the 1990s what is the appropriate monetary policy response to a stock market bubble? One answer is that monetary policy should respond symmetrically to deviations in stock prices from economic fundamentals (Cecchetti et al., 2000), that is, monetary policy should be tight as the apparent bubble grows and expansionary after the bubble pops. As discussed below this symmetric response describes US monetary policy to the apparent stock market bubble in the 1920s and the initial response to the crash in October 1929. Another answer is that monetary policy should respond asymmetrically to a stock price boom: neutral monetary policy with respect to the stock market during a boom and then expansionary if the stock market boom turns into a bust. This describes the monetary policy the FED followed from the mid–1990s to today and perhaps is the consensus view among central bankers.

In this chapter, after a review of the literature, we discuss what economists know about what causes stock price bubbles and whether monetary policy can prick or pop a bubble. Then we explore the events influencing and the responses to events of monetary policy in the 1920s up to the end of 1930 as a case study of how a central bank responded to an apparent stock market bubble and the consequences of its response. We then discuss what light this historical episode can shed on the question of whether a symmetric or asymmetric monetary policy response to stock bubbles is more appropriate.

## 2 MONETARY POLICY AND STOCK PRICES: A REVIEW OF THE LITERATURE

One influential study on the topic of monetary policy and the stock market is Bernanke and Gertler (1999) who make a number of important points. One is that monetary policy should only be concerned with stock prices if 1) stock prices are sometimes driven by non-fundamentals and 2) changes in the value of stocks have an economically significant impact on the economy. For the first point Bernanke and Gertler cite a number of historical episodes where booms and busts in stock prices are difficult to reconcile in terms of economic fundamentals: for example the US from 1925 to 1930, Japan in the late 1980s, and the US in the late 1990s to name a few.

On the second point they observe that economic booms and busts are correlated with the stock price booms and busts. An asset price boom increases aggregate demand due to increases in consumption via the wealth effect and increases in investment via 'balance sheet effects'. The result of the increase in aggregate demand is higher output growth and higher inflation. After a stock price bust the process reverses itself resulting in a recession or slowing growth and disinflation or even deflation. Bernanke and Gertler simulate a dynamic new Keynesian model with financial accelerator effects that includes stock prices that are determined by economic fundamentals as well as a bubble. The bubble component is modeled to capture feedback effects that occur when investors drive stock prices higher and base their buying decision solely on observing rising prices in the past. In their model the bubble can burst at any point in time with a given exogenous probability.

In Bernanke and Gertler's simulations the stock bubble grows for five periods and then crashes. The simulations show that by aggressively focusing on inflation targeting when setting short–term nominal interest rates in a Taylor rule specification of monetary policy, a central bank can minimize the effects of an expanding asset price bubble and its eventual burst. Further they show that including stock prices in the Taylor rule does not help to minimum fluctuations in output and inflation. In fact, Bernanke and Gertler's simulations show that when the observed asset price boom contains both an unobservable boom in profit fundamentals as well as an unobservable bubble, then a Taylor rule that includes stock prices results in more variable output growth and inflation than a monetary rule that focuses on just inflation and the output gap.

Given the difficulty the FED actually had in the 1990s of performing the signal extraction problem of separating the observed stock prices into an economic fundamental component and a bubble component, the Bernanke and Gertler (1999) results strongly support monetary policy focusing on inflation and output gaps and not directly on the stock market. Focusing on inflation rather than directly on stock prices may help solve the stock price signal extraction problem: a pure stock market bubble by increasing aggregate demand results in higher inflation, while a stock market boom driven by economic fundamentals, such as productivity and profit–enhancing technological innovations, also increases aggregate supply and hence has a smaller or no impact on inflation. Hence Bernanke and Gertler (1999) argue that a central bank dedicated to a policy of flexible inflation targeting should pay little attention to asset price inflation because a proper setting of interest rates to achieve the desired inflation target will stabilize output growth and inflation as well as stock prices.

A second important paper in this literature is Cecchetti et al. (2000). In this paper the authors simulate the Bernanke and Gertler (1999) model and find that including deviations of stock price from economic fundamentals in the Taylor rule, along with inflation and the output gap, reduces the variability of output growth and inflation. Bernanke and Gertler (2001) explain the differences in Cecchetti et al. (2000) results as due to Cecchetti et al. assuming that stock prices are only driven by a bubble and that a bubble pops after five periods with probability one, rather than having a given probability of popping in any given period. As Bernanke and Gertler state, Cecchetti et al. are correct in finding that central banks should include stock prices in their monetary policy rules '...if the central bank 1) knows with certainty that the stock market boom is driven by non-fundamentals and 2) knows exactly when the bubble will burst, both highly unlikely conditions'. Clearly in the 1990s, the FED was uncertain how much of the asset price boom was due to fundamentals and how much was a bubble. And certainly Greenspan and everyone else had no idea when the bubble would burst.

Cecchetti et al. (2003) defend their claim that monetary policy can improve the performance of the economy by reacting to estimates of 'asset price misalignments' directly as well as to inflation and the output gap. They motivate their position by appealing to the intuition provided by Poole (1970) who showed that if financial shocks (shocks to the LM curve) dominated real spending shocks (shocks to the IS curve) then monetary policy minimizes the fluctuations to output by keeping nominal interest rates constant rather than the money supply. In the context of the stock market Cecchetti et al. take the position that if non-fundamental shocks (bubble or financial shocks) dominate fundamental (technology) shocks in the stock market, then including stock prices in a monetary policy rule will yield superior economic performance. However they agree that:

> ...[if] the central bank has no possibility to differentiate between underlying sources of movements in endogenous variable, then it is quite possible that it is best to ignore certain variables when monetary policy is formulated. This would be the case for example when stock prices have increased but we do not know whether this is due to a positive productivity shock in the economy or to a financial bubble. There is no controversy here.

Still Cecchetti et al. (2003) go on to argue that stock prices and asset prices in general contain information that is potentially useful in the setting of monetary policy and should not be ignored and that further central banks can reasonably estimate 'asset price misalignments'.

Blanchard (2000) for the sake of argument assumes that the central bank knows that there is a bubble in the stock market. In other words, suppose that the FED has decided that the price of stocks exceeds economic fundamentals and that the bubble will eventually collapse and stock prices will return to fundamentals. Blanchard asks the question, how should monetary policy respond under these assumptions? While Blanchard (2000) finds the analysis of Bernanke and Gertler powerful, he argues that if investment depends on the bubble, among other economic factors, then with output at its natural level, an increase in investment can occur only by an equivalent decrease in consumption. Thus, while flexible inflation targeting, as suggested by Bernanke and Gertler (1999), dampens the inflationary impact of a bubble, it does not deal with the potential change in the composition of output. A stock price bubble tilts composition of spending more in favor of investment and thus the bubble may cause excessive capital accumulation. When ultimately the bubble bursts this excessive capital accumulation deters firms from investment and postpones economic growth. Thus inflation targeting does not address issues related to the impact of a bubble on the *composition of output* and the long-run impact of the bubble on capital accumulation and growth.

Bordo and Jeanne (2002) make a similar argument to Blanchard (2000). Their idea involves the risk that excessive optimism about a 'new economy' leads to excessive debt accumulation. They state that:

> ...letting a boom go unchecked entails the risk that it will be followed by a bust, accompanied by a collateral induced credit crunch. Restricting monetary policy can be thought of as an insurance against the risk of a credit crunch. On the other hand, this insurance does not come free: restricting monetary policy implies immediate costs in terms of lower output and inflation.

Bordo and Jeanne suggest that restrictive monetary policy in the face of a stock market boom is optimal '...when the risk of a bust is large and monetary authorities can defuse it at a relatively low cost'. They make their case within the context of a two period model which is consistent with standard undergraduate textbook macro and in the spirit of dynamic New Keynesian models. In their framework, borrowers' ability to borrow depends on the value of their collateral relative to debt. If the ratio of collateral over debt is sufficiently low, borrowers are credit constrained and there is a fall in economic activity. In the first period borrowers borrow based on their subjective probability that the second period productivity and profits will be a high, that is, that a 'new economy' will occur. If borrowers think the probability is high they borrow a lot. In the second period actual productivity is learned and asset prices and hence borrowers' collateral adjusts accordingly. If productivity turns out to be low, asset prices and the value of collateral falls. If asset prices fall enough and if first period debt accumulation is sufficiently high a credit crunch occurs and second period output falls.

Bordo and Jeanne argue that if the central bank judges that borrowers are too optimistic in the first period, i.e. borrowers subjective probability of a 'new economy' occurring in the second period is unreasonably high, monetary policy should be restrictive to reduce first period debt accumulation and thus reduce the probability of a credit crunch and economic slump in the second period. This judgment by central bankers involves a trade off between lower output in the first period in exchange for higher output in the second period. Bordo and Jeanne state '[a]...more difficult question is whether (and when) the conditions for [such] a proactive monetary policy are met in the real world. We view this question as very much open and deserving of further empirical research'. Essentially Bordo and Jeanne advocate the need for discretionary monetary policy where policy makers assess the probability of extreme events and take into account the balance sheets of economic agents rather than just looking at inflation forecasts and output gaps in a linear way when implementing monetary policy.

A number of other papers have contributed to the debate on monetary policy and the stock market. Cogley (1999) claims that deliberate attempts to puncture asset price bubbles may destabilize the economy and thus monetary policy may generate instabilities that are similar to the ones arising from the burst of a bubble. He also discusses the example of the US in the 1920s that we discuss below. As Greenspan (2004) states concerning the 1990s, 'the notion that a well-timed incremental tightening could have been calibrated to prevent the late 1990s bubble while preserving economic stability is almost surely an illusion'. Filardo (2001) explores the role of monetary policy in an economy with asset bubbles by developing a small-scale macroeconomic model and running various simulations. He finds that if there is no uncertainty about the role of asset prices in determining output and inflation then monetary policy should respond to asset prices. However, if the monetary authority is sufficiently uncertain about the macroeconomic consequences of stock prices then it is preferable for monetary policy to remain neutral.

Given this review of the literature what can be said about the answer to the question: should monetary policy react to an asset price bubble? The answer is that it depends on whether central bankers can distinguish between stock price booms driven by economic fundamentals and those driven by bubbles. Bernanke and Gertler (1999, 2001) think that in the real world central bankers cannot make this separation and hence just set interest rates to target inflation and the output gap. Their argument is that before the collapse of the stock bubble, it is difficult to argue that monetary policy should proactively respond to the apparent bubble if it is not clear how to identify a bubble and estimate its size.

Cecchetti et al. (2000, 2003) on the other hand think that central bankers may be able to separate bubbles from fundamentals depending on the circumstances. One thing on which there is agreement is that after a stock price bubble bursts, monetary policy should always act in order to stabilize the economy and if a burst bubble threatens the financial system, a central bank should play its traditional role of lender of last resort.

## 3　WHAT CAUSES ASSET PRICE BUBBLES AND CAN MONETARY POLICY POP THEM?

There is debate among economists as to whether or not asset price bubbles even exist and if they exist what causes them. During asset price booms typically there are differences of professional opinion over whether the boom is due to fundamentals or a bubble. Clearly bubbles are easier to identify *ex post* rather than *ex ante*. For example, it is difficult to find economists who would argue today that the stock market increase in Japan in the late 1980s or the Nasdaq increase in the late 1990s reflected only fundamentals. The fact that in both cases these markets declined significantly is *ex post* evidence of the existence of a bubble, yet there was no consensus among economists prior to its dramatic collapse that a bubble was present in these two markets.

Another issue is, assuming stock price bubbles exist, whether it is possible for monetary policy to 'pop', 'prick' or 'deflate' them? The assumption of at least some economists is that monetary policy can deflate a bubble or prevent then from happening. Recently Krugman (2004) writing about Alan Greenspan's monetary policy and the US stock market in the 1990s says '... over the last three years millions of American workers lost their savings or suffered the indignity and financial hardship of prolonged unemployment – pain that could have been avoided if Greenspan had burst the bubble before it grew so big'. As we show below, a review of the theoretical models of bubbles provides little support for the idea that monetary policy can pop a bubble, however it may slow the growth of a bubble. Attempting to slow the growth of a bubble using restrictive monetary policy has the costly side–effect of slowing economic activity. The case of the 1920s discussed below gives an example of the difficulty in popping an apparent stock market bubble and the economic costs of attempting to do so.

In a broad sense, economists have developed two alternative models of stock prices, rational and irrational. The rational model is the efficient market hypothesis where stock prices are the present discounted value of expected future dividends, that is, 'economic fundamentals'. Expectations are assumed to be rational and so are correct up to zero mean serially uncorrelated forecast error. In an efficient market, the stock price, at any point in time, reflect solely economic fundamentals. Further, if the stock market is efficient then central bankers have no comparative advantage over private agents in determining fundamentals and hence the appropriate level of stock prices. In this case as Bernanke and Gertler (1999) point out, there is no need for a central bank to be concerned with stock and instead should just focus on controlling inflation and stabilizing the output gap. So any case to be made for central bankers responding to stock prices assumes that at least episodically the stock market is not efficient, that is, actual stock prices can deviate from a price based solely on fundamentals, which is what is meant by the term 'bubble'.

There are two 'theoretical' approaches to thinking about bubbles: rational bubbles (which are consistent with rational expectations) and bubbles driven by 'euphoria' or 'animal spirits'. The rational bubble literature (see Blanchard and Fischer, 1989 for an introduction) is motivated by the observation that in solving the difference equations which arise from asset price arbitrage conditions, the efficient market solution, or rational expectations equilibrium, is not the only solution. There is also a 'rational bubble' solution in which asset prices can rationally deviate from economic fundamentals, if the deviation, that is the bubble, is expected to grow at rate of return on the riskless asset.

Blanchard and Fischer (1989) provide an example of rational bubble that bursts with a given probability that is similar to bubble specification used by Bernanke and Gertler (1999). The current stock price, $q_t$, is the sum of a fundamental component $q_t^*$, and a bubble $b_t$:

$$q_t = q_t^* + b_t \qquad (8.1)$$

where $q_t^*$ is the expected discounted value of future dividends. The bubble term is modeled as:

$$b_{t+1} = \begin{cases} [\pi(1 + r)]^{-1} b_t + e_{t+1} & \text{with probability } \pi \\ e_{t+1} & \text{with probability } (1 - \pi) \end{cases} \qquad (8.2)$$

where r is the riskless interest rate, $e_{t+1}$ is white noise, $\pi$ is the probability the bubble persists and $1-\pi$ is the probability the bubble bursts. This specification satisfies the property of a rational bubble since $E_{t+1} b_{t+1} = (1 + r)^{-1} b_t$.

Unfortunately, this model of a rational speculative bubble tells us little or basically nothing about what causes asset price bubbles and whether or not monetary policy can burst them. The cause of the bubble in this model is exogenous and so is the bursting of the bubble. Hence in this framework monetary policy cannot burst a bubble (that occurs exogenously). Monetary policy can dampen the growth in stock prices by raising interest rates. This reduces the fundamental stock price value by decreasing the rationally expected present value of dividends both by the direct effect of raising interest rates and by the effect that raising interest rates has on economic activity. Also equation (8.2) implies that higher interest rates can dampen stock prices by making a rational bubble grow more slowly. Figure 8.1 simulates equation (8.2) for 8 quarters with $\pi = 0.8$ and interest rates rising from 2% to 10% in 200 basis point increments, assuming the bubble does not burst. While higher interest rates make the bubble grow more slowly, the simulations in Figure 8.1 imply that large increases in interest rates have a relatively small negative impact on the path of the bubble.

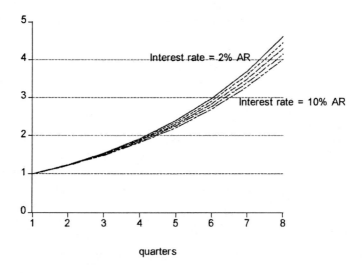

quarters

*Figure 8.1    Simulated bubble from equation (8.2)*

Irrational bubble models, that is, the idea that asset bubbles are driven by 'euphoria' or 'animal spirits', date back at least to Keynes (1936). Shiller (2000, 2001) gives a more recent discussion along these lines of the US stock market boom of the 1990s. He lists a set of conditions that he argues potentially caused the asset price bubbles to occur. Shiller claims that an asset price bubble is essentially a ponzi scheme. People trade based on the past behavior of prices and changes in fundamentals play little or no role in influencing their decision to buy stocks. According to Shiller (2000, 2001), events that precipitate irrational asset price booms in general include a belief that rising prices in the past imply rising prices in the future. This belief passes among investors in a way similar to an epidemic and generates herd behavior on behalf of investors. In addition Shiller (2001) argues that asset price bubbles are usually associated with a belief in a new economic era: 'Major speculative bubbles, as I argue in Irrational Exuberance, are always supported by some superficially-plausible popular theory that justifies them, and that is widely viewed as having sanction from some authoritative figures. These may be called new-era theories'. New-era theories occurred in the 1990s and also in the 1920s as discussed below. Shiller provides no explanation for what ultimately causes stock price crashes other than that the boom is not sustainable. Monetary policy plays little role in Shiller's discussion of stock market bubbles or busts.

Monetary policy may help create an economic environment that helps cause stock market bubbles. First, periods of stock price booms are often associated with periods of low inflation. Low inflation creates an economic environment of stability that encourages investments and growth. To the contrary, periods of very high inflation and in extremes cases, periods of hyperinflation totally discourage investments and growth. Second, low inflation leads to low interest rates, ceteris paribus. Again, low interest rates stimulate both real investment and also consumption. Third, the combination of low inflation and low interest rates contributes to higher rates of investment in new potentially highly profitable technologies. These changes in fundamentals begin to move the equity market higher, since low interest costs and new profitable technology combine to generate above normal profits. Fourth, higher profits are not enough to cause acceleration of equity prices into a bubble. For a broadly defined bubble to materialize, first solid fundamentals are needed for few years to justify the early rises in equity prices, but additional catalysts are to get an asset price bubble going.

The 1920s and 1990s in the US and the 1980s in Japan and the discussion of Shiller (2000) suggest that the invention of a new exciting technology plays the role of such a catalyst. By a new exciting technology we mean widespread advances that affect a significant portion of the whole economy. Radio, telephones, airplanes, chemicals and other factors created the US boom of the 1920s. Automobiles, television sets and electronics propelled Japans' growth in the 1980s and finally, personal computers, software, communications, biotechnology and the internet fueled the last US bubble in the 1990s. This creates and supports the idea that a new economic era has arrived and the rising stock prices support the idea of a new era. The irony for central bankers is that by creating economic stability and low inflation, monetary policy may also be creating an environment in which asset price bubbles can occur.

Finally, Greenspan (2004) offers one additional insight in the formation of bubbles. He argues that the success of the FED to bring down inflation during the 1980s and early 1990s set up powerful expectations that inflation could be controlled over the business cycle and thus economic volatility would remain lower than in the past. In such a low inflation setting, interest rates were expected to remain below their long-run averages. Greenspan concludes: 'Perhaps the greatest irony of the past decade is that the gradually unfolding success against inflation may well have contributed to the stock market bubble of the latter part of the 1990s'.

## 4   THE FED AND THE STOCK MARKET IN THE 1920s

In this section we explore the events influencing and the responses to events of monetary policy in the 1920s up to the end of 1930 as a case study of how a central bank responded to an apparent stock market bubble and the consequences of its response. Then we discuss what light this historical episode can shed on the question of whether a symmetric or asymmetric monetary policy response to stock bubbles is more appropriate.

In the context of the question: should monetary policy respond to a stock market bubble, the 1920s are an interesting case: Cogley (1999) takes the position that the 1920s and 1930s are evidence of the damage that can be done by monetary policy responding to a bubble, while Bordo and Jeanne (2002) argue the 1920s' FED did not do enough to diffuse the bubble.

Figure 8.2 shows the key macroeconomic variables from 1920 to 1930. The quarterly data are from Balke and Gordon (1986) and the monthly data are from the NBER historical macro series database and FRED. The top two graphs of Figure 8.2 show two measures of output: industrial production and real GNP. The shaded areas correspond to NBER dates for four economic contractions in the 1920s: January 1920 to July 1921, May 1923 to July 1924, October 1926 to November 1927 and finally August 1929 to March 1933.

Industrial production (which the FED measured at the time) and real GNP (which was not measured at the time) are highly correlated and match the NBER dates for recessions in 1920–1921, 1923–24, 1926–1927, the peak prior to the Great Depression in the third quarter (August) of 1929. The second column of Table 8.1 gives the summary statistics for the quarterly growth rate of real GNP by economic contraction and expansion from 1920 to 1929. Over the period real GNP grew from 1921:1 to the peak in 1929:3 (August) at an average rate of 4.7%. The level of real GNP increased 160%. Over the same period the year to year growth rate of industrial production averaged 5.7% with the level increasing 197%. Hence the 1920s were a period of impressive economic growth as well as having four recessions. The economic growth was fueled in part by the new technologies of electric appliances and the automobile, the real costs of which were falling over the period. These new technologies provided credence to the idea of a 'new economy era'.

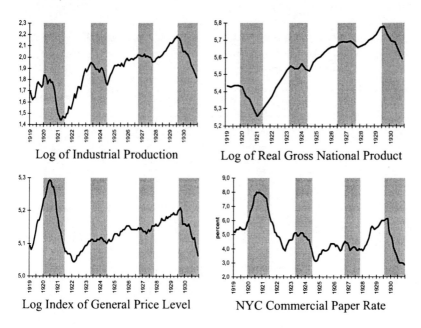

Log of Industrial Production          Log of Real Gross National Product

Log Index of General Price Level          NYC Commercial Paper Rate

*Figure 8.2     Measures of economic activity 1919–1930**

*Note:*    * Shaded areas are NBER dates for contractions. Measures are in logs.
*Sources:* FRED, Balke and Gordon (1986), NBER Historical Data.

The lower left graph in Figure 8.2 shows log of the price level during the period. There is no sustained inflation during this period as there is after World War I but rather the price level fluctuates rather dramatically. Inflation associated with World War I is followed by deflation in the early 1920s. From 1922 on, the price level has an upward trend until the beginning of the Great Depression. The third column of Table 8.1 gives monthly rate of inflation by economic contraction and expansion from 1920 to 1929. From July 1921 to August 1928 median monthly inflation equals zero, while average inflation increases during the period over each phase of the business cycle. The lower right graph in Figure 8.2 shows the behavior of the commercial paper rate. A comparison of the commercial paper rate with the upper left graph in Figure 8.4 shows that the commercial paper rate tracked the discount rate set by the New York Federal Reserve Bank.

Figure 8.3 shows the path of the Dow-Jones Industrial stock price index from 1919 to 1933. The fourth column of Table 8.1 gives the monthly growth rate of the DOW by economic contraction and expansion from 1920 to 1929.

*Table 8.1    Summary statistics by contraction and expansion 1920 to 1929, quarterly percent for real GNP and monthly percent changes for inflation and the Dow*

| | Growth Rate Real GNP | Inflation | Growth Rate of the Dow |
|---|---|---|---|
| **Sample: 1920:01 1921:07 Peak to trough** | | | |
| Mean | -1.522895 | -0.735589 | -2.280305 |
| Median | -1.931731 | -1.227009 | -0.862360 |
| Maximum | 9.018342 | 2.150621 | 3.470917 |
| Minimum | -8.607277 | -3.815177 | -10.290080 |
| Standard deviation | 3.979116 | 1.684201 | 4.573008 |
| **Sample: 1921:07 1923:05 Trough to peak** | | | |
| Mean | 2.111111 | 0.106050 | 1.400545 |
| Median | 2.751525 | 0.000000 | 1.538084 |
| Maximum | 5.872605 | 1.273903 | 5.428741 |
| Minimum | 3.447730 | -1.273903 | -5.152887 |
| Standard deviation | 2.863309 | 0.646621 | 2.964519 |
| **Sample: 1923:05 1924:07 Peak to trough** | | | |
| Mean | -1.232896 | 0.000000 | -0.086755 |
| Median | -1.557592 | 0.000000 | 0.331126 |
| Maximum | 2.291381 | 0.607905 | 6.182181 |
| Minimum | -4.503042 | -0.607905 | -5.152887 |
| Standard deviation | 2.024499 | 0.456769 | 3.525579 |
| **Sample: 1924:07 1926:10 Trough to peak** | | | |
| Mean | 0.901314 | 0.149275 | 1.759483 |
| Median | 1.044333 | 0.000000 | 2.314532 |
| Maximum | 3.910389 | 1.197619 | 6.995231 |
| Minimum | -1.731086 | -0.604231 | -9.357557 |
| Standard deviation | 1.681465 | 0.500232 | 3.794813 |
| **Sample: 1926:10 1927:11 Peak to Trough** | | | |
| Mean | -0.440468 | 0.041408 | 1.172250 |
| Median | -0.394696 | 0.000000 | 1.731706 |
| Maximum | 1.186535 | 1.162804 | 6.041663 |
| Minimum | -2.399399 | -0.589972 | -5.417062 |
| Standard deviation | 1.074161 | 0.583109 | 3.200468 |
| **Sample: 1927:11 1929:08 Trough to Peak** | | | |
| Mean | 0.968071 | 0.230523 | 2.898951 |
| Median | 1.004641 | 0.000000 | 1.887325 |
| Maximum | 2.093274 | 1.136376 | 10.519890 |
| Minimum | -1.026901 | -0.576370 | -2.244133 |
| Standard deviation | 0.869545 | 0.541278 | 3.582199 |

The US stock market boomed from 1925 to 1929. The business press in the 1920s was optimistic about the future growth prospects of the economy and echo the 'new era' language used to describe the stock market boom of the

1990s. In addition, there was an optimistic belief in Federal Reserve System's ability to stabilize the economy (Shiller, 2000). The 1926–1927 recession did not stop the boom and after the economy starting expanding again in November 1927 the boom accelerated. Cogley (1999) argues using the historic average of the price earnings ratio, that '...stock prices were not obviously overvalued at the end of 1927'. Kindleberger (1989) claims the bubble began in March 1928 and beginning in 1928 the FED became concerned about what it perceived to be excessive stock market speculation.

During 1920s the monetary policy of the Federal Reserve System was influenced by both international and domestic events and the FED's responses to these events were filtered through the ideology of the gold standard and the real bills doctrine. Figure 8.4 shows four measures of monetary policy: the discount rate, monetary base, gold reserves (part of the monetary base at the time) and the M2 measure of the money supply.

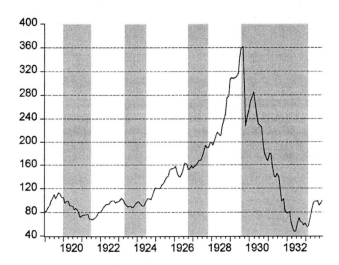

*Figure 8.3    Dow Jones Industrial Stock Price Index (1919–1933)*[*]

*Note:*    [*] Shaded areas are NBER dates for contractions.

While the US had remained on the gold standard during World War I its European trading partners had not. The ideology of the gold standard held that leaving the gold standard to fight a war was just a temporary policy and not a change of 'regime' (Temin, 1989). After the war it was assumed that countries would return to gold. In 1925 the UK chose to return to gold at the pre-war parity rate. At the pre-war parity rate the British pound turned out to be overvalued relative to the franc and the dollar and consequently the UK ran balance of payment deficits with France and the US. Historical accounts of the period suggest the Federal Reserve System helped the UK's return to gold by lowering its discount rate prior to 1925. From the NBER historical data, (see Figure 8.4) the average monthly discount rate at the Federal Reserve Bank of New York has a downward trend from 1920 to the end of 1924. But the downward trend stops in 1925, the year the UK returned to gold, with an increase from 3% to 3.50% by March 1925. From 1926 to February 1928 the discount rate fluctuated between 3.50% and 4%. The historical accounts of monetary policy in this period also focus on the influence of the FED's gold reserves on the setting of the discount rate. For example the loss of gold reserves in 1925 stopped the downward trend of the discount rate. The FED was willing to help the Bank of England so long as it did not lose too much gold.

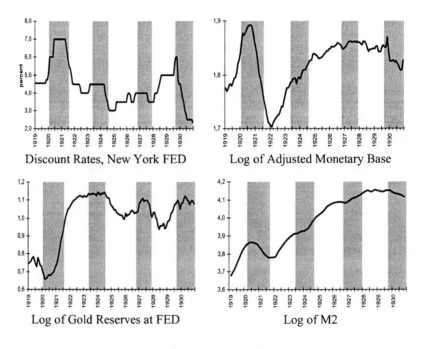

Figure 8.4   *Measures of Monetary Policy, 1919–1930*[*]

*Note:*   [*] Shaded areas are NBER dates for contractions.
*Sources:* FRED, Balke and Gordon (1986), NBER Historical Data.

Consistent with historical accounts, Figure 8.4 clearly shows that monetary policy turns contractionary in 1928: the discount rate increases by over 200 basis points from 1927 to September 1929 and the growth rate of the monetary base and M2 goes from positive to essentially zero during this period. According to Hamilton (1987), '...in terms of magnitudes consciously controlled by the Federal Reserve, it would have been difficult to design a more contractionary policy' than the monetary contraction of 1928. The switch to contractionary policy by the FED is attributed, by economic historians, to two causes (Temin, 1989; Eichengreen, 1996). The first reason for the switch in policy was to stop the decline in gold reserves. This reason is consistent with the gold standard ideology of maintaining sufficient gold reserves to maintain convertibility. The second reason was to stop speculation in the stock market. This reason was in line with the real bills doctrine that held that bank loans should only be made to finance real economic activity and not to finance financial speculation. By 1927 the FED had become concerned of what it thought was excessive bank loans to finance speculation in the stock market that conflicted with the real bills doctrine (Eichengreen, 1996). The New York FED responded in March 1928 by increasing the discount rate in a series of steps peaking in October 1929 at 6%. The FED also discouraged banks from lending to finance speculation. The result can be seen in the measures of monetary policy in Figure 8.4: the growth of the monetary base and M2 essentially go to zero.

What is particularly interesting for the issues of monetary policy and the stock market is that the contractionary monetary policy beginning in 1928 did not arrest the stock market boom. In fact the DOW continued to increase for an additional 19 months, with the DJIA increasing by 77% after the shift to a contractionary monetary policy. In addition, Figure 8.2 shows that the economy boomed along with the stock market in 1928. Industrial production peaked in August 1929 and then the stock market crashed in October 1929. Hence the impact of monetary policy on real economic activity occurred, as always, with a lag. Interestingly in this case, with the slower growth in the economy showing up a couple of months prior to the stock market crash, the economy led the stock market.

The FED responded to the stock market crash by cutting the discount rate to 150 basis points by the end of 1929. If such an expansionary monetary policy had continued there was a good chance that the Great Depression may have just been another recession. Instead a series of monetary and fiscal policy mistakes led to the Great Depression (see for example Temin, 1989).

Bordo and Jeanne (2002) argue that the 1920s and 1930s are an example of a boom–bust cycle in stock prices that was very costly in terms of loss of output. They suggest if monetary policy had '...diffused the stock market boom in 1928 rather than following the policies that it did, the outcome would have been very different'. In contrast Cogley (1999) in reviewing the 1920s argues that '...rather than illustrating the dangers of standing on the sidelines, the events of 1928–1930 actually provide a case study of the risks associated with a deliberate attempt to puncture a speculative bubble'. The economic history literature on the Great Depression suggests that the monetary contraction of 1928 in response to the stock market bubble was the initial cause of the Great Depression (see for example Temin, 1989 and Eichengreen, 1996). As mentioned above, Hamilton (1987) says that in the late 1920s monetary policy was very restrictive. Further in theoretical models of bubbles, which perhaps are not very well developed, it is not clear that monetary policy can burst or pop a bubble. Finally the fact that the stock market continued to expand dramatically after the monetary policy turned contractionary, suggests that monetary policy cannot pop bubbles.

The late 1920s serve as an example of the FED responding to a perceived speculative bubble by enacting a contractionary monetary policy. The contractionary monetary policy beginning in 1928 resulted in a recession that began in August 1929 and perhaps contributed to the crash of October 1929. Stopping the stock market bubble, if monetary policy was indeed at least part of the cause of the crash, involved causing a recession that due to other monetary and fiscal policy mistakes evolved into what is now called the Great Depression. The contractionary monetary policy of 1928–29 turned out to be the initial shock that led to the Great Depression.

## 5   CONCLUSIONS

So how should monetary policy respond to the stock market? Simulations of New Keynesian Macro models (Bernanke and Gertler, 1999, 2001; Cecchetti et al. 2000, 2003) suggest that if central bankers can separate how much of a stock price boom is driven by bubbles and how much is due to economic fundamentals, then monetary policy should respond to a stock market bubble. However, perhaps a majority of economists and central bankers believe that central bankers cannot separate bubbles from fundamentals.

Even if central bankers could identify a bubble, the theoretical literature on bubbles gives no support for monetary policy actually popping bubbles, although in rational bubble models restrictive monetary policy can slow the growth of a bubble. The US experience in the 1920s gives an example of a central bank attempting to pop what was perceived to be a speculative bubble. Monetary policy was highly restrictive from 1928 to September 1929 and is cited by economic historians as the initial cause of the Great Depression. However, monetary policy in the late 1920s was not successful in stopping the stock market boom. Stock prices continued to rise dramatically for over a year and a half after monetary policy turned restrictive. Only after the economy began contracting did the stock market boom turn to a bust in October 1929. Interestingly enough, we have not had a situation of a serious bubble bursting (except the 19 October 1989 one–day decline of the S&P 500 Index by about 20%) with continued strong economic fundamentals. The US crash of 1929 and 2000 and the Japanese crash of 1989 were all followed by deteriorating fundamentals. However, the lessons learned from 1929 in the US and 1989 from Japan have helped the FED reduce the deterioration of the real economy during 2000–2001.

Historical episodes are heavily weighted to cases where a central bank has at best been successful at slowing an asset price boom while at the same time causing a recession. Examples of this include the case of Germany in the 1920s (Temin, 1989) where the central bank slowed the asset price boom and at the same time depressed the economy. Japan in the late 1980s is another example of monetary policy attempting to deflate a financial boom which also at least contributed to Japan's economic slowdown in the early 1990s. The US in the 1920s as discussed above is a third example.

Thus, using monetary policy to deflate an asset bubble without causing an economic slowdown or contraction appears to be at least very hard and maybe impossible. Bernanke (2002) claims that: 'designing the appropriate monetary policy to deflate a bubble is equivalent to using an axe to perform brain surgery'. Perhaps this is why central bankers resort to 'jaw–boning'. For example in each of the three US stock market peaks in the 20th century, Federal Reserve Officials warned that the stock market was overvalued (Shiller, 2000, p. 224). Perhaps the hope of these announcements was to convince investors to stop bidding up stocks without a central bank having to raise interest rates. However it is clear that jaw–boning may not. After Greenspan's announcement of 'irrational exuberance' in 1996, the US stock market continued to expand. Even backing up cheap talk with contractionary monetary policy failed to work in the late 1920s until after the economy started contracting.

Empirical evidence suggests that monetary policy has a strong impact on real economy activity and at best a weak impact on growth of stock market bubbles but not their bursting. A stock market crash can have a weak impact on real economic activity, at least with the appropriate response of monetary policy. For example, the October 1987 crash apparently had little effect on the economy. In fact, based on the 1987 crash experience Temin (1989) argues that the 1929 crash contributed little to the economic downturn of the Great Depression.

Are there any examples where monetary policy was neutral during a stock market bubble where the bubble bursts and then a recession occurs? Perhaps the 2000 recession is such an example. It is hard to imagine that an aggressively contractionary monetary policy in the late 1990s would have prevented a recession in 2000! The recession that did occur was mild as measured by real GDP. The bursting of the US stock market bubble in 2000 resulted in a decline in stock market wealth in the trillions of dollars that along with a collapse in investment spending caused a recession that was mild perhaps due to the timely and aggressive monetary easing of the Federal funds rate from 6.50% to 1% beginning in January 2001.

Hence, the weight of the theoretical literature and the case of the 1920s suggest that monetary policy should not react solely to the stock market but rather should stay focused on maintaining price stability and maximum sustainable economic growth. Using monetary policy to attempt to pop asset price bubbles seems to be a case where the side–effects of the cure are potentially worse than the disease itself. This conclusion supports Greenspan and Bernanke's (2002) claim that there is no low-risk, low-cost incremental monetary tightening that can reliably deflate a bubble. Hence an asymmetric response of monetary policy to the stock market is appropriate: neutral in stock market booms unless they cause inflation, and monetary ease after a stock market bust to dampen the effect on output and if needed to provide liquidity to financial markets as the lender of last resort.

## REFERENCES

Balke, Nathan S. and Gordon, Robert J. (1986), 'Appendix B Historical Data', in Robert J. Gordon (ed.), *The American Business Cycle: Continuity and Change*, Chicago: University of Chicago Press.
Bernanke, Ben (2002), 'Asset-Price "Bubbles" and Monetary Policy', *Remarks before the New York Chapter of the National Association for Business Economics*, New York, October 15.
Bernanke, Ben and Mark Gertler (1999) 'Monetary Policy and Asset Price Volatility', *Federal Reserve Bank of Kansas City Economic Review*, **4**, 17–51.
Bernanke, Ben and Mark Gertler (2001), 'Should Central Banks Respond to Movements in Asset Prices?', *American Economic Review*, **91** (2), 253–257.
Blanchard, Olivier (2000), 'Bubbles, Liquidity Traps, and Monetary Policy: Comments on Jinushi et al. and on Bernanke', in *Japan's Financial Crisis and its Parallels to the US Experience,* Institute for International Economics.
Blanchard, Olivier and Stanley Fischer (1989), *Lectures on Macroeconomics*, Boston, MA: The MIT Press.
Bordo, Michael and Olivier Jeanne (2002), 'Boom – Busts in Asset Prices, Economic Instability and Monetary Policy', *NBER Working Paper*, No. 8966.
Cecchetti, Stephen, Hans Genburg, John Lipshy and Sushil Wadhwani (2000), *Asset Prices and Central Bank Policy – Geneva Reports on the World Economy No. 2*, London: International Center for Monetary and Banking Studies.

Cecchetti, Stephen, Hans Genberg and Sushil Wadhwani (2003), 'Asset Prices in a Flexible Inflation Targeting Framework', in William Hunter, George Kaufman and Michael Pomerleano (eds), *Asset Price Bubbles: The Implications for Monetary, Regulatory and International Policies*, Boston, MA: The MIT Press.

Cogley, Timothy (1999), 'Should the FED Take Deliberate Steps to Deflate Asset Price Bubbles?', *Federal Reserve Bank of San Francisco Economic Review*, 1, 42–52.

Eichengreen, Barry (1996), *Globalizing Capital: A History of the International M System*, Princeton, NJ: Princeton University Press.

Filardo, Andrew J. (2001), 'Should Monetary Policy Respond to Asset Price Bubbles? Some Experimental Results', in G. Kaufman (ed.), *Asset Price Bubbles: Implications for Monetary Policy and Regulatory Policies*, New York: JAI Press, 99–118.

Greenspan, Alan (2002), 'Issues for Monetary Policy', *Remarks Before the Economic Club of New York*, December 19, 2002.

Greenspan, Alan (2004), 'Risk and Uncertainty in Monetary Policy', *Remarks Before the American Economic Association*, San Diego, California, January 3.

Hamilton, James (1987), 'Monetary Factors in the Great Depression', *Journal of Monetary Policy*, **19**, 145–169.

Hayford, Marc and A.G. Malliaris (2001), 'Is the Federal Reserve Stock Market Bubble–Neutral?', in George Kaufman (ed.), *Asset Price Bubbles: Implications for Monetary and Regulatory Policy*, Amsterdam: Elsevier Science, 229–243.

Hayford, Marc and A.G. Malliaris (2004), 'Monetary Policy and the US Stock Market', *Economic Inquiry*, **42** (3), 387–401.

Hayford, Marc and A.G. Malliaris (2005), 'How Did the FED React to the 1990s Stock Market Bubble? Evidence From an Extended Taylor Rule', *European Journal of Operational Research*, **163** (1), 20–29.

Keynes, John M. (1936), *General Theory of Employment, Interest and Money*, New York: Harcourt Brace.

Kindleberger, Charles (1989), *Manias, Panics and Crashes*, New York: John Wiley & Sons.

Krugman, Paul (2004), 'The Maestro Slips Out of Tune', *The New York Times Magazine*, June 6.

Poole, William (1970), 'Optimal Choice of Monetary Policy Instruments in a Simple Stochastic Macro Model', *Quarterly Journal of Economics*, **88**, 197–216.

Shiller, Robert (2000), *Irrational Exuberance*, Princeton, NJ: Princeton University Press.

Shiller, Robert (2001), 'Bubbles, Human Judgment and Expert Opinion', *Cowles Foundation Discussion Paper*, No. 1303.

Temin, Peter (1989), *Lessons from the Great Depression*, Boston, MA: The MIT Press.

PART FIVE


ACCESSION COUNTRIES
AND EMU

# 9. The Internationalization of the Euro: Trends, Challenges and Risks

**George Michalopoulos**

## 1 INTRODUCTION

The creation of internationally used money capable of challenging the dominance of the dollar has always been the hidden agenda behind the adoption of the common European currency. From the very beginning of the conception of the European monetary integration, the European leaders believed that the internationalization of the euro would be able to generate substantial economic and political benefits. Thus, the issue of the international prospects of the euro has been strongly debated since the period leading up to its introduction in 1999. The key question of the debate has been whether the euro can ever become an equally important international currency as the dollar or even take the lead in the international monetary system.

Many researchers, in the eve of the introduction of the euro, predicted that it would soon be able to rival the dollar dominance in the international financial markets (for example, Portes and Ray, 1998). However, the achievements of the euro since its birth in 1999, although significant, have not justified such optimistic predictions. Initially, the weakening of the euro vis-à-vis the dollar, during the 1999–2002 period gave rise to views which shed doubts about the ability of the new currency to rival the dollar. Neaime and Paschakis (2002), for example, argued that the euro would challenge the dominance of the dollar only if the economic strength of the euro zone exceeds that of the USA in the long run. Others claimed that the euro could not threat the dominance of the dollar in the foreseeable future, because a weaker institutional framework compared to the dollar surrounds it. Salvatore (2000), for example, argues that the absence of a federal government in the euro zone puts a limit to financial integration because it prevents the creation of a large unified market for government securities. Bergsten (2002) supports the view that the euro zone dissipates much of the potential of the international position of the euro because of the lack of institutional cohesiveness, which does not allow Euroland to act together and speak with a single voice to the rest of the world. On similar grounds, Cohen (2003, p. 575) supports the view that the euro '…is fated to remain a distant second' to the dollar in the international markets. The main reasons for this, he argues, are the anti-growth bias build into EMU institutions and the ambiguous governance structure in the EU.

This chapter discusses the opportunities and challenges that the internationalization process of the euro currently faces. In the section that follows, the paper evaluates the extent of the international use of the euro. The next three sections deal with the key factors limiting the internationalisation process of the euro, namely the insufficient financial integration, the problems related to monetary policy in the euro area, and the quality of governance within the EU. Finally, there is a discussion of the challenges that the euro faces in relation to the current economic and monetary developments at the global level.

## 2   THE INTERNATIONAL POSITION OF THE EURO: WHAT ACHIEVEMENTS?

Before evaluating the international position of the euro, it is useful to review the key drivers of the international use of a currency. The literature highlights four key factors, which influence the degree of internationalization of a currency in the long run (see for example, Frankel, 1999; Issing, 2003), namely:

1.  the size of the share that the issuing country possesses in global GDP and world trade,
2.  the size and the depth of the issuing country's financial markets,
3.  the perceived quality of the currency and its long–run performance in terms of stability, and
4.  history, since inertia in the use of currencies favour the dominant currency of the past.

Issing (2003) emphasizes the role of the issuing country's institutions in ensuring currency stability and financial market soundness, both of which are necessary for the internationalization of a currency. He notes that '… the country with a wise fiscal authority, a sound legal and judicial system, efficient regulatory authorities (i.e. banking supervision, anti-trust, etc.), and with a monetary authority geared towards price stability is more likely to have its currency used as international money' (Issing, 2003, p. 2).

Although the international position of a currency critically depends on the ability of the issuing country to ensure currency stability in the long run, it is rather immune to the short–run fluctuations of the currency value (within the floating exchange rate system). The large swings of the dollar during the 1970s and 1980s, for example, did not affect the extent of its international use. On the contrary, the outstanding long–run performance of Germany in maintaining monetary stability led to the establishment of the mark as the second most important international currency since the 1970s.

Table 9.1 shows the relative economic size and economic performance of the US and the euro area. The two regions show comparable economic power in the world economy. The euro area GDP is about 75% of the US GDP. However, the contribution of the euro area to the international trade is three times that of the USA. Furthermore, with the possible future enlargement of the euro area to include some of the sizeable economies of the rest of the EU, the economic power that surrounds the euro will be substantially increased. The optimistic predictions on the future of the euro rest on the logic that, since the EU shows comparable economic power with the USA, the euro will enjoy similar degree of internationalization with the dollar eventually.

*Table 9.1    Economic size and performance: the EU versus USA (2003)*

| | USA | Euro Area | EU (25) |
|---|---|---|---|
| **As in 2003** | | | |
| Population (% of world population) | 4.7 | 5.0 | 7.4 |
| Share in world GDP (%) | 21.1 | 15.7 | 22.2 |
| Share in world exports in goods and services (%) | 11.0 | 34.5[*] | 43.8[*] |
| Average annual rate (1994–2003) | | | |
| Growth rate (%) | 3.3 | 1.9 | 2.2 |
| Inflation rate (%) | 2.0 | 2.2 | 2.2 |
| Unemployment rate (%) | 5.2 | 9.6 | 9.5 |

*Note:*    [*] The intra-EU trade is included.

*Source:* IMF, World Economic Outlook (2004), EU Commission (2004); author's calculations.

However, past experience shows that economic size alone may not be sufficient for upgrading the international role of a currency. The Swiss franc, for example, has traditionally enjoyed a significant degree of internationalization despite the relatively small economic size of Switzerland. On the contrary, the economic size of Japan did not yield an analogous international role for its currency. Therefore, it is the combination of the aforementioned factors (i.e. size, trade, financial markets, price stability, history) that underpins the internationalization process of a currency. Furthermore, besides these economic factors, the importance of the international political stance of the issuing country needs to be stressed. History shows that the dominant world currencies (i.e. sterling, dollar) have been backed by strong political power in the international field. For example, the political supremacy of the USA in the international fora by the end of World War II was clearly reflected in the adoption of the Gold Exchange Standard at Bretton Woods which effectively put the dollar at the centre of the world economy.

After discussing the key drivers of the international usage of currencies, an attempt is made to review the achievements of the euro so far. Due to the short period of its existence and due to the availability of limited data on the international use of currencies one cannot draw safe conclusions about the performance of the euro in the long run. Moreover, the period that followed its introduction in 1999 was characterized by increased global economic and financial instability: first, there was the creation of the 'new economy bubble', the increased capital flows towards the USA and the long period of the euro weakness (1999–2002); then it was the burst of the bubble and the developments that followed the 2001 terrorist attack on the USA. One could imagine that increased uncertainty might have worked against the internationalization of the newly introduced currency and in favour of the established currencies.

Table 9.2 summarizes the key indicators of the international use of the euro relative to other competing currencies and relative to the EMS currencies it replaced.

## 2.1    The Euro and the International Trade

Survey data on the use of invoice currencies are quite rare and non-regular. According to Table 9.2, on the eve of the introduction of the euro, the dollar was used as invoice currency in more than the half of the world trade, with the key EMS currencies enjoying a share of 25%. Although recent data on invoicing behaviour in trade globally are not available, the European Central Bank provides some aggregate data on trade invoicing, for a group of countries[1]. The ECB on the basis of such data concludes that the use of the euro in the euro area external trade has increased since its introduction to reach a share of about 50% in 2002 (ECB, 2002, 2003). In line with Grassman's rule, the share of the euro in the euro area exports to the non–euro area countries is larger compared to imports. However, the use of the euro has substantially increased in both the exports and imports of the euro

Table 9.2  *International use of currencies (% share in total)*

| | 1995 | End 1997 or 1998 | | | End 2001 or 2002 | | |
|---|---|---|---|---|---|---|---|
| | International Trade | Official Foreign Exchange Reserves | Global Debt Securities Market | Foreign Exchange Markets[a] | Official Foreign Exchange Reserves (2002)[b] | Global Debt Securities Market | Foreign Exchange Markets[a] |
| Dollar | 52 | 61 | 54 | 44 | 65 | 46 | 45 |
| EMS currencies | 25[c] | 16[c] | 20[c] | 27 | – | – | – |
| Euro | – | – | – | – | 19 | 24 | 19 |
| DM | 13.2 | 13 | 11 | 15 | – | – | – |
| Pound | 5.4 | 4 | 8 | 6 | 2 | na | na |
| Yen | 4.7 | 5 | 8 | 11 | 5 | 18 | 11.3 |

*Notes:*

[a] The share of each currency is divided by two, so that all shares add up to 100%. The currency shares in the forex market add up to 200% of total turnover because two currencies participate in each market transaction.
[b] Data revised by IMF in November 2003 (see ECB, 2003).
[c] The main currencies participating the EMS.

*Sources:* Data from Frankel (2000); ECB (2002, 2003); author's calculations.

area[2]. There is evidence that the trade of the new EU members and the accession countries is also increasingly invoiced in euro. It is worth mentioning that the share of the euro in the Japanese exports (imports) to (from) the EU increased from 44% to 54% (from 17% to 31%), during the 2000–2002 period[3].

These developments indicate that the use of the euro in international trade has increased. However, this increase is mainly because of the heavier use of the euro in trade both within the EU and with neighbouring countries. The dollar actually holds a significant share of the international trade of each country. A factor that works against the euro and in favour of the dollar, in this respect, is the use of the latter for quotation in the international commodity markets. As a consequence the invoicing of energy goods and raw materials is in terms of dollars exclusively. Thus, for example, a significant portion of the euro area trade in energy goods and raw materials is in terms of dollars[4]. This advantage of the dollar will probably continue to be in effect as long as international prices continue to be expressed in that currency.

## 2.2    The Euro and the Financial Markets

The degree of use of the euro in global bond markets has been more than satisfactory. Table 9.2 shows the relative shares of the key currencies in the denomination of the debt securities in the global markets (domestic and international). There is clear evidence that not only has the euro inherited the role of the EMS currencies in these markets, but also it has increased its share; about a quarter of the global stock of debt was denominated in the euro in 2002, compared to a share of 46% for the dollar. Particularly, the share of the euro in the international supply of debt securities was quite close to the dollar share in the same period (38% relative to 44% for the dollar)[5].

However, euro–denominated debt is characterized by a strong regional focus. This feature contrasts with the strong international character of the dollar–denominated debt. In particular:

1.  Non–resident issuers of debt–denominated in euro are concentrated in few industrialized economies (such as the USA or the UK), while only a few emerging economies (mainly those which are geographically close to the EU) make use of the euro for the same purpose.
2.  On the demand side, euro–denominated bonds are mostly held by investors in non–euro area European countries. There is almost zero demand for them from financial institutions in the USA and Canada, while demand from Asian investors is small but growing

3.  Up to two–thirds of the non–euro area financial activity related to euro debt takes place in the City of London.

Unlike the developments in the debt markets, the euro presence in the foreign exchange markets does not show equal dynamism. The dollar is the dominant vehicle currency, while the euro has not achieved a much larger share compared to the DM (see Table 9.2).

Many economists argue that the existence of high transaction costs that characterize trading in euro assets undermine the euro's prospects of becoming an important vehicle currency. Hau, Killeen and Moore (2002) suggest that the euro forex markets exhibited less liquidity and higher transaction costs relative to the DM. Cohen (2003) attributes the existence of high transaction costs in the European financial markets to limited financial integration.

ECB (2003), however, supports the view that for the foreign exchange market, the high transaction costs of the euro/dollar trading compared to the DM/dollar trading is not because of thinner markets but because of the existing quoting convention (i.e. the so called 'pip' or 'granularity' hypothesis).

According to Kenen (2002), efficient information management and cost optimization calls for single currency dominance in relation to vehicle currency function. McKinnon (2002) for similar reasons describes the function of the international money as a 'necessary natural monopoly'. For these reasons the dollar share in the forex market will not be reduced, unless trading costs in the euro fall substantially below those for the dollar.

## 2.3 The Official Use of the Euro

The official use of the euro is quite limited compared to the dollar. The dollar is by far the key currency of denomination of official reserves. In addition, its share in the global foreign exchange reserves has increased since the introduction of the euro. In contrast, the share of the euro in total reserve holdings is smaller compared to the share of the EMS currencies it replaced. This development mainly reflects the elimination of the intra-euro area holdings of predecessor currencies from the measurement of official reserves.

Kenen (2002), Portes and Rey (1988) and McKinnon (2002) argue that the private use of a currency is the key driver for its official use. Monetary authorities prefer to use the currency that enjoys the vehicle function for official intervention. Moreover, when the currency peg option is adopted, authorities tend to use the reference currency for intervention. Consequently, the foreign exchange holdings are mainly denominated in the currency used for intervention. Thus, the dominance of the dollar in the official reserve holdings can be explained by mainly two facts: first, the dollar functions as the key vehicle currency in the global foreign exchange markets, and second, it is widely used as an anchor currency for a large number of countries world wide from Latin America to South East Asia. Asian countries, in particular, give a considerable boost to the official use of the dollar. Japan and other Asian countries account for more than 50% of the global reserve holdings; they also show a strong preference towards holding reserves in dollar-denominated financial assets. For example, evidence from a group of emerging Asian countries that report the composition of their reserves reveals that the average holdings of dollar and euro assets in total reserves are about 60% and 6% respectively[6].

On the contrary, the use of the euro as an anchor currency is limited to countries that are geographically close to the EU or countries with some kind of institutional arrangements with the EU (e.g. EMS members, accession countries, Mediterranean countries, the CFA Franc Zone). As a result, these countries hold the bulk of the official reserves in euro assets. According to the ECB, by 2003, more than a quarter of the countries that follow an exchange rate regime were using the euro as an anchor currency[7]. Thus, the official use of the euro, although regional, cannot be characterized as negligible.

The analysis presented above suggests that the performance of the euro has yielded mixed results. On the one hand, the significant use of the euro in the wider region that surrounds the euro area refutes the pessimistic predictions which suggested that the euro would not survive in international markets. On the other hand, however, it has not provided justification to the optimistic predictions suggesting that, given the economic size of the EU, the euro would soon challenge the dominance of the dollar. Academics and financial analysts have identified certain features that represent important drawbacks in the internationalization process of the euro. Criticism was focused on three features of the functioning of the euro, namely: a) the insufficient integration of the euro area financial markets, b) the particularities of the ECB's monetary policy, and c) the nature of the economic and political governance in the euro area.

## 3   FINANCIAL MARKET INTEGRATION AND THE EURO

Cohen (2003) stressed the negative consequences of limited financial integration in the EU for the internationalization process of the euro. He supported that financial markets in Europe are largely fragmented due to: a) the absence of Europe-wide regulation on many aspects of finance, b) inefficiencies in the regulatory system, c) inconsistent implementation of regulation agreed at the EU level, and d) due to differences in the euro area settlements systems. Financial market fragmentation in the EU keeps transaction costs in asset trading at high levels. Thus, the use of the euro as a vehicle currency is more costly relative to its rival currencies.

Hartmann and Issing (2002) argue that key structural features of the euro area financial system limit the potential role of the euro as a world currency. For example, the euro area financial system is based more on the bank loan finance rather than the security finance, compared to the US financial system. This characteristic restricts the size of the euro area capital markets. Moreover, European stocks are traded on a large number of stock exchanges, while insufficient consolidation in the securities settlements industry hampers cross-border trading. They claim that, due to these reasons, economies of scale in securities trading within the EU are limited and transaction costs are higher compared to the US case.

A report by the Economic and Financial Committee also highlighted the problem of the high costs in cross–border financial transactions within the EU (EU Commission, 2002, p. 4). In 2001, the average charge for a cross–border payment of €100 was €24, a bit higher compared to the 1993 level. It also claimed that the costs per transaction in cross-border securities trades are much larger (perhaps in the order of eight to ten times) than in the national trades[8]. The report attributed these inefficiencies to obstacles to cross-border wholesale market activity, caused by the lack of convergence in the areas of market practices' regulation, supervisory practices, competition policies and taxation.

Salvatore (2000) argued that due to the absence of a federal government in the euro area the government securities markets would never be fully integrated. This is due to the fact that securities issued by different governments have different risk characteristics and thus are not perfect substitutes. It is claimed, for example, that due to the size and the liquidity of the US Treasury bills market, transaction costs are very low. The US T-bills for large holders are, essentially, interest-bearing money since they can be converted into cash at virtually no cost. Thus, many analysts doubt whether the euro area will be able to achieve a comparable T-bills market in the near future.

In short, the evidence suggests that the financial market integration in EU is far from complete. However, financial market integration has to be seen as an ongoing process. The single market project and the introduction of the euro have been the most decisive moves towards financial integration. Especially, the adoption of the single currency is responsible for the creation of a largely integrated money market in the euro area; it also has led to a considerable growth of the bond markets in the EU; and it has created an impetus towards the consolidation of the EU stock exchanges, as the case of the Euronext indicates.

It is now realized that financial integration is essential for economic growth in the EU, and that the introduction of the euro is not sufficient for ensuring full financial market integration. Thus, the expressed strong will of the EU leadership for the immediate adoption of policies capable of removing the obstacles to financial market integration creates much optimism on the issue. The Barcelona Council in 2002 called for the immediate implementation of the proposals of the Lamfalussy report on financial market integration. It expressed its strong commitment to implementing the Financial Services Action Plan (a blueprint for financial integration) for achieving fully integrated capital and financial services markets by 2005. The majority of the measures proposed by the Plan have been finalized already. Such action has greatly raised expectations on the issue of financial integration in the EU.

## 4   MONETARY POLICY, THE ECB AND THE INTERNATIONAL ROLE OF THE EURO

The institutional arrangements within the euro area impose a neutral stance towards the international role of the euro. Thus, there is no explicit consideration about the internationalization process of the euro. However, the performance of the euro area in the monetary sphere is crucial for the future of the euro. As the ECB admits, credibility in the monetary policy making in the euro area plays a key role in the internationalization of the euro.

There has been considerable criticism on both the institutional framework of the euro and the performance of the ECB in monetary policy making. Many authors argue that the institutional structure of the ECB poses certain difficulties to the internationalization of the euro. Cecchetti and O'Sullivan (2003), for example, argue that the real power in the decision making within the ECB lies with the governors of the 12 national central banks (NCBs) who dominate the ECB Governing Council. The fact that a country has one vote on the Governing Council creates a pull towards the median country and a possibility of compromising the target of price stability for the area. In addition, NCBs have an important input in the preparation and compilation of information (monetary statistics, economic forecasts) used by the ECB.

Unlike the ECB, the monetary institutional framework in the USA gives the sense that the Board of Governors of the Federal Reserve and not the regional federal banks is in control. The Board of Governors supervises regional Federal Reserve Banks, while its staff provides the bulk of information relevant to monetary policy making. Therefore, such a structure leaves less ambiguity about the process of monetary policy making compared to the ECB case. It is also argued that the operation framework of the ECB is characterized by less clarity: the fact that in the euro area all NCBs are involved in the open market operations simultaneously makes ECB system of providing liquidity particularly cumbersome. It has been argued that these features of monetary policy making create an environment of high uncertainty for the euro.

Following a similar line of argumentation, Schroeder (2003) suggests that the ECB institutional framework is a necessary but not sufficient condition for achieving the target of monetary stability. National preferences towards inflation play an important role. Since most of the member countries show higher tolerance to inflation compared to Germany, majority voting in the ECB Governing Council suggests that inflation performance in the euro area will be worse than the past inflation performance of Germany. This logic implies that the euro will be less stable in the long run compared to the DM, and thus less favourable as an international currency.

For similar reasons, Begg et al. (1998) and Gros (2003) suggest that the balance of power in the ECB should shift from national governors to the Executive Board of the ECB. If the Executive Board gets the real power in stirring monetary policy, a smaller number of people will be in control, and thus, the flexibility and efficiency of ECB decision making will be improved.

A second line of criticism refers to the policy strategy adopted by the ECB. Many authors related the weakness of the euro during the 1999–2002 period to problems of credibility caused by high uncertainty about the functioning of the ECB and its policies (Neaime and Paschakis, 2002). The criticism mainly focuses on the two-pillar monetary policy strategy followed by the ECB. Although the ECB puts the first pillar (targeting monetary aggregates) on the top of the list, M3 targeting is claimed to be ineffective. The target of M3 growth of 4.5% has not been met since 2001: M3 increased by 7.2% and 8% in 2002 and 2003 respectively. Herr (2002) and Bibow (2001) claimed that, during the period of the weak euro, the ECB formulated predominately an exchange rate oriented policy (in support of the euro) without clearly informing the public. Thus, the ECB strategy cannot be characterised as clear. Arestis and Sawyer (2003) argue that such a lack of clarity in the making of ECB policy has been confusing to financial markets, and this had negative repercussions for the euro.

Some economists argue that the ECB institutional framework exhibits strong anti-growth bias (Cohen, 2003; Arestis and Sawyer, 2003). It is claimed that the institutional arrangements give excessive emphasis to price stability relative to the goal of full employment and growth. Thus, the ECB has been reluctant to respond to recession by lowering interest rates. It is also claimed that the one-size-fits-all monetary policy of the ECB makes dealing with (asymmetric) economic shocks by individual member countries a very difficult exercise. Therefore, the ECB policy in conjunction with the fiscal constraints set by the Stability and Growth Pact (SGP) are regarded as negative factors that seriously undermine the growth potential of the euro area. The negative impact on economic growth would lead to low yields on euro–denominated assets, thus limiting the international use of the European currency. For example, many authors (especially in the financial press) attributed the weakness of the euro during the first years of its existence to the inactive stance of the ECB to the recession of that period. Kenen (2002), after analysing ECB behaviour in the same period, argued that ECB interprets its mandate too strictly, handling the issue of price stability with excessive caution. However, he claims that the ECB cannot be blamed for the weakness of the euro.

The recovery of the euro since mid–2002 indicates that its earlier weakness was the reflection of the temporary real economic conditions prevailing in the euro area and the USA (mainly), rather than due to any institutional flaws in the monetary policy of ECB. In particular, the higher productivity levels in the USA and the shift of the international portfolio investments to US securities are the key explanations for the depreciation of the euro vis-à-vis the dollar[9]. If long-term price stability matters for the internationalization of the euro there is no evidence that the ECB has done badly. The average inflation rate in the euro area in the 1999–2003 period was at 2%, i.e. on the ECB official target, despite the fact that during this period the introduction of the euro has been a source of uncertainty in the area.

Similarly, with respect to the external value of the euro, there is no evidence that the ECB policy has been generating excessive instability. Table 9.3 shows the volatility of the effective exchange rate of the euro in both nominal and real terms relative to that of the dollar and the DM for the periods 1980–1989, 1990–98 and 1999 to date. It can be concluded that there has been a noticeable increase in the volatility of the euro since 1999, relative to that of the synthetic euro in the 1990–98 period. The increase in volatility can be attributed mainly to increased financial instability caused by a series of extraordinary events such as the bursting of the 'new economy' stocks bubble, the September 11 terrorist attack, and the war in Iraq. However, the volatilities of the nominal and the real effective exchange rates of the euro were clearly lower compared to those of the dollar in the recent period. Thus, there is no indication that the new European currency exhibits a disadvantage relative to the dollar in terms of internal (price level) or external (exchange rate) stability.

In addition, experience has helped ECB to improve its communication with the public. The ECB increasingly speaks with a single voice and works towards increasing the transparency of the monetary policy (Eichengreen,

2003). The disproportional emphasis given in the past to the first pillar of its monetary policy strategy (i.e. the M3 target) is gradually reduced. In its latest Annual Report, the ECB clarifies the way in which it integrates information resulting from the analysis of the two pillars, to make judgements on the risks to price stability. It admits that the assessment of the short– to medium–run risks to price stability is based on the 'economic analysis' (i.e. analysis of cost and pricing behaviour, economic activity etc.). It uses, however, 'monetary analysis' (i.e. information contained in monetary aggregates) to identify the longer-term trends underlying price developments. The ECB believes that '...[t]he undisputed relationship between money growth and inflation in the medium to long term provides monetary policy with a firm and reliable nominal anchor beyond the horizons conventionally adopted when constructing inflation forecasts on the basis of standard macroeconomic models'[10].

*Table 9.3     Volatility* of the effective exchange rates for the euro, dollar and the DM, (1980–2004)*

|         | Euro |      | US Dollar |      | DM |      |
|---------|---------|------|---------|------|---------|------|
|         | **Nominal** | **Real** | **Nominal** | **Real** | **Nominal** | **Real** |
| 1980–89 | 1.50 | 1.51 | 2.09 | 2.11 | 0.88 | 1.06 |
| 1990–98 | 1.19 | 1.26 | 1.71 | 1.68 | 0.81 | 1.03 |
| 1999–04 | 1.49 | 1.50 | 1.68 | 1.76 | – | – |

*Note:*     * The volatility index is the standard deviation of the monthly changes of the effective
         exchange rates, defined as the differences of the natural logarithm of the series
         multiplied by 100. The effective exchange rates are according to the IMF definitions.
         Pre-1999 data for the euro refer to the 'synthetic euro'.

*Source*: International Financial Statistics.


# 5   GOVERNANCE OF THE EURO AREA

A strong concern is expressed about the effectiveness of the economic and political governance in the euro area. First, it is widely agreed that there is insufficient coordination of economic policies within the euro area. Second, there are problems related to the political and institutional deficits in the EU. Finally, there is the issue of the lack of external representation of the euro area.

According to the Working Group on the Economic Governance formed for the needs of the European Convention, improved coordination between the economic policies of the member states is necessary. The Working Group also argued that '…in order to ensure economic growth, full employment and social cohesion, …(coordination) should extend to bringing macroeconomic policy within the shared competences of the Union and the Member States'[11].

In particular, fiscal policy coordination, which relies on the rules set by the SGP, is considered as problematic. The problems related to SGP have been extensively discussed in the literature. In a nutshell, it is argued that the SGP is inflexible; it is a one-size-fits-all policy rule that fails to take into account the specific circumstances of each member state. It is also characterized by strong anti-growth bias: its strict application reduces the counter–cyclical ability of the fiscal policy or it could even force policy makers to act in a pro-cyclical manner, thus aggravating economic cycle (Cohen, 2003; Arestis and Sawyer, 2003; Wyplosz, 2001).

The decision of the Ecofin Council in November 2003 to hold the excessive deficit procedure for Germany and France 'in abeyance' and not to apply sanctions shows that the implementation of the SGP is, also, problematic. An effective coordination is necessary to ensure consistency between the monetary and fiscal policy. Monetary policy cannot be independent of fiscal policy developments. Loose fiscal policies might lead to the adoption of tighter ECB policy to keep inflation low. In the long run, they might lead to higher debt to GDP ratios in the euro area, thus increasing the costs related to keeping inflation at low levels.

The EU institutions agree that there is no need to change either the Treaty or the SGP with respect to fiscal policy coordination or to introduce new budgetary objectives and rules.[12] The attempted reform focuses on improving the implementation process. In particular, there is willingness to make the assessment of fiscal policies more flexible by paying attention to cyclical characteristics of the deficits and to country–specific circumstances (e.g. overall debt, growth potential etc.). Whether such reform will be enough it will be shown in the future.

Next to improving the euro area fiscal policies, action has to be taken for enhancing economic policy coordination in other areas, especially in those related to structural reforms. In line with the so–called 'Lisbon Strategy', it is necessary for the euro area to undertake further action in adopting coordinated policies aiming at capital market integration and improving competition in goods and services markets. Particular attention should be paid, to improving the functioning of the labor markets by increasing flexibility, improving labor mobility and making the wage–bargaining process more sound. Improving the structure of the economy is necessary if the euro area is to maintain compatible levels of competitiveness with the USA and Japan.

The issue of policy coordination relates to the institutional deficits of the EU. It is often argued that there is no clear answer to the question of who is in charge of the euro area. In particular, there is no clarity concerning the delegation of authority among national governments and institutions at the EU level. For an effective policy coordination of economic policies a certain degree of 'Europeanization' of policies is required. However, many problems arise because 'Europeanization' contradicts the long-standing principle of subsidiarity in the EU (Boyer, 2000). A dramatic demonstration of such a contradiction took place when in November 2003 the Ecofin Council decided not to apply sanctions to Germany and France as determined by the 'excessive deficits procedure', and, later, when the Commission brought this decision before the European Court of Justice, challenging its legitimacy. The seriousness of this episode is reflected in the anxiety of the ECB warning insisting that '... the failure of the ECOFIN Council to follow the rules and procedures foreseen in the Stability and Growth Pact risked undermining the credibility of the institutional framework and confidence in the soundness of public finances of countries across the euro area'[13].

Such conflicts in EU decision making give support to the view that the institutional deficits result in an economic and political environment for the euro characterized by higher uncertainty compared to its rival currencies, namely the dollar and the yen. This represents a clear disadvantage for the euro. Decision making in the sphere of economic governance of the dollar or the yen is in the hands of a single government. On the contrary, economic decision making affecting the euro lies in the hands of national governments as well as the EU institutions. In addition, policy actions decided at the EU level are often the result of an agreement reached within the EU institutions after painful, time-consuming negotiations characterized by disagreements and conflicts among national policies.

Therefore, further institutionalization of policy coordination is necessary for reducing uncertainty in policy making. For example, it is argued that the fiscal policy coordination can be more effective if it is based on institutions rather than on fiscal rules. Thus, the establishment of an independent Fiscal Policy Committee with a clear mandate in making decisions about the deficits and the evolution of debt could give a viable solution to problems related to the SGP (Wyplosz, 2001).

Finally, there is a need for upgrading coordination in the area of the external representation of the EU. Such a task requires upgrading the existing institutional framework. Bergsten (2002, p. 307) notes that although the EU is the dominant player in the international trade, it speaks '...with multiplicity, even a cacophony of voices...' on issues such as trade negotiations or economic policy coordination in the G7 or the IMF. According to McNamara and Meunier (2002), a single voice for the euro is necessary for mainly two reasons: first, for defending the value of the euro in foreign exchange markets, and second for increasing EU power in the fora of international policy coordination, the construction of a new financial architecture and the management of global financial crises. Gros (2002) notes that the EU aim of creating economic and political stability in Europe does not seem to be sufficient when global instability exists. Thus, the EU should act as an influential actor on the global financial and economic stage. He argues that the absence of the EU from the international efforts to contain the volatility of the emerging markets in the late 1990s, and its inability to use its economic instruments (aid, trade preferences, etc.) under a coherent strategy to promote stability in the Middle East show that it remains a non-actor on the global stage. According to Gros, this can be changed only if the EU decides to allow for coordination of its economic instruments with a strengthened Common Foreign and Security Policy (CFSP).

## 6  FUTURE CHALLENGES FOR THE EURO

The euro as a global currency is currently facing important challenges. These challenges are related to certain developments that take place at the international as well as the EU level. On the one hand, conditions in the international stage become more favourable for the euro; on the other hand, the recent EU enlargement generates opportunities and risks.

First, the external conditions for the euro in the near future are expected to be more favourable compared to those of the recent past. Since the introduction of the euro, the prevailing perception has been that the US performance in the areas of productivity growth and the quality of economic management was superior compared to the EU. This perception was mainly responsible for the increased demand of the US securities and the strong dollar of the 1999–2002 period. However, this perception is now changing. The EU economy gradually moves to recovery after suffering a prolonged recession. On the contrary, in the US economy expectations are less optimistic now compared to those prevailing three to four years ago. Recent research suggests that the productivity in the EU and the USA in the long run grow at similar rates. Any differences in the past can be explained by differences in the economic cycle or differences in the average hours worked per person[14]. In addition, recent economic policies in the USA have resulted in strong internal and external imbalances. The federal budget deficit is estimated at 4.5% of GDP for 2004 and is expected to remain high for the next few years. The current account deficit exceeded 5% of GDP in 2004, despite the sharp depreciation of the dollar in 2003. The economic situation in the USA suggests that a prolonged period of dollar weakness is possible in the future. Brook et al. (2004), by conducting simulations using the OECD Interling model, show that a further depreciation of the effective exchange rate of the dollar by more than 20% might be necessary if the deficit is to be reduced by 2% within the current decade.

A prolonged period of dollar weakness could help the euro gain larger shares in the global financial markets. Since the private use of an international currency is the key factor supporting its official use, such development would have positive repercussions to the official use of the euro also.

Second, in the internal front, the EU enlargement offers a unique opportunity for the euro to dominate in terms of economic size and trade volumes. However, the process of the widening of Euroland entails risks as well. There are many areas that raise concern. To start with, most of the new candidate members for Euroland are characterized by substantially different economic structure relative to current members. In particular, the Central and Eastern European Member Countries (CEEMCs) are relatively poor in terms of GDP per capita, with large agricultural sectors in terms of employment. The share of the agricultural employment for these countries is about four times larger than in the current euro area. The financial sector in CEEMCs is also problematic. The capital markets are small in size and banking is the dominant form of intermediation. The level of financial intermediation amounts to only one-third of the euro area average[15]. It is even lower compared to other emerging market economies with compatible income levers. Such divergence in real terms poses certain risks for the euro. CEEMCs have to make significant progress not only in nominal convergence but also more importantly in real convergence, if their EMU participation is to be without serious problems. Their convergence process needs to be cautious to minimize the risks for the euro. For example, a hasty participation in the ERM II in the presence of structural problems or macroeconomic imbalances might lead to exchange rate crises. In this case, the CEEMCs would not only harm their convergence process but they would also jeopardize the stability of the euro.

Moreover, a trade–off between nominal and real convergence might be at work for these countries: too much tightening of fiscal and monetary policies to speed up nominal convergence might lead to lower public investment, slower structural adjustments, higher unemployment and thus to real divergence. In such a case, one cannot rule out that public opinion may gradually turn against the EMU participation, weakening the commitment of public administration, and, thus, making the whole process extremely fragile. Again, negative developments in the accession to EMU would lead to increased uncertainty for the euro.

Finally, the recent enlargement of the EU could lead to aggravation of the governance problems discussed above. It has been argued that as the members of the union increase, decision-making procedures become more unwieldy, even if the distribution of preferences remains unchanged. In order to solve the problem, the EU has to find the right balance between widening and deepening (Wyplosz, 2003; Boyer, 2000). The new constitution agreed by the EU leaders in June 2004, represents an important step towards improving the governance within the EU. It extends majority voting, gives the EU a legal personality enabling it to sign international agreements, commits the EU to progressive framing of a CFSP and upgrades the role of the European Parliament[16]. Whether the adoption of the new constitution will be a sufficient for solving the key problems related to governance within the EU remains to be seen.

## 7   CONCLUSION

The chapter reviews the achievements of the euro on its way to becoming a fully-fledged international currency. It concludes that the euro has become an important international currency with regional character since it is used mainly in the wider region that surrounds the euro area. However, the euro remains second to the dollar, which is by far the main international currency with global use.

The key factors that limit the internationalization process of the euro are examined. In particular, the chapter discusses problematic areas of the euro, related to the limited financial market integration in the EU, the monetary policy making and the economic governance of the euroland. It is suggested that while there is an ongoing improvement in other areas, the complexity of economic governance in the EU poses a real disadvantage for the euro relative to the dollar in the long run. However, it is argued that recent developments in the USA (e.g. dollar weakness, macroeconomic imbalances) and in the EU (e.g. the process of enlargement and institutional change) offer a unique opportunity for upgrading the international role of the euro. This opportunity can only be exploited if the EU works towards the creation of a sound framework of economic and political governance of the euro.

## NOTES

[1]   It includes most of the euro area countries, the new EU member countries, the UK and Japan.

[2]   For example, during the 2000–2002 period, the share of the euro in the exports to non–euro area increased from 48% to 55% for France, from 49% to 58% for Spain, and from 40% to 49% for Portugal. Similarly, the share of the euro in the imports from the non–euro area, during the same period, increased from 35% to 53% for France, from 44% to 55% for Spain, and from 47% to 58% for Portugal.

[3]   See ECB, 2003, p 32.

⁴  In 2002, energy goods and raw materials amounted to 21% of the euro area's total goods imports and the 5% of total exports.
⁵  The share refers to the broadly defined international debt securities, i.e. those issued by non-residents plus domestic issues targeting international markets. See ECB, 2002.
⁶  See ECB, 2003, p. 47.
⁷  From a total of 150 countries, 41 were using the euro as an anchor. See ECB, 2003.
⁸  See 'Report by the Economic and Financial Committee on EU financial Integration' EU Commission, *Economic* Papers, 171, May 2002, p. 4. The report bases its estimations on the findings of the 'Giovannini Group' Report.
⁹  See for example discussion in Frankel, 2000.
¹⁰  See the ECB Annual Report 2003, p. 19.
¹¹  See Work Group VI on Economic Governance Report, p. 3.
¹²  See the ECB Annual Report 2003.
¹³  See the ECB Annual Report 2003, p. 131.
¹⁴  See for example discussion in '*The Economist*', 2004, June 19, p. 75–77.
¹⁵  See the ECB Annual Report 2003.
¹⁶  Wyplosz (2003) discusses some areas such as the task allocation process which are not properly addressed in the new constitution

# REFERENCES

Arestis, Philip and Malcolm Sawyer (2003), 'Making the Euro Work', *Challenge*, **46** (2), 80–96.
Begg David, Paul de Grauwe, Francesco Giavazzi, Harald Uhlig and Charles Wyplosz (1998), *The ECB: Safe at Any Speed? Monitoring the European Central Bank 1. A CEPR Report*, CERP
Bergsten, C. Fred (2002), 'The Euro Versus the Dollar: Will There Be a Struggle for Dominance?', *Journal of Policy Modeling*, **24**, 307–14.
Bibow, Jörg (2001), 'Easy Money Through the Back Door: The Markets Vs. the ECB', *Working Paper*, No. 323, The Levy Economics Institute of Bard College.
Boyer, Robert (2000) 'The Unanticipated Fallout of European Monetary Union: The Political and Institutional Deficits of the Euro', in C. Crouch (ed.), *After the Euro: Shaping Institutions for Governance in the Wake of European Monetary Union*, Oxford: Oxford University Press, 24–88.
Brook, Anne–Marie, Franck Sédillot and Patrice Ollivaud (2004), 'Channels for Norrowing the US Current Account Deficit and Implications for Other Economies', *Organisation for Economic Co–operation and Development, Economics Department Working Papers*, No. 390.
Cecchetti, Stephen G. and Roisin O'Sullivan (2003), 'The European Central Bank and the Federal Reserve', *Oxford Review of Economic Policy*, **19** (1), 30–43.
Cohen, Benjamin J. (2003), 'Global Currency Rivalry: Can the Euro Ever Challenge the Dollar?', *Journal of Common Market Studies*, **41** (4), 575–95.
Eichengreen, Barry (2003), 'The Euro Through a Glass Darkly', *Institute of European Studies, Working Paper*, No. 12.
ECB (2002), *Review of the International Role of the Euro*, December.
ECB (2003), *Review of the International Role of the Euro*, December.
Frankel, Jeffrey A. (2000), *EMU and the Euro: An American Perspective*, Brescia, Italy: Fontazione Lucchini.
Gros, Daniel (2002), 'Europe as a Global Economic Actor', *CEPS Policy Brief*, **20**, April.

Gros, Daniel (2003), 'Reforming the Composition of the ECB Governing Council in View for Enlargement: An Opportunity Missed!', *CEPS Policy Brief*, **32**, April.

Hartmann, Philipp and Otmar Issing (2002), 'The International Role of the Euro', *Journal of Policy Modeling*, **24**, 315–45.

Hau, Harald, William Killeen and Michael Moore (2002), 'The Euro as an International Currency: Explaining First Evidence from the Foreign Exchange Markets', *Journal of International Money and Finance*, **21**, 351–83.

Herr, Hansjörg (2002), 'ECB Monetary Policy during the "Weak Euro" Period of 1999/2001: Theoretical Approach and Reality', *Intereconomics*, Nov./Dec., 321–27.

Issing, Otmar (2003), *The Euro – A Stable International Currency*, Frankfurt: European Central Bank.

Kenen, Peter B. (2002), 'The Euro Versus the Dollar: Will There Be a Struggle for Dominance?', *Journal of Policy Modeling*, **24**, 347–54.

McKinnon, Ronald (2002), 'The Euro Versus the Dollar: Resolving a Historical Puzzle', *Journal of Policy Modeling*, **24**, 355–59.

McNamara, Kathleen R. and Sophie Meunier (2002), 'Between National Sovereignty and International Power: What External Voice for the Euro?', *International Affairs*, **78**, 849–68.

Neaime Simon and John Paschakis (2002), 'The Future of the Dollar–Euro Exchange Rate', *North American Journal of Economics and Finance*, **13**, 56–71.

Portes Richard and Helene Rey (1998), 'The emergence of the euro as an international currency', *Economic Policy*, **13** (26), 307–343.

Salvatore, Dominick (2000), 'The Euro, the Dollar, and the International Monetary System', *Journal of Policy Modeling*, **22** (3), 275–79.

Schroeder, Juergen (2003), 'The European Central Bank (ECB) and the International Role of the Euro', *Journal of Asian Economics*, **14**, 209–18.

Wyplosz, Charles (2001), *Fiscal Policy: Institutions Vs. Rules*, Report, Geneva: Graduate Institute for International Studies and CEPR.

Wyplosz, Charles (2003), 'The Challenges of a Wider and Deeper Europe', Paper presented at the East–West conference 'The Economic Potential of a Larger Europe – Keys to Success', Vienna, 2–4, Nov.

# 10. Linkages in the Term Structures of the EU Accession Countries

## Minoas Koukouritakis and Leo Michelis

## 1 INTRODUCTION

The enlargement process of an economic union is an important issue in the theory and practice of economic integration. In the framework of the European Union (EU), enlargement has been a concern since the foundation of the European Economic Community by the Treaty of Rome in 1957. The Treaty states explicitly that one of its main objectives is the continuous and balanced expansion. Indeed the current EU is the result of various expansions since 1957.

After growing in size from the original six to twelve and then to fifteen member states, the EU has recently experienced its biggest expansion ever in terms of scope and diversity. On 1 May 2004 ten countries joined the EU. These countries are Cyprus, the Czech Republic, Estonia, Hungary, Latvia, Lithuania, Malta, Poland, the Slovak Republic and Slovenia. In order to successfully join the EU these countries had to satisfy certain economic and political criteria, which include being stable democracies, respect human rights and the rule of law as well as having a functioning market economy.

The Maastricht Treaty has laid down explicit nominal convergence criteria that must be satisfied before a candidate country can join the European Monetary Union (EMU) successfully. One criterion concerns the convergence of long–term interest rates to the average interest rate of the three EMU countries with the lowest inflation rates. In this chapter we investigate interest rate linkages among the new and old EU countries using the expectations hypothesis of the term structure (EHTS) of interest rates. According to the EHTS, the interest rate on a long–run government security is an average of the current short rate and the expected future rates on securities of shorter maturity. If future short rates are expected to be constant over time, then the yield curve will be a horizontal line at the level of the current short rate. If future short rates are expected to rise, then the yield curve will be upward–sloping, while if future short rates are expected to fall, the yield curve will be downward–sloping. Thus, the EHTS provides a plausible link between short– and long–term interest rates over time.

Clearly the EHTS has important policy implications. The term structure is a channel through which government policies can affect the long–term prospects of an economy. For example, if a government adopts policies that lower the expected future short rates, then the long–term interest rate will be lower and consequently, investment and economic growth will be higher.

Even though most studies to date have been concerned with testing the EHTS for a specific country or group of countries[1], the decomposition of the term structure into its transitory (i.e. the $I(0)$ cointegration relation) and permanent (i.e. the $I(1)$ common trend) component can be equally useful and insightful. The cointegration relation which captures the spread between the long and short rates, contains information about the effects of short–run monetary policies, while the common trend contains information about long–run macroeconomic conditions and expectations about the course of future government policies. The interdependence among the transitory or the permanent components for a group of countries can thus reveal information about the degree of policy convergence among the countries. This is useful information for applied economists and policy makers.

Hafer, Kutan and Zhou (1997) used the multivariate cointegration and common trends' techniques of Gonzalo and Granger (1995) to study linkages in the term structures of interest rates in four EU countries: Belgium, France, Germany and the Netherlands. Using a sample of monthly observations from 1979:3 to 1995:6, they found that the EHTS holds for these countries. Also, by decomposing each term structure into its transitory and permanent components, these authors found that the long–term interest rate is the source of the common trend in each country, and that the common trends are cointegrated across countries and thus move together over time, but no single country dominates the common trends. Holmes and Pentecost (1997) reported similar results for six EU countries (Belgium, France, Germany, Italy, the Netherlands and the UK), using a sample of monthly observations from 1974:1 to 1996:3.

In this chapter we contribute to the existing literature in three ways. First, we use the most recent data available from the early 1990s to the present and the VECM approach of Johansen (1988, 1991, 1994, 1995) to test the EHTS of interest rates for the ten new EU member states.

Second, we use the Gonzalo Granger methodology to identify and estimate the common trend that drives the cointegrating relation between long and short rates in each country. Hypothesis testing in this framework provides information as to which interest rate contains the common trend. This is useful information for the design of monetary policies of the ten new EU countries.

Third, using multivariate Granger causality and Johansen cointegration tests, we investigate the possibility of short–run and long–run interdependence among the term structures of the countries in our sample. This is also useful information, since interdependence among the term structures of interest rates means interdependence among the monetary policies of these countries.

The rest of the chapter is organized as follows. In Section 2 we briefly describe the EHTS of interest rates and outline the models for cointegration and common trends that we use in the chapter. In Section 3 we describe the data and analyze the empirical results. Briefly, the evidence suggests that the EHTS holds for all countries of our sample, except for Malta. Our results also indicate that the short–run monetary policies are set independently for most of the new EU countries, while the long–run monetary policies are only weakly interdependent. In Section 4 we make some concluding remarks.

## 2  THEORETICAL FRAMEWORK

### 2.1  The EHTS of Interest Rates

The EHTS of interest rates states that the yield to maturity of an $n$-period bond $R_{n,t}$ will equal an average of the current and future rates on a set of $m$-period short yields $r_{m,t}$, with $m < n$, plus the term premium. The relationship can be expressed in the following form

$$(1 + R_{n,t})^n = \varphi_{n,t}^* \prod_{i=0}^{n-1} (1 + E_t r_{m,t+i}) \qquad (10.1)$$

where $\varphi_{n,t}^*$ is a possible non-zero but stationary $n$-period term premium and $E_t$ is the expectations operator conditional on information up to and including time $t$. The equality in equation (10.1) is established by the condition of no arbitrage opportunities to investors willing to hold both short–term and long–term bonds. Log-linearizing equation (10.1) we get

$$R_{n,t} = \varphi_{n,t} + (1/n) \sum_{i=0}^{n-1} E_t r_{m,t+i} \qquad (10.2)$$

where $\varphi_{n,t} = \log(\varphi_{n,t}^*)$. Equation (10.2) indicates that the yield of the $n$-period bond and the $m$-period short yields are functionally related. For the subsequent analysis it is convenient to re-express equation (10.2) as

$$R_{n,t} - r_{m,t} = \varphi_{n,t} + (1/n)\sum_{i=1}^{n}(r_{m,t+i-1} - r_{m,t}). \qquad (10.3)$$

The left–hand side of equation (10.3) represents the spread between the *n*-period (long term) yield and the *m*-period (short term) yield. Assuming that the yields are *I(1)* and cointegrated the right–hand side of equation (10.3) is stationary. It follows that the left–hand side of equation (10.3) is stationary and that $(1,-1)'$ is a cointegration vector linking the long–term and short–term interest rates. In what follows, we analyze the time series and cointegration properties of the long–term and short–term interest rates, given the insights of equation (10.3).

## 2.2   The Cointegration and Common Trends Models

This section outlines the basic maximum likelihood theory of cointegration and the models that are employed in the subsequent empirical analysis. The maximum likelihood theory of cointegration assumes that the stochastic variables are integrated of order one, or *I(1)*, and that the data–generating process is a Gaussian[2] vector autoregressive model of finite order *k*, or VAR(*k*), which may possibly include some deterministic components. Let $Y_t$ be a *p*-dimensional column vector of *I(1)* variables. Then the VAR(*k*) can be written in a vector error-correction model (VECM) form as

$$\Delta Y_t = \Pi Y_{t-1} + \sum_{i=1}^{k-1}\Gamma_i \Delta Y_{t-i} + \mu_0 + \mu_1 t + \varepsilon_t, \quad t = 1,...,T \qquad (10.4)$$

where $\Pi$ and $\Gamma_i$ are (*p* x *p*) matrices of coefficients, $\mu_0$ and $\mu_1$ are (*p* x 1) vectors of constant and trend coefficients respectively and $\varepsilon_t$ is a (*p* x 1) multivariate normal random error vector with mean vector zero and variance matrix $\Omega$ that is independent across time periods.

The hypothesis of cointegration can be stated in terms of the rank of the long–run matrix $\Pi$ in equation (10.4). Under the hypothesis of cointegration, this matrix can be written as

$$\Pi = \alpha\beta' \qquad (10.5)$$

where $\alpha$ and $\beta$ are (*p* x *r*) matrices of full rank. If *r*=0, then $\Pi$=0, which means that there is no linear combination of the elements of $Y_t$ that is stationary. The other extreme case is when the rank of the $\Pi$ matrix equals *p*. In this case $Y_t$ is a stationary process. In the intermediate case, when $0 < r < p$ there are *r* stationary linear combinations of the elements of $Y_t$ and *p* - *r* non stationary common trends.

Under the hypothesis $\Pi = \alpha\beta'$, the relation between $\alpha$ and the deterministic term $\mu_t = \mu_0 + \mu_1 t$ is crucial for the properties of the process $Y_t$. To see this, first decompose $\mu_0$ and $\mu_1$ in the directions of $\alpha$ and $\alpha_\perp$, where $\alpha_\perp$ is a ($p$ x ($p$ -$r$)) matrix that is the orthogonal complement to $\alpha$:

$$\mu_i = \alpha\beta_i + \alpha_\perp\gamma_i, \quad i=0,1 \tag{10.6}$$

where $\beta_i = (\alpha'\alpha)^{-1}\alpha'\mu_i$ and $\gamma_i = (\alpha'_\perp\alpha_\perp)^{-1}\alpha'_\perp\mu_i$. Next, following Johansen (1994), consider the following five submodels, which are ordered from the most to the least restrictive:

| | |
|---|---|
| Model 0: | $\mu_i = 0$ |
| Model 1*: | $\mu_i = \alpha\beta_0$ |
| Model 1: | $\mu_i = \alpha\beta_0 + \alpha_\perp\gamma_0$ |
| Model 2*: | $\mu_i = \alpha\beta_0 + \alpha_\perp\gamma_0 + \alpha\beta_1 t$ |
| Model 2: | $\mu_i = \alpha\beta_0 + \alpha_\perp\gamma_0 + (\alpha\beta_1 + \alpha_\perp\gamma_1)t$ |

The interpretation of these models becomes clear in the context of the solution of $Y_t$ in equation (10.4). The solution is given by

$$Y_t = C\sum_{i=1}^{t}\varepsilon_i + \tfrac{1}{2}\tau_2 t^2 + \tau_1 t + \tau_0 + W_t + A \tag{10.7}$$

where $W_t$ is a stationary process, $A$ is a vector such that $\beta'A = 0$, $C = \beta_\perp(\alpha'_\perp\Gamma\beta_\perp)^{-1}\alpha'_\perp$, $\Gamma = I_p - \sum_{i=1}^{k-1}\Gamma_i$, $\beta_\perp$ is a ($p$ x ($p$ -$r$)) matrix of full rank that is orthogonal to $\beta$ and $\tau_2 = C\mu_1$.

Using equation (10.7), Johansen (1994) shows that the five submodels imply different behavior for the process $Y_t$ and the cointegrating relations $\beta'Y_t$. Briefly, in Model 0, $Y_t$ has no deterministic trend and all the stationary components have zero mean. In Model 1*, $Y_t$ has neither quadratic nor linear trend. However, both $Y_t$ and the cointegrating relations $\beta'Y_t$ are allowed a constant term. In Model 1, $Y_t$ has a linear trend, but the cointegrating relations $\beta'Y_t$ have no linear trend. In Model 2*, $Y_t$ has no quadratic trend but $Y_t$ has a linear trend that is present even in the cointegrating relations. In Model 2, $Y_t$ has a quadratic trend but the cointegrating relations $\beta'Y_t$ have only a linear trend.

Because of the normality assumption, one can easily test for the reduced rank of the $\Pi$ matrix using the maximum likelihood approach. This procedure gives at once the maximum likelihood estimators (MLE) of $\alpha$ and $\beta$ and the eigenvalues needed in order to construct the likelihood ratio test. The MLE of

$\alpha$ and $\beta$ are obtained by regressing $\Delta Y_t$ and $Y_{t-1}$ on $\Delta Y_{t-1}...\Delta Y_{t-k}$ and $\mu_t$ (allowing for the restrictions imposed by each of the five models). These auxiliary regressions give residuals $R_{0t}$ and $R_{1t}$ respectively, and residual product matrices

$$S_{ij} = T^{-1} \sum_{t=1}^{T} R_{it} R'_{jt}, \quad i,j=0,1. \tag{10.8}$$

Solving the eigenvalue problem

$$\left| \lambda S_{11} - S_{10} S_{00}^{-1} S_{01} \right| = 0 \tag{10.9}$$

for eigenvalues $1 > \hat{\lambda}_1 > ... > \hat{\lambda}_p > 0$ and eigenvectors $\hat{V} = (\hat{v}_1...\hat{v}_p)$, normalized such that $\hat{V}'S_{11}\hat{V} = I$, one gets the MLE of $\alpha$ and $\beta$ as $\hat{\alpha} = S_{01}\hat{\beta}$ and $\hat{\beta} = (\hat{v}_1...\hat{v}_r)$, where $(\hat{v}_1...\hat{v}_r)$ are the eigenvectors associated with the $r$ largest eigenvalues of equation (10.9).

In testing the null hypothesis that $rank(\Pi) \leq r$ against the alternative hypothesis that $rank(\Pi) = p$, the likelihood ratio statistic, also called the Trace statistic by Johansen and Juselius (1990), is given by

$$Trace = -T \sum_{i=r+1}^{p} \ln(1 - \hat{\lambda}_i). \tag{10.10}$$

The testing is performed sequentially for $r=0,...,p-1$ and it terminates when the null hypothesis is not rejected for the first time.

It is also possible to test the null hypothesis that $rank(\Pi) = r$ against the alternative that $rank(\Pi) = r+1$. In this case, the likelihood ratio statistic, which is called the $\lambda_{max}$ statistic, is given by

$$\lambda_{max} = -T \ln(1 - \hat{\lambda}_{r+1}). \tag{10.11}$$

Of course, the $\lambda_{max}$ statistic is equal to the Trace statistic when $p-r=1$.

MacKinnon, Haug and Michelis (1999) have computed highly accurate critical values for the Trace statistic in equation (10.10) and the $\lambda_{max}$ statistic in equation (10.11), using the response surface methodology. These critical values differ substantially from those existing in the literature, especially when the dimension of the VECM is large; e.g., compare to Osterwald-Lenum (1992). Since we deal with large dimensional systems in this study, we use these new critical values for testing hypotheses[3].

In respect to the common trends, it is clear from equation (10.7) that the common trends in $Y_t$ are contained in the first term of that expression. Given the definition of $C$, Johansen (1995) defines the common trends by the cumulated disturbances $\alpha_\perp' \sum_{i=1}^{t} \varepsilon_i$. Assuming that the common trends are a linear combination of $Y_t$, in the form $f_t = \alpha_\perp' Y_t$, Gonzalo and Granger (1995) derived the MLE of $\alpha_\perp$ as the eigenvectors corresponding to the *(p-r)* smallest eigenvalues of the problem

$$\left| \lambda S_{00} - S_{01} S_{11}^{-1} S_{10} \right| = 0.$$ 

(10.12)

Solving equation (10.12) for eigenvalues $1 > \hat{\lambda}_1 > ... > \hat{\lambda}_p > 0$ and eigenvectors $\hat{M} = (\hat{m}_1, ... \hat{m}_p)$, normalized such that $\hat{M}'S_{00}\hat{M} = I$, one gets the MLE of $\alpha_\perp$ as $\hat{\alpha}_\perp = (\hat{m}_{r+1} ... \hat{m}_p)$.

Given this framework, it is easy to test whether or not certain linear combinations of $Y_t$ can be common trends. Null hypotheses on $\alpha_\perp$ have the following form

$$H_0 : \alpha_\perp = G\theta$$

(10.13)

where $G$ is a $p \times m$ known matrix of constants and $\theta$ is an $m \times (p-r)$ matrix of unknown coefficients such that $p-r \le m \le p$. To carry out the test, one solves the eigenvalue problem

$$\left| \lambda G'S_{00}G - G'S_{01}S_{11}^{-1}S_{10}G \right| = 0$$

(10.14)

for eigenvalues $1 > \hat{\lambda}_1^* > ... > \hat{\lambda}_m^* > 0$ and eigenvectors $\hat{M}^* = (\hat{m}_1^* ... \hat{m}_m^*)$, normalized such that $\hat{M}^* (G'S_{00}G)\hat{M}^* = I$. Choose $\hat{\theta}_{m \times (p-r)} = (\hat{m}_{(m+1)-(p-r)} ... \hat{m}_m)$ and $\hat{\alpha}_\perp = G\hat{\theta}$. The likelihood ratio test statistic for testing $H_0$ is given by

$$L = -T \sum_{i=r+1}^{p} \ln \left[ (1 - \hat{\lambda}_{i+(m-p)}^*) / (1 - \hat{\lambda}_i) \right]$$

(10.15)

In the next section, we use the *L*-statistic in (10.15) to test the statistical significance of $\alpha_\perp$ of the long–term and the short–term interest rate of the EU accession countries. A significant $\alpha_\perp$ implies that the respective interest rate is weakly exogenous and dominates the common trend in the cointegrating system.

## 3   DATA AND EMPIRICAL RESULTS

### 3.1   Data

We collected data for the ten new EU member states. Due to lack of data availability we worked only on two interest rates for each country: either treasury bill yields (short term) and government bond yields (long term) or short–term and long–term commercial banks' lending rates. Our sample consists of monthly data of varying time spans for different countries determined by data availability. All interest rates are expressed in natural logarithms.

For Cyprus the time span is 1997:1 to 2003:12. Monthly average treasury bill rates were obtained from the International Financial Statistics (IFS) of the IMF, 2004. Monthly average government bond yields were obtained from the Central Bank of Cyprus and refer to bonds with maturity greater than five years. For the Czech Republic the time span is 1993:8 to 2003:12. Treasury bill rates and long–term government bond yields were obtained from the IFS. This IFS data series begins at January 2000. For the period 1993:8-1999:12 we used long–term government bond yields obtained from the Central Bank of the Czech Republic.

No data on treasury bill rates or government bond yields are available for Estonia, Latvia, Lithuania and Slovenia. For this reason, we used commercial banks' lending rates instead. For Estonia the time span is 1994:1 to 2003:12. Three-month lending rates were obtained from the Main Economic Indicators (MEI) of the OECD, 2004, and ten-year lending rates were taken from the Central Bank of Estonia. For Latvia short–term and long–term lending rates were obtained from the MEI and the time span is 1993:1 to 2003:12. For Lithuania six to twelve months and over five years lending rates were taken from the Central Bank of Lithuania and the time span is 1997:1 to 2003:12. For Slovenia the time span is 1996:1 to 2003:12 and the short–term and long–term lending rates were obtained from the Central Bank of Slovenia.

For Hungary the time span is 1997:1 to 2003:12. The three-month treasury bill rates and the five-year government bond yields were obtained from the Central Bank of Hungary. For Malta the time span is 1993:1 to 2003:12. Monthly average treasury bill rates were obtained from the IFS, while five-year monthly average government bond yields were taken from the Central Bank of Malta.

For Poland the time span is 1994:2 to 2003:12. The one-year treasury bill rates and the over two years government bond yields were obtained from the Polish Ministry of Finance. In the case of the Slovak Republic the time span is 1994:12 to 2003:12. The one- to six-months treasury bill rates were taken from the Central Bank of the Slovak Republic. For government bond yields the IFS data series (line 61) for the Slovak Republic begins at September 2000 and refers to ten-year government bond yields. For the period 1994:12-2000:8 we collected data from the Central Bank of the Slovak Republic.

## 3.2    Testing for the EHTS

In this section we report and analyze the unit root and cointegration results between the short–term and the long–term interest rates for each country. Evidence of cointegration would validate empirically the EHTS of interest rates.

*Table 10.1    Augmented Dickey Fuller tests for a unit root*[a]

| Country | Short–term interest rate | | Long–term interest rate | |
|---|---|---|---|---|
| | Level | First Difference | Level | First Difference |
| Cyprus | -0.39 | -8.87* | -0.44 | -4.95* |
| Czech Republic | -1.02 | -6.70* | -1.02 | -10.25* |
| Estonia | -2.56 | -9.04* | -1.49 | -8.41* |
| Hungary | -1.67 | -8.96* | -1.40 | -7.20* |
| Latvia | -2.07 | -4.15* | -1.47 | -6.48* |
| Lithuania | -1.82 | -12.62* | -0.87 | -3.53* |
| Malta | 0.68 | -6.42* | -1.57 | -4.35* |
| Poland | -3.92* | - | -4.11* | - |
| Slovak Republic | -2.82 | -11.47* | -0.98 | -9.90* |
| Slovenia | -1.36 | -9.78* | -1.23 | -8.95* |

*Note:*     [a]The entry in each cell is the ADF test statistic. *denotes rejection of the unit root hypothesis at the 5% level of significance. For the countries of the table, the sample sizes are 84 for Cyprus, 125 for the Czech Republic, 120 for Estonia, 84 for Hungary, 132 for Latvia, 84 for Lithuania, 132 for Malta, 119 for Poland, 109 for the Slovak Republic and 96 for Slovenia.

Before testing for cointegration, we tested each time series for unit roots using the Augmented Dickey Fuller test at the 5% level of significance. The results are presented in Table 10.1. To select the appropriate lag length for the ADF test regression, we used the Akaike's information criterion.As shown in Table 10.1, we fail to reject the unit root hypothesis in the long and short rates in all countries except Poland. In all the cases where the unit root hypothesis was not rejected, we also tested for a second unit root. As shown in Table 10.1, this hypothesis was rejected in all cases. Based on these results we proceeded with cointegration analysis using the VECM in equation (10.4) above, where $Y_t = (R_{n,t}, r_{m,t})'$.

To select the appropriate lag length, $k$, in equation (10.4), we set up a separate VECM for each country and used the likelihood ratio test. Under the hypothesis $\Gamma_k=0$, the likelihood ratio test is asymptotically distributed as $\chi^2$ with $p^2$ degrees of freedom (see Johansen 1995, p. 21). Further, to determine which submodel describes best each set of variables, we tested the submodels against each other using the likelihood ratio tests in Johansen (1995, pp. 161–162). These tests are also distributed as $\chi^2$ with degrees of freedom determined by the pairs of models being tested as follows:

$$0 \underset{r}{\subseteq} I^* \underset{p-r}{\subseteq} I \underset{r}{\subseteq} 2^* \underset{p-r}{\subseteq} 2.$$

Table 10.2 reports the cointegration results between the long and short rates for each of the new EU countries (except Poland). Based on the Trace and the $\lambda_{max}$ statistics at the 5% level of significance, we find evidence of one cointegrating vector between the short–term and the long–term interest rates in all the countries, except Malta. Clearly, this is indirect evidence in favor of the EHTS of interest rates in all countries in this sample, except for Malta.

Table 10.3 reports the parameter estimates of the cointegration vectors, normalized on the long rate, for the countries for which the EHTS holds (i.e. Cyprus, the Czech Republic, Estonia, Hungary, Latvia, Lithuania, the Slovak Republic and Slovenia). Numbers in parentheses are likelihood ratio test statistics which are distributed as $\chi_1^2$ asymptotically, under the null hypothesis that each component of the cointegration vector is insignificantly different from zero. As shown in Table 10.3, the parameters of the cointegrating vectors ($\beta_i$) are statistically significant in all cases, which means that the short–term and the long–term interest rates enter significantly into each cointegration vector. We also tested the hypothesis $H_0$: $\beta_R+\beta_r=0$, when $(\beta_R,\beta_r)=(1,-1)$. Equivalently, we tested whether or not the spread between the long–term and short–term interest rates belongs in the cointegration space of the term structure, as suggested by the EHTS. Using the likelihood ratio test statistic at the 5% level of significance, this hypothesis is rejected for Cyprus, Hungary, Latvia and Slovenia, but it cannot be rejected for the Czech Republic, Estonia, Lithuania and the Slovak Republic. Consequently, only the latter group of countries satisfies the EHTS exactly.

The parameter estimates of the adjustment coefficients $\alpha_R$ and $\alpha_r$ are also presented in Table 10.3. These are the coefficients of the error–correction terms in the VECM and their subscripts denote the variable that adjusts to deviations from the long–run equilibrium relation between the two rates. As shown in Table 10.3, $\alpha_R$ is statistically significant and $\alpha_r$ is statistically insignificant at the 5% level, for the three Baltic countries (i.e., Estonia, Latvia and Lithuania). This implies that, for this group of countries, the long–

term interest rate is an endogenous variable which adjusts to deviations from its long–run equilibrium with the short rate. At the same time, the short rate is a weakly exogenous variable, changes of which have a permanent effect on both the long rate and the short rate. On the other hand, $\alpha_R$ is statistically insignificant and $\alpha_r$ is statistically significant for Cyprus, the Czech Republic, the Slovak Republic, Slovenia and Hungary. Hence for the latter group of countries, the evidence suggests that the short–term interest rate adjusts to deviations from the long–run equilibrium, while the long rate is weakly exogenous, affected primarily by fundamental factors such as the future state of the economy and expectations about the future path of government policies.

These empirical findings are reinforced by direct tests on $\alpha_\perp$, the components of the common trend in each country. In order to test the statistical significance of $\alpha_\perp$, we compute the $L$-statistic in equation (10.15) for specific choices of the $G$ matrix. In particular, to test the null hypothesis that the long–term interest rate has a permanent component in the common trend of a country, we set the $G$ matrix to

$$G = \begin{bmatrix} 1 \\ 0 \end{bmatrix}.$$

Alternatively, to test the hypothesis that the short–term interest rate has a permanent component in the common trend, we set the $G$ matrix to

$$G = \begin{bmatrix} 0 \\ 1 \end{bmatrix}.$$

*Table 10.2    Trace and $\lambda_{max}$ statistics[a]*

| (p-r) | Trace | $\lambda_{max}$ | Trace | $\lambda_{max}$ | Trace | $\lambda_{max}$ | Trace | $\lambda_{max}$ |
|---|---|---|---|---|---|---|---|---|
| | **Cyprus** | | **Czech Republic** | | **Estonia** | | **Hungary** | |
| 2 | 20.14* | 19.25* | 13.95* | 11.81* | 16.30* | 14.39* | 12.81* | 11.41* |
| 1 | 0.89 | 0.89 | 2.15 | 2.15 | 1.91 | 1.91 | 1.39 | 1.39 |
| $k^b$ | 4 | | 1 | | 3 | | 2 | |
| Model | 0 | | 0 | | 0 | | 0 | |
| | | | | | | | | |
| (p-r) | **Latvia** | | **Lithuania** | | **Malta** | | **Slovak Republic** | |
| 2 | 29.81* | 24.23* | 22.59* | 17.23* | 3.16 | 1.89 | 23.37* | 23.25* |
| 1 | 5.58 | 5.58 | 5.37 | 5.37 | 1.28 | 1.28 | 0.12 | 0.12 |
| $k^b$ | 6 | | 5 | | 3 | | 3 | |
| Model | 1* | | 1* | | 0 | | 0 | |

| (p-r) | Trace | $\lambda_{max}$ | | 5% critical values for Model 0 | | 5% critical values for Model 1* | |
|---|---|---|---|---|---|---|---|
| | **Slovenia** | | | | | | |
| 2 | 18.25* | 15.56* | | 12.32 | 11.23 | 20.25 | 15.88 |
| 1 | 2.69 | 2.69 | | 4.13 | 4.13 | 9.17 | 9.17 |
| $k^b$ | 3 | | | | | | |
| Model | 0 | | | | | | |

Notes:  [a]The value reported at the top of each column is for $r=0$, so that $p-r=p$, where $p=2$ (i.e. the number of interest rates included). * denotes rejection of the null hypothesis of at most $r$ cointegrating relations at the 5% level of significance.
[b]$k$ indicates the lag length.

Table 10.3 reports the computed $L$-statistics. For the countries for which $\alpha_R$ is statistically significant (i.e., the three Baltic states), the null hypothesis that the short–term interest rate, $r$, has a permanent component in the common trend cannot be rejected at the 5% level of significance.

On the other hand, for the countries with a significant $\alpha_r$ (i.e. Cyprus, the Czech Republic, Hungary, the Slovak Republic and Slovenia), the null hypothesis that the long–term interest rate, $R$, has a permanent component in the common trend cannot be rejected at the 5% level of significance. For Hungary the null hypothesis cannot be rejected at the 10% level of significance. For these countries the short–term interest rate adjusts to deviation from the long–run equilibrium, while the long–term interest rate is not affected by past disequilibria and thus 'drives' the common trend.

Table 10.3    Testing for the term structure of interest rates[a]

| | $\beta_R$ | $\beta_r$ | $H_0$: $\beta_R+\beta_r=0$ | $\alpha_R$ | $\alpha_r$ | $\alpha_\perp^R$ | L-stat | $\alpha_\perp^r$ | L-stat |
|---|---|---|---|---|---|---|---|---|---|
| Cyprus | 1.00** (18.29) | -1.15** (18.32) | 18.28** | -0.09 (0.56) | 0.44** (16.55) | -27.70 | 0.57 | -5.90** | 16.52 |
| Czech Republic | 1.00** (9.60) | -1.04** (9.66) | 1.99 | -0.06 (1.31) | 0.07** (7.65) | -11.46 | 1.31 | -8.92** | 7.64 |
| Estonia | 1.00** (11.82) | -1.01** (12.43) | 0.03 | -0.09** (9.27) | 0.09 (2.41) | -3.41** | 9.27 | -3.68 | 2.41 |
| Hungary | 1.00** (10.02) | -0.93** (10.01) | 8.75** | -0.09 (0.57) | 0.25* (3.12) | -11.39 | 0.57 | -4.10* | 3.13 |
| Latvia | 1.00** (18.65) | -0.69** (18.43) | 16.06** | -0.51** (16.77) | 0.10 (1.13) | 1.84** | 16.77 | 9.36 | 1.13 |
| Lithuania | 1.00** (6.08) | -1.25** (11.52) | 0.42 | -0.19** (11.82) | -0.00 (0.01) | -0.17** | 11.82 | 12.70 | 0.01 |
| Slovak Republic | 1.00** (22.07) | -0.99** (20.63) | 0.04 | -0.07 (2.24) | 0.14** (7.47) | -4.64 | 2.24 | -2.52** | 12.14** |
| Slovenia | 1.00** (6.61) | -1.07** (7.11) | 12.34** | 0.06 (2.34) | 0.13** (11.32) | -28.87 | 2.35 | 7.47 | 11.33 |

Note: [a] R and r denote the long-term and short-term interest rate respectively. β are the parameters of the cointegrating vectors, normalized on the long-term interest rates. α are the adjustment coefficients and $\alpha_\perp$ are their orthogonal complements. Numbers in parentheses are likelihood ratio statistics for $H_0$: $\beta_r=0$ or $H_0$: $\alpha_r=0$. Numbers in the row of $H_0$: $\beta_R+\beta_r=0$ are likelihood ratio test statistics. L-statistics are for the null hypothesis that the respective interest rate (either R or r) determines the common trend. ** (*) denotes rejection of the null hypothesis at the 5% (10%) level of significance.

### 3.3    Short–run Interdependence

In this section we analyze short–run interdependence among the term structures of the new EU member states using Granger causality tests. In order to include all the countries in our analysis, the time span is restricted to 1997:1–2003:12 in this and the next section.

Fluctuations in the transitory component (or the spread) of the term structure are often thought to be caused by changes in monetary policy. If these fluctuations are related across the countries, then it is possible that policy actions are interdependent in the short run. Since the transitory components of the term structures are stationary, we test for such interdependence explicitly by conducting causality tests based on multivariate VAR models among the cointegrating relations. The appropriate lag length for each VAR model was selected using the likelihood ratio test.

The causality results are reported in Table 10.4. The test results contain pairwise causality tests and joint causality tests that include all the countries in a given group of countries. The first panel of Table 10.4 includes results for all the new EU member states, except Poland for which the interest rates are stationary and Malta for which the EHTS does not hold. It is clear from this panel that there is weak short–run interdependence among the term structures of the countries in this group. Only eight out of fifty-six possible pairwise test statistics (excluding the own effects) and two out of eight joint test statistics are significant at the 5% or 10% level of significance. For example, only the Slovak Republic's spread is influenced by changes in the spreads of the Czech Republic and Latvia, both pairwise and jointly, at the 5% level. Similar results hold for Slovenia with respect to Estonia and Hungary.

The second panel of Table 10.4 reports the results for the group of the Central European countries: the Czech Republic, Hungary, the Slovak Republic and Slovenia. In this case, there is evidence of greater short–run linkages among the term structures. The Wald test statistics are significant in four out of ten pairwise tests and three out of four joint tests. Except for Hungary changes in the spreads of the other Central European countries jointly influence those of the Czech Republic, the Slovak Republic and Slovenia in the short run. These findings are expected, given the historic and economic links in the latter group of countries and the relative independence of Hungary, which in recent times has followed policies tied more closely to Western Europe than to Central Europe.

The third panel of Table 10.4 includes the three Baltic countries. As shown in the last column of this panel, changes in the spreads of Latvia and Lithuania jointly affect the spread of Estonia at the 10% level of significance. The spread of Lithuania is influenced only by changes in the spread of

*Table 10.4*   Testing for short run interdependence: Multivariate Granger Causality tests[a]

| Dependent variable | Explanatory variables (lag length = 1) | | | | | | | | |
|---|---|---|---|---|---|---|---|---|---|
| | CY | CZ | EE | HU | LV | LT | SK | SV | Joint |
| CY | 40.56** | 0.10 | 1.16 | 1.95 | 0.78 | 0.03 | 0.13 | 0.03 | 3.95 |
| CZ | 3.42* | 90.80** | 0.13 | 0.08 | 2.18 | 0.48 | 0.00 | 2.00 | 8.59 |
| EE | 1.74 | 0.50 | 28.73** | 0.31 | 1.75 | 0.39 | 0.01 | 2.32 | 8.56 |
| HU | 3.28* | 2.40 | 1.76 | 57.73** | 0.02 | 0.23 | 2.60 | 0.38 | 8.11 |
| LV | 1.52 | 1.44 | 0.45 | 1.93 | 67.93** | 0.04 | 3.86* | 0.27 | 8.55 |
| LT | 0.01 | 0.08 | 1.56 | 0.47 | 0.02 | 118.64** | 0.99 | 3.52* | 9.53 |
| SK | 0.04 | 4.72** | 0.03 | 0.28 | 4.34** | 1.98 | 2.75* | 0.10 | 17.13** |
| SV | 0.55 | 1.83 | 13.78** | 2.79* | 0.44 | 0.05 | 0.56 | 54.83** | 20.40** |
| df[b] | 1 | 1 | 1 | 1 | 1 | 1 | 1 | 1 | 7 |

continued overleaf

Notes:

[a]  The number in each cell is the Wald test statistic which, under the null, is asymptotically distributed as $\chi^2$.

[b]  df stands for the degrees of freedom of the Wald statistic. ** (*) denotes rejection of the null hypothesis $\Gamma_k=0$ at the 5% (10%) level of significance. CY is for Cyprus, CZ for the Czech Republic, EE for Estonia, HU for Hungary, LV for Latvia, LT for Lithuania, SK for the Slovak Republic and SV for Slovenia.

*Table 10.4    (continued)*

| Dependent variable | Explanatory variables (lag length = 2) | | | | |
|---|---|---|---|---|---|
| | CZ | HU | SK | SV | Joint |
| CZ | 116.59** | 1.23 | 5.10* | 3.59 | 12.28* |
| HU | 1.80 | 51.51** | 5.69* | 1.93 | 9.18 |
| SK | 8.11** | 1.12 | 7.56** | 2.18 | 14.43** |
| SV | 1.11 | 1.45 | 13.35** | 129.99** | 18.34** |
| df | 2 | 2 | 2 | 2 | 6 |

| Dependent variable | Explanatory variables (lag length = 1) | | | |
|---|---|---|---|---|
| | EE | LV | LT | Joint |
| EE | 39.76** | 2.14 | 1.99 | 5.22* |
| LV | 0.84 | 86.90** | 0.61 | 1.11 |
| LT | 4.12** | 0.06 | 212.95** | 4.13 |
| df | 1 | 1 | 1 | 2 |

Estonia, while the spread of Latvia is unaffected by changes in the spread of Estonia and Lithuania. Clearly, the term structures of the three Baltic countries are loosely linked to each other, which reflect their independent monetary policies.

In summary, the above results indicate weak short–run linkages among the term structures of the new EU countries including the subgroup of the Baltic states. The results also indicate more links among the spreads in the subgroup of the five Central European countries.

### 3.4  Long–run Interdependence

In this section, we examine the long–run interdependence among the term structures by analyzing linkages among their common trends in a cointegration framework.

The common trends are often thought to capture information about future economic and monetary policies. Following Hafer and Kutan (1994) we can claim that there are strong long–run linkages among these policies in a group of $p$ countries, if there exist $r=p-1$ cointegrating relations among the commontrends. On the other hand, if $0 < r < p-1$, then there is only partial interdependence among the future policies of the countries concerned. In this sense, interdependence means that the countries' policies have converged enough, so that the permanent components of their term structures tend to move toward a long–run equilibrium and do not drift too far apart over time.

The cointegration results for the common trends for different groups of countries are reported in Table 10.5[4]. The Trace and $\lambda_{max}$ statistics refer to the same groups of countries as in the previous section. As shown in the first panel of Table 10.5, the Trace and the $\lambda_{max}$ statistics indicate four and two cointegration vectors respectively, at the 5% significance level, among the eight common trends of the new EU countries. For the four Central European countries, both statistics indicate one cointegration vector among the four common trends. Similarly for the three Baltic countries, both statistics indicate one cointegration vector among the three common trends. Overall, the above results indicate weak long–run interdependence among the term structures in these groups of countries, and consequently, only partial long run convergence of their monetary policies.

## 4  CONCLUSIONS

In this chapter we investigated empirically the term structure of interest rates among the ten new EU countries. Since the interest rates follow random walks, we evaluated the expectations hypothesis of the term structure using cointegration analysis and common trends techniques. Further we analyzed short–run and long–run interdependence among the term structures of these countries.

*Table 10.5    Testing for long–run interdependence: Trace and $\lambda_{max}$ statistics*

| (p-r) | CY, CZ, EE, HU, LV, LT, SK, SV Trace | $\lambda_{max}$ | CZ, HU, SK, SV Trace | $\lambda_{max}$ | 5% critical values for Model 1[*] Trace | $\lambda_{max}$ |
|---|---|---|---|---|---|---|
| 8[a] | 234.47[*] | 69.61[*] | | | 169.54 | 53.15 |
| 7 | 164.86[*] | 50.62[*] | | | 134.70 | 47.06 |
| 6 | 114.24[*] | 36.34 | | | 103.84 | 40.95 |
| 5 | 77.90[*] | 28.05 | | | 76.96 | 34.80 |
| 4 | 49.85 | 19.17 | 64.54[*] | 40.63[*] | 54.09 | 28.58 |
| 3 | 30.69 | 16.88 | 23.91 | 16.17 | 35.19 | 22.30 |
| 2 | 13.81 | 7.26 | 7.74 | 5.14 | 20.25 | 15.88 |
| 1 | 6.55 | 6.55 | 2.59 | 2.59 | 9.17 | 9.17 |
| k[b] | 2 | | 2 | | | |
| Model | 1[*] | | 1[*] | | | |

*continued overleaf*

*Table 10.5     (continued)*

| (p-r) | EE, LV, LT | | 5% critical values for Model 0 | |
|---|---|---|---|---|
| | Trace | $\lambda_{max}$ | Trace | $\lambda_{max}$ |
| 3 | 38.65* | 27.16* | 24.28 | 17.80 |
| 2 | 11.49 | 8.81 | 12.32 | 11.23 |
| 1 | 2.69 | 2.69 | 4.13 | 4.13 |
| k | 1 | | | |
| Model | 0 | | | |

*Notes:*
[a]  The value reported at the top of each column is for $r=0$, so that $p-r=p$, where $p$ is the number of common trends included. * denotes rejection of the $H_0$ at most $r$ cointegrating relations, at a 5% significance level.
[b]  $k$ indicates the lag length.

Our empirical findings indicate that the EHTS holds for all the new EU countries, except for Malta. For Cyprus, the Czech Republic, Hungary, the Slovak Republic and Slovenia, the long–term interest rate is weakly exogenous and drives the common trend in each term structure. On the other hand, for the three Baltic states, the short–term interest rate is weakly exogenous and has a permanent component in the common trend.

Our results also indicate weak short–run and long–run interdependence among the term structures of the new EU states and the subgroups of the Eastern European and Baltic states. This evidence, in turn, implies that these countries set their monetary policies independently, both in the short run and the long run.

Our analysis has been focused on term structure linkages among the new EU member states. This is a useful exercise as it provides valuable knowledge about the degree of monetary convergence in these countries. More insights can be gained by analyzing the term structures of these countries in relation to some core EU countries such as France and Germany. We intend to undertake this research in the near future.

## NOTES

[1]   The empirical literature is large and, in general, supportive of the EHTS of interest rates. Among others, Hall, Anderson and Granger (1992) used monthly data from 1970:3 to 1988:12 to analyze the term structure of 12 yield series on USA Treasury bills. Using multivariate cointegration methods and the vector error–correction model approach (VECM), these authors found evidence supportive of the EHTS for the US. Hardouvelis (1994) used monthly data of different time spans to investigate empirically the EHTS for the G7

countries: Canada, France, Germany, Italy, Japan, the UK and the USA. Based on OLS regression and VAR techniques, he found that the EHTS holds for all countries except the USA. Gerlach and Smets (1997) studied the term structures in a sample of 17 countries with time spans between 10 and 30 years, and monthly data for 1-month, 3-month, 6-month and 12-month euro rates. Using cross-sectional regression analysis, they concluded that for most of the countries the EHTS is compatible with the data. Jondeau and Ricart (1999) adopted the VECM approach to test the EHTS on French, German, UK and US euro rates. Using monthly data for 1-month, 3-month, 6-month and 12-month euro rates from 1975:1 to 1997:12, they could not reject the EHTS for French and UK rates, but they rejected it for German and US rates.

[2] The Gaussian assumption is not necessary, but it is convenient for the derivation of asymptotic results.

[3] The latest edition of EViews 5 has also adopted the MacKinnon et al. (1999) critical values.

[4] The appropriate lag length $k$ for the VECM and the submodel that describes best each set of variables were chosen following the same procedures as in Section 3.2 above.

# REFERENCES

Gerlach, Stefan and Frank Smets (1997), 'The Term Structure of Euro–Rates: Some Evidence in Support of the Expectations Hypothesis', *Journal of International Money and Finance*, **16** (2), 305–21.

Gonzalo, Jesus and Clive W.J. Granger (1995), 'Estimation of Common Long–Memory Components in Cointegrated Systems', *Journal of Business and Economic Statistics*, **13** (1), 27–35.

Hafer, Rik W. and Ali M. Kutan (1994), 'A Long Run View of German Dominance and the Degree of Policy Convergence in the EMS', *Economic Inquiry*, **32** (4), 684–95.

Hafer, Rik W., Ali M. Kutan and Su Zhou (1997), 'Linkages in the EMS Term Structures: Evidence from Common Trend and Transitory Components', *Journal of International Money and Finance*, **16**, 595–607.

Hall, Anthony D., Heather M. Anderson and Clive W.J. Granger (1992), 'A Cointegration Analysis of Treasury Bill Yields', *Review of Economics and Statistics*, **74** (1), 116–26.

Hardouvelis, Gikas A. (1994), 'The Term Structure Spread and Future Changes in Long and Short Rates in the G7 Countries', *Journal of Monetary Economics*, **33** (2), 255–83.

Holmes, Mark J. and Eric J. Pentecost (1997), 'The Term Structure of Interest Rates and Financial Integration in the ERM', *International Journal of Finance and Economics*, **2** (3), 237–47.

Johansen, Soren (1988), 'Statistical Analysis of Cointegration Vectors', *Journal of Economic Dynamics and Control*, **12**, 231–54.

Johansen, Soren (1991), 'Estimation and Hypothesis Testing of Cointegration in Gaussian Vector Autoregressive Models', *Econometrica*, **59** (6), 1551–80.

Johansen, Soren (1994), 'The Role of the Constant and Linear Terms in Cointegration Analysis of Nonstationary Variables', *Econometric Reviews*, **13**, 205–29.

Johansen, Soren (1995), *Likelihood-Based Inference in Cointegrated Vector Autoregressive Models*, Oxford: Oxford University Press.

Johansen, Soren and Katarina Juselius (1990), 'Maximum Likelihood Estimation and Inference on Cointegration with Applications to the Demand for Money', *Oxford Bulletin of Economics and Statistics*, **52** (2), 169–210.

Jondeau, Eric and Roland Ricart (1999), 'The Expectations Hypothesis of the Term Structure: Tests on US, German, French, and UK Euro–Rates', *Journal of International Money and Finance*, **18** (5), 725–50.

MacKinnon, James G., Alfred A. Haug and Leo Michelis (1999), 'Numerical Distribution Functions of Likelihood Ratio Tests for Cointegration', *Journal of Applied Econometrics*, **14** (5), 563–77.

OECD (2004), *Main Economic Indicators*, Paris: OECD.

Osterwald–Lenum, Michael (1992), 'A Note with Quantiles of the Asymptotic Distribution of the Maximum Likelihood Cointegration Rank Test Statistics', *Oxford Bulletin of Economics and Statistics*, **54** (3), 461–71.

# Index